VEKHI

Vekhi—also known under the English title *Landmarks* or *Signposts*—is a collection of essays first published in Moscow in 1909. Writing from various points of view, the authors reflect the experience of Russia's failed 1905 revolution—a failure to be blamed not only on the repressive forces of the autocracy but also on the intellectual bankruptcy of the intelligentsia and the Russian nation's inability to use freedom constructively. They saw as their task the construction of the moral, religious, philosophical under-pinnings of a new, liberal order in Russia.

Condemned by Lenin, rediscovered by dissidents, and widely circulated in post-Soviet Russia today, the *Vekhi* essays have tremendous resonance. This new edition of Shatz and Zimmerman's highly praised translation will afford invaluable insights to anyone who wants to grasp the terms of discussion in the postrevolutionary Russia of today.

Also from *M.E. Sharpe*

RUSSIAN THOUGHT AFTER COMMUNISM
The Recovery of a Philosophical Heritage
Edited by James P. Scanlan

REMAKING RUSSIA
Voices from Within
Edited by Heyward Isham
With an Introduction by Richard Pipes

VEKHI

❧Landmarks❧

A Collection of Articles about the Russian Intelligentsia

NIKOLAI
BERDIAEV

SERGEI
BULGAKOV

MIKHAIL
GERSHENZON

A. S.
IZGOEV

BOGDAN
KISTIAKOVSKII

PETR
STRUVE

SEMEN
FRANK

Translated and edited by
MARSHALL S. SHATZ
and
JUDITH E. ZIMMERMAN

With a Foreword by
MARC RAEFF

M.E. Sharpe
Armonk, New York
London, England

Translations originally serialized in *Canadian Slavic Studies*
(vol. 2, no. 2, to vol. 5, no. 3)
and reissued in a revised edition in 1986 by
Charles Schlacks, Jr., Publisher, Irvine, California.

Library of Congress Cataloging-in-Publication Data
Vekhi. English.
Vekhi = Landmarks / [Nikolai Berdiaev . . . et al.]; translated by
Marshall S. Shatz and Judith E. Zimmerman; with a foreword
by Marc Raeff.
p.   cm.
Includes bibliographical references and index.
Contents: Philosophical verity and intelligentsia truth / Nikolai
Berdiaev—Heroism and asceticism (reflections on the religious
nature of the Russian intelligentsia) / Sergei Bulgakov—Creative
self-consciousness / Mikhail Gershenzon—On educated youth (notes
on its life and sentiments / A.S. Izgoev—In defense of law (the
intelligentsia and legal consciousness) / Bogdan Kistiakovskii—The
intelligentsia and revolution / Petr Struve—The ethic of
nihilism (a characterization of the Russian intelligentsia's moral
outlook) / Semen Frank.
ISBN 1-56324-390-3   ISBN 1-56324-391-1
1. Russia—Intellectual life—1801–1917. 2. Intellectuals—Russia.
I. Berdiaev, Nikolai, 1874–1948. II. Shatz, Marshall S.
III. Zimmerman, Judith E. IV. Title. V. Title: Landmarks.
DK255.V4413   1994
001.1´0947—dc20   94-26039
CIP

Printed in the United States of America

The paper used in this publication meets the minimum requirements of
American National Standard for Information Sciences—
Permanence of Paper for Printed Library Materials,
ANSI Z 39.48-1984.

♾

MV (c)   10   9   8   7   6   5   4   3   2   1
MV (p)   10   9   8   7   6   5   4   3   2   1

CONTENTS

FOREWORD

Marc Raeff

An orthodoxy that has long held sway over the values and ideas of an intellectual elite will eventually wear itself out and lose its power to shape society's public life. This is especially the case when the society has undergone a rapid and profound transformation under the impact of such forces as scientific discoveries, new values and interests from abroad, changing aesthetic styles and spiritual needs, economic innovation, political upheaval. The resulting sense of dissatisfaction and unease will spur some among the intellectual leadership "to put on a new thinking cap," to quote Alfred North Whitehead. Such a change occurred in Western Europe and the United States after World War I and again in the 1960s; we are witnessing a similar development today in the former Soviet world.

A "new thinking cap" cannot be created *ex nihilo*, however. It has to make use of available fabrics and patterns, some of them drawn from older traditions. Even so, it may not be immediately and universally accepted; many will reject it as alien or subversive. In some instances the new ideas advanced by an intellectual avant-garde will be forced underground, only to be rediscovered and put to use by later generations. Such was the fate of the ideas and values propounded by the authors of *Vekhi*, or Landmarks, a collection of essays published in Moscow in 1909, during another time of intellectual crisis.

Why did some of the leading intellectuals in Russia feel the need for a new way of thinking in 1909? The informative introduction to this excellent translation of *Vekhi* by Marshall S. Shatz and Judith E. Zimmerman gives the essential facts of the collection's origins and reception. Here I would like to offer only a few general reflections.

At the turn of the present century the majority of Russia's intellectual elite —the intelligentsia—had failed to adjust its *mentalité* to the far-reaching social and economic changes brought about in the 1860s and 1870s by the Great Reforms of the reign of Alexander II, in particular the emancipation of the serfs. Without venturing a critical assessment of the accomplishments, as well as the failures, of the Great Reforms, it may be said that, as a result, by 1900 Russian society had undergone a radical transformation, and its rapid momentum had not slowed down as yet. On the other hand, the intelligentsia's basic outlook had remained very much a pre-reform one, rooted in the simple-minded belief in a scientism that was now challenged by new orientations in the natural sciences. It had also remained uncritically beholden to what Leonard Schapiro called the "mystique of revolution," a single-minded dedication to the overthrow of autocracy without giving much thought to constructive alternatives. In a sense the intelligentsia's rigidity of thought was due to its rejection of the liberal solutions and compromises demanded by a society rapidly developing industrial capitalism with its attendant economic and social complexities. Paradoxically, although the traditional intelligentsia's outlook had been shaped under the influence of West European ideas and experiences, there was a refusal to accept the aesthetic and philosophic innovations (symbolism, neo-Kantianism, pragmatism) that were flowing in from Europe and America. These new currents rejected the philosophic assumptions of materialist positivism and proclaimed the primacy of an idealist metaphysics and a revolutionary aesthetics and science. What most shocked Russia's radical intelligentsia, however, was the revival of religious concerns on the one hand and respect for legal and national values on the other.

The revolution of 1905 and its authoritarian aftermath created a still deeper rift in the ranks of Russia's intellectual elite. Those events confirmed the radical intelligentsia in its traditional "mystique of revolution" and social philosophy, while another element now distanced itself from politics and focused on spiritual and professional concerns. How this new trend might have evolved we will never know, for the imperial regime's inability to cope with the world war precipitated its collapse and the virtual disintegration of the Russian polity, making it possible for the most extreme party of the revolutionary intelligentsia to seize control. The Bolshevik government proceeded to promote its own intellectual orthodoxy, rooted in the outlook of the mid-nineteenth century, and eventually imposed the rigid framework of Soviet totalitarianism on all of Russian cultural life.

By the 1980s Soviet orthodoxy had, in its turn, become untenable. The dissident movement, although it undermined the stranglehold of official thinking, did not provide genuinely novel and constructive alternatives. This was not surprising, for the regime had isolated the intellectual elite both from foreign influences and from non-Leninist prerevolutionary ideas. As the Soviet system lost its nerve, wavered, and then collapsed, the need for intellectual alternatives became apparent. It was quite natural to turn to Russia's pre-1917 heritage, prompting the rediscovery of *Vekhi*. Disenchantment with the Soviet "experiment" of social engineering fostered mistrust of any political program or blueprint for total socioeconomic transformation, and so the *Vekhi* appeal for a liberal politics of compromise, gradualism, and the rule of law now found a sympathetic reception in the Russian intelligentsia. The end of the harsh Soviet antireligious campaigns has opened the way for a religious revival and demand for ecclesiastical reform quite similar to those advocated by the *Vekhi* authors. The pervasive sense of breakdown of the family and of individual morality has endowed with particular relevance the *Vekhi* appeal for a return to spiritual and moral values and to a respect for the supreme dignity of the responsible individual. Finally, Soviet "internationalist imperialism" has given way to awareness of the desirability of a return to historic traditions and the pursuit of strictly national political goals, although not always in the tolerant and cosmopolitan spirit of the *Vekhi* authors.

The profound social revolution—by whatever means and at whatever cost—that was carried out by the Soviet regime also brought about a restructuring of the intelligentsia and its relationship to a people that had acquired literacy and access to education. But it did not eliminate, so it would seem, the existence of a deep gulf between the intelligentsia and the people. The latter still harbor distrust, or even hatred, of the so-called Soviet intelligentsia, the professional and cultural elite that was the main helpmate of the Bolsheviks in implementing their programs and plans. One of the central themes of the *Vekhi* authors was the intelligentsia's need to overcome its alienation from the Russian people. This theme, too, is relevant today.

Little wonder, then, that the *Vekhi* essays have been reprinted several times in Russia in recent years and have become a wellspring of opinions and ideas in the ongoing debate over the best way for Russia to emerge from the murky heritage of the Soviet period. The goal of a political culture rooted in spiritual values and embodied in free moral individuals respectful of national traditions and liberal political practices has no less appeal in the 1990s than it had in 1909. Indeed, it is a message from which the West could benefit as well as Russia.

INTRODUCTION

Marshall S. Shatz and Judith E. Zimmerman

Vekhi (Landmarks, sometimes translated Signposts), this small volume of seven essays, was an expression of profound anxiety over Russia's future on the part of some of prerevolutionary Russia's most thoughtful intellectuals. Four years prior to its publication, in 1905, their country had experienced its first major revolution. The *Vekhi* authors were among those who had long struggled against the repressive tsarist regime and had dreamed of a new era of individual freedom and national renewal. By 1908, when the collection was planned, they perceived instead a nation that had been unable to move forward from oppression to political liberty, personal autonomy, and orderly development. The fault, they believed, lay with the men and women who had claimed political and intellectual leadership of the Russian people, the "intelligentsia." Hence, *Vekhi* took the form of a many-sided and sharply worded criticism of the intelligentsia's beliefs. Each of the authors investigated some facet of the intelligentsia's world-view: its approach to philosophy, education, law and religion; its concept of culture; its image of the state and the people; its ideological positions and its political behavior. In all cases the authors found the intelligentsia's values and assumptions faulty and demanded no less than a recasting of its entire intellectual and spiritual framework. If the intelligentsia did not make fundamental changes in its outlook, *Vekhi* warned, it would not only fail to achieve democracy and social justice, which had long been its cherished goals; it would destroy civilized life in Russia.

The *Vekhi* authors had anticipated that the volume would create a sensation, and they were not disappointed. It was designed to be a challenge to Russian public opinion, and so it was perceived by its first readers. Within a year the book had gone through five editions and had elicited hundreds of reviews, commentaries, and analyses. The entire spectrum of the Russian press participated in the controversy, and discussions of the book appeared in newspapers and magazines ranging from Siberia to St. Petersburg, from far right to extreme left, from underground publications to government journals. Literary societies devoted their meetings to *Vekhi*, and a variety of public figures took a stand on it. In addition to speeches and articles, several pamphlets and three book-length symposia dealt specifically with *Vekhi*. Intelli-

Nikolai Berdiaev

gentsia spokesmen rightly perceived the book as an attack on both their views and their political record, and it seemed as if every one of them had to express his own hostility and anger.

Vekhi would hardly have had so stormy a reception had it emanated from the conservatives who habitually criticized the intelligentsia. *Vekhi*, however, was the work of men who had long been associated with it. Most of them had begun their own political lives as Marxist socialists; they had been closely identified with the struggle against the autocratic government, and some had suffered arrest, loss of job, and exile for their convictions. Their indictment of what they considered to be the intelligentsia's errors was in part a self-indictment, and this enhanced the work's moral authority.

Mikhail Osipovich Gershenzon (1869–1925) edited the volume and also contributed one of its articles.[1] Born in Kishinev, Bessarabia, the son of an unsuccessful Jewish businessman, Gershenzon became a well-known literary critic and historian. A professional man of letters, he contributed articles and reviews to several journals, and in 1908 he was one of the editors of the journal *Critical Survey* [Kriticheskoe obozrenie].

Gershenzon's most important works were biographical studies of members of the intellectual circles of the 1830s and 1840s, and the theme of alienation that runs through those studies was related to his criticism of the contemporary intelligentsia. Ideologically, he stood apart from his collaborators in some important respects. Unlike them, he was an admirer of the philosophy of Lev Tolstoi and so did not really believe in political action, since he felt individual moral improvement was more important than institutional change. He also found Tolstoi's cult of simplicity attractive, and so when making value judgments he trusted a somewhat anti-intellectual "wholeness" over analysis and rationalism. The other *Vekhi* authors, more active politically than Gershenzon, were unsympathetic to Tolstoi's cultural views.

Nikolai Aleksandrovich Berdiaev (1874–1948) had already traversed a long intellectual journey, and in 1909 was just beginning the phase of his career that would make him one of the outstanding Russian philosophers of the twentieth century.[2] He had grown up in the cosmopolitan atmosphere of a wealthy gentry family in Kiev. In his student days at Kiev University he had joined a Marxist group, and for this he was exiled to the Far North. Subsequently he rejected Marxism and was drawn into the circle of symbolist writers and religious thinkers grouped around the novelist Dmitrii Merezhkovskii and his wife, the poet Zinaida Hippius. They propounded a "new religious consciousness," which rejected Christianity for a "Third Testament of the Holy Spirit," one that would overcome what they felt was Christianity's one-sided spirituality and restore the flesh to its rightful, sacred place in human life.[3] In 1908 Berdiaev broke with the Merezhkovskiis and began his evolution toward the somewhat more conventional Christianity that marked his mature thought. He was a most prolific writer and by 1909 had

Sergei Bulgakov

Photo courtesy of Susan Eva Heuman

Bogdan Kistiakovskii

already published five books and more than fifty articles.

Sergei Nikolaievich Bulgakov (1871–1944) was another thinker who was only on the threshold of his intellectual maturity when he participated in *Vekhi*.[4] The son of an Orthodox priest, he had lost his faith in Christianity as a young man, and he began his career as a Marxist economist. After doing research in Western Europe he taught political economy in Kiev and at the same time began to move back to the Christianity of his childhood. In 1905–6, after the 1905 revolution had made political activity legal for the first time, he attempted to create a specifically Christian party. In 1907 he was elected to Russia's fledgling legislature, the State Duma, where he regarded himself as a Christian socialist; in practice, however, he was affiliated with the liberal Constitutional Democratic ("Kadet") Party. Disillusioned with politics after 1907, he began to produce the theological work that dominated the rest of his career. In 1918 his religious evolution culminated in his ordination as an Orthodox priest.

A.S. Izgoev (pseudonym of Aleksandr Solomonovich Lande, 1872–1935) was born in Irbit, in the Urals region, and attended Novorossiisk and Tomsk universities.[5] He was a liberal journalist and Kadet Party activist with a Marxist background. After 1905 he was a member of the staff of both the Kadet newspaper *Speech* [Rech'] and Struve's journal, *Russian Thought* [Russkaia mysl']. He became a member of the Kadet Central Committee in 1906, and unlike the other *Vekhi* contributors, he remained actively involved in the party through the revolution of 1917. His article in *Vekhi* was part of a continuing concern with student life and youth attitudes.

Bogdan Aleksandrovich Kistiakovskii (1868–1920) was a student of sociology and constitutional law.[6] In 1908–9 he was one of the co-editors of *Critical Survey*. The legal and constitutional characteristics of a liberal political system were among his major intellectual concerns. His early work shows traces of Marxist influence, although he was never a member of the Social Democratic Party. A moderate Ukrainian nationalist, Kistiakovskii was also interested in the creation of a political system in which minority rights would be expanded within the framework of the Russian Empire.

Petr Berngardovich Struve (1870–1944) was a prominent liberal editor and journalist.[7] He had been one of the first important Marxist theorists in Russia and had taken a major part in the Marxist polemic against Populism. Never orthodox in his Marxism, however, he was first a revisionist and then drifted away from Marxism altogether to a liberalism that both was statist and included elements of socialism. In 1902 he had emigrated to Stuttgart, where he edited the influential émigré liberal newspaper *Liberation* [Osvobozhdenie]. When the revolution of 1905 permitted him to return to Russia he became active in the Kadet Party, was elected to its Central Committee, and served in the Second Duma. After the dissolution of the Duma in 1907 he withdrew from party politics, and in the years before 1917 he taught economics in St.

Petr Struve

Semen Frank

Petersburg and edited one of the leading "thick journals" of the day, *Russian Thought.*

Semen Liudvigovich Frank (1877–1950) was the youngest of the *Vekhi* authors.[8] He was brought up in a middle-class Jewish household in Moscow and was attracted to Marxism while still in secondary school. While an economics student at the university he was expelled for participation in a Marxist circle, and therefore had to complete his studies in Germany, which he did between 1899 and 1901. After he returned to Russia he abandoned Marx for Nietzsche. In the following years Frank served as Struve's assistant on several newspapers and magazines, including *Liberation* and *Russian Thought.* He found his true vocation, philosophy, only after the appearance of the *Vekhi* volume. In 1912 Frank converted to Christianity, but it is not clear just what influence Christianity exercised on his mature outlook.

Gershenzon conceived of *Vekhi* as a means "to tell the Russian intelligentsia the bitter truth about itself."[9] His position on the journal *Critical Survey* put him in touch with many of Russia's leading non-Marxist thinkers, and he used these contacts to put together his group of collaborators. Early in October 1908 he sent letters to a number of philosophers, inviting them to participate in the venture. His primary contact in St. Petersburg was Frank, who was also writing regularly for *Critical Survey.* Frank served as the liaison with Struve, suggested Izgoev's participation, and argued vigorously for the special contributions that Berdiaev and Bulgakov could make to the project.[10] By mid-November, at a meeting in Moscow, Gershenzon, Struve, Kistiakovskii, and Bulgakov had drawn up the final list of contributors and the topics on which they would write.[11]

The *Vekhi* contributors were chosen primarily on the basis of their record of criticism of the intelligentsia, and not as the spokesmen for an alternative set of beliefs. They did not constitute a "school" in any sense, and they disagreed on many issues. Thus, there were contradictions in the volume that puzzled many of its readers. Yet despite their disagreements, at the time *Vekhi* was published these men had known one another for nearly ten years, and they had followed similar patterns of development from Marxism through philosophical idealism to liberalism, and in some cases beyond. They had, moreover, frequently collaborated with one another on newspapers and journals. There is, thus, a certain logic in treating the *Vekhi* authors as a group and searching for unifying threads in their thought. Gershenzon himself, however, must be excluded from attempts to generalize about the *Vekhi* authors, since his views differed so substantially from those of his collaborators.

The *Vekhi* authors' intellectual evolution took place against the background of cultural ferment known as Russia's Silver Age.[12] Music, dance, fine arts, and poetry all made bold departures in the two decades before World War I: Stravinsky and Diaghilev caused riots in Paris with their *Rite of Spring*, Chagall was painting fiddlers on the roofs of his native Vitebsk, and modern literature was dissolving the realism of the nineteenth century. Culturally it was one of the richest periods of Russian history and the first time Russia was part of the European avant garde.

The *Vekhi* authors were sympathetic observers of artistic modernism. But with the exception of Berdiaev they tended to maintain a certain distance from the philosophy that accompanied it. The prevailing mood in Russian modernist circles was apocalyptic: many believed that the end of the world was at hand and that the violence of the time heralded the Second Coming. Spiritualism, occultism, and theosophy all had their adherents, while the mission of the followers of Nikolai Fedorov was to bring the dead back to life. Sexuality was also celebrated—in Merezhkovskii's and Berdiaev's Third Testament of the Holy Spirit, the overt sexual content of *Rite of Spring*, and the first public emergence of homosexuality. It was all too heady, and the *Vekhi* men tended to derive their own modernism from the more sober confines of the Western university world, and especially from German philosophy and social science. They were concerned with politics and institutions, not eschatology.

The one leader of Silver Age thought whom the *Vekhi* men did acknowledge was the religious philosopher Vladimir Solov'ev (1853–1900). But only Berdiaev and Bulgakov were genuine followers of Solov'ev—and they interpreted his legacy in very different ways. For the others it was Solov'ev's combination of mystical religion with a reaffirmation of liberal principles in civic life that was so important. They rendered homage because his example proved that religion was not necessarily accompanied by reaction and obscurantism.

Despite their disagreement with many of the representatives of the new trends of the Silver Age, it is worth reiterating that the *Vekhi* authors were modernists themselves. Those in the avant garde spoke the same language, even if they frequently used it to argue with each other.

In contrast to *Vekhi*, most *intelligenty* still spoke the language of the nineteenth century. Their outlook was characterized by materialism, utilitarianism, scientism, and crude rationalism, or—to use the general term often applied to this set of attitudes—"positivism." By the time *Vekhi* appeared, its authors had already spent a decade criticizing the positivist outlook that had held sway over the intelligentsia for generations. The positivist tradition extended, they believed, from mid-nineteenth-century figures such as Belinskii, Bakunin, and Chernyshevskii, to contemporary Populists and Social Democrats. Their own evolution away from this traditional stance had begun for Berdiaev, Bulgakov, Struve, and Frank—whose articles form the real core of *Vekhi*—in the 1890s, when they were all part of the small group of Marxist revisionists who were called "Legal Marxists."[13] Like the German revisionists, Legal Marxists adopted the Social Democratic social and political program, while discarding revolutionism and most of the philosophical underpinning of Marx's original doctrine. They were particularly dissatisfied with Marxism's materialism—the belief that the universe is made of matter which can be known by human observers. The revisionists took an idealist position instead, arguing, in the first instance, that whatever the nature of external reality may be, it is unknowable; the human mind can grasp only its own image of it, and not the underlying reality (if there is one). After they had abandoned Marxism altogether, these four future *Vekhi* authors moved on to metaphysical idealism, the belief that there are nonmaterial realities—ideals or Divinity—which provide life with its meaning.

The philosophical break with Marxist materialism was based on the idealism of Immanuel Kant. The four former Marxists were joined by Kistiakovskii at this stage of their development. Their recourse to Kant was paralleled by a renewed interest in German idealism on the part of more academic thinkers, and in 1903 they collaborated with other political writers and professional philosophers in a collection of articles entitled *Problems of Idealism* [Problemy idealizma].[14] The rejection of positivism in *Problems of Idealism* makes this work a precursor of *Vekhi*.

Although they were able to use cultural and philosophic concepts in a sophisticated manner, the journalism of the *Vekhi* authors normally had a political content. Their idealism provided legitimation for a political liberalism based on individual rights, a position that they defended from the beginning of the twentieth century to about 1907. Their ideology in these years was virtually identical to that of the Kadet Party (founded in 1905, with antecedents stretching back several years). It was also in these years that Izgoev, the Kadet journalist and politician, began to collaborate with the other *Vekhi* men.

The revolution of 1905 and its aftermath shook the faith of the *Vekhi* authors in the liberal and democratic potential of the Russian people. At the time the volume appeared, most of its authors had moved into alignment with a new political group, the Progressists. This was the first Russian party to assert that the commercial and industrial class should play the leading role in the country's development. While strongly oppositional, the Progressists rejected traditional Russian liberalism's stress on social welfare. Moreover, their hope that a party of the elite could manipulate a mass following implied a lack of respect for the moral and political autonomy of each citizen. For the *Vekhi* authors, it marked a significant retreat from their earlier Kantian idealism and its notion that every individual must always be perceived as an end in himself.

The *Vekhi* men believed that 1905 disproved many of the tenets of the traditional radical faith. Unlike the socialists and many of the liberals, they did not feel that the revolution failed to achieve political liberty and social justice simply because the autocracy had been able to bring superior force to bear against it. Rather, failure had resulted from the Russian nation's inability to use freedom constructively. The people were anarchic and immature, and their leaders, the intelligentsia, had encouraged their worst instincts instead of educating them to political responsibility. The intelligentsia's traditional radicalism lacked the positive values and realistic understanding of human nature necessary for genuine progress. The *Vekhi* contributors believed that the violence and lawlessness of 1905 was a foretaste of the utter disaster Russia would undergo if the intelligentsia did not drastically revise its approach to the solution of the nation's problems. The mood of disappointment and apathy that affected much of the intelligentsia in the aftermath of the revolution's failure appeared to create the appropriate conditions for such self-examination and "repentance." What was not spelled out in *Vekhi*, but did appear in the authors' other writings of the same period, was that the new ideology the intelligentsia should adopt was that of a genuine bourgeoisie, or, failing that, the intelligentsia itself should be replaced by new bourgeois spokesmen.[15]

* * *

The content of *Vekhi* cannot be analyzed in detail here, but it will be useful to identify briefly some of the major themes that recur throughout the work.

Individualism is one important thread. It had long been a major concern of the *Vekhi* authors, who insisted that any legitimate politics must be based on recognition of the absolute value and autonomy of the individual human beings who constitute the society. In the past, they had used this argument to legitimate political and social democracy. Now, however, the notion of individualism was transformed in a manner that de-emphasized politics, while sharply attacking the programs of the left. They no longer evaluated political doctrines on the basis of the respect each accorded the individual; instead, they now judged political groups by the ethical and intellectual qualities of their members and the people they influenced. The foundation of political life, they argued, was the personality structure and ethical values of the individuals who made up the society. Thus, they attacked the intelligentsia for concentrating on political, social, and economic change while disregarding individual ethical improvement. *Vekhi*'s authors did not altogether neglect political and social justice, as many of their critics claimed; numerous statements in the articles recognized the pressing need for concrete reforms. But they had decisively shifted their emphasis.

The authors believed that the intelligentsia's ideology threatened individual values in three respects. First, it denied the existence of absolute ethical standards, replacing them with notions of "class morality" and "class justice." This moral relativism had shown its dangerous potential with dismaying clarity during the revolution, when members of radical groups readily engaged in criminal acts and terror tactics. Second, the intelligentsia's tendency to view justice in strictly utilitarian and materialist terms risked sacrificing the welfare of living individuals to the welfare of an abstraction: "the proletariat," "the peasantry," "the people." Finally, by justifying any activity that seemed to further its goals, the intelligentsia's ideology fell into the trap of allowing the ends to justify the means.

A second major thread that runs throughout *Vekhi* is recognition of the weakness of civic culture in Russia. The authors did not have very satisfactory language for this concept, but they seem to have been calling for the propagation of those values that make civil society possible. Each in his own way, the authors recognized Russia's need for a solid, structured, autonomous set of political and social institutions that could stand between the oppressive government, on the one hand, and the undifferentiated mass of the people, on the other, that is, between autocracy and anarchy. Such an institutional structure would provide the nation with a capacity for self-organization that it had historically lacked. Hence, *Vekhi* criticized the intelligentsia for its negative attitude toward the main elements of this structure: the state, the rule of law, national consciousness, historical tradition, and so on; hence, also, the book's rejection of revolution in favor of gradualism, political education, and respect for historical continuity. The authors' concern with institutional guarantees of rights and liberties and their desire to build on the constitutional arrangements granted in 1905–6 were part of this general outlook. It was also the source of the respect for Western Europe which each of the articles displayed. While several of the authors criticized the intelligentsia for its habit of adopting without question the latest Western intellectual fads, all regarded the West as a model for the kind of sturdy, historically conditioned institutional structure that would permit Russia to attain both freedom and progress.

A third, closely related theme is the concept of culture, which all the contributors except Gershenzon shared. They believed that each society's intellectual, aesthetic, and spiritual creations—its art, literature, philosophy, and religion—form an organic unity which gives that society its unique identity and which has its own absolute value. To reduce cultural creativity to a mere reflection of economic and social forces, as in the notion of "class culture," or to view it simply as an instrument for achieving material welfare, was to deprive society of an essential instrument of self-consciousness and its members of a dimension of human life. The *Vekhi* authors called this reductionism "nihilism," and one of their major charges against the intelligentsia's world-view was that it was fundamentally anticultural. Along with autonomous social and political institutions, they believed, Russia needed a firm cultural structure, based on her own national traditions, within which all classes of the population could engage in constructive, creative activity.

Finally, tying together and subsuming all these themes was a fourth thread derived from the authors' philosophical development. The intelligentsia's world-view dismayed them by the way it reduced all moral, institutional, and cultural values to relative status, subordinating and, if necessary, sacrificing them to utilitarian political, social, and economic objectives. The transformation of the intelligentsia's consciousness that they deemed essential required, above all, recognition of the absolute nature of those values and their obligatory claim on man. By 1909 the authors, each in his own way, had reached the conclusion that only belief in the existence of a suprahuman order in the universe could provide the necessary sanction for absolute values. This explains the metaphysical and religious motifs that recurred throughout *Vekhi*. They took different forms in the different articles and were more explicit in some than in others, but they lent the book much of its real unity. In this way *Vekhi* reflected the philosophical and religious quests of the Silver Age and attempted to apply them to Russia's political needs in the post-1905 era.

* * *

Surprisingly few of the commentators on *Vekhi* probed these broad themes very deeply, and most read into the book only what they wished to see. For example, Lev Tolstoi, now the great sage of Russia, granted an interview on the subject. He found the book overly intellectual, he said, and on the whole less illuminating than a letter he had just received from a simple Tashkent peasant.[16] (Since Tolstoi's philosophy was one of *Vekhi*'s targets, his aloofness is understandable.) To Lenin it proved that the bourgeois liberals had repudiated genuine reform; he insisted that *Vekhi* was the voice of the Kadet Party, even though many Kadets bitterly denounced it.[17] In general, the representatives of the right wing of public opinion, such as the journalist Aleksandr Stolypin, brother of the prime minister Petr Stolypin, were surprised and delighted by *Vekhi*. The left, on the other hand, greeted its appearance with anger and derision.[18]

Much of the criticism was not only tendentious but disappointingly superficial. *Vekhi*'s readers were not informed of the rather haphazard way the collection had been put together, and many of the critics limited their comments to the inevitable inconsistencies among the authors. They also attacked Gershenzon, perceiving him as the central figure in the collection, although, as we have seen, his position was in fact anomalous. The passage most frequently singled out for censure was Gershenzon's assertion that the intelligentsia had to "bless" the government for protecting it with bayonets from the people's hostility. So loud was the outcry over this statement that Gershenzon found it necessary to qualify it in the second edition, while Struve publicly repudiated it as "morally and politically inaccurate and historically absurd."[19]

To a number of commentators, Gershenzon's statement in the Preface that the "common platform" of the *Vekhi* authors was their recognition of the "primacy of spiritual life over the external forms of community" was an expression of political quietism. An attentive reading of the articles themselves would have revealed that each of the authors—including Gershenzon—explicitly called for social and political change. It was not apparent, though, how they proposed to translate moral and spiritual reform into practical activity. Frank wrote later that there had been some thought of following *Vekhi* with a sequel that would have made positive recommendations, but this project was not carried out.[20] Finally, all the critics noticed that the "intelligentsia," supposedly the central focus of the book, was not defined with any degree of uniformity. Each author had his own definition, and these definitions generally contradicted each other. The points the authors were making would emerge only on sympathetic reading, and this the critics were utterly unwilling to give them.

Vekhi claimed to stand above politics; its critics denounced it in partisan terms. But the book's moral and cultural critique did in fact mask a predominantly political motive. The critics correctly perceived that it was an attack on the tradition that had unified the various opposition groups in the "liberation movement" that fought the autocracy up to the revolution of 1905. That movement had been based on the assumption that all who fought against the autocracy, liberals and socialists alike, shared a common cause, and that the differences among them were matters to be dealt with only after the primary aim of ending political oppression had been accomplished. The *Vekhi* authors condemned Russia's socialist parties, which in their view were almost solely concerned with encouraging revolutionary violence and class hatred. The liberals, probably the only people they hoped to convince by their work, should acknowledge that their own goals of political freedom and individual autonomy were incompatible with a political approach aimed at the disintegration of the country's social and political cohesion.[21] Political change should be a matter of educating the populace to the responsibilities of citizenship, not arousing it to spontaneous violence.

As it turned out, most liberals, well aware that they lacked substantial popular support, were unwilling to break their connection to the liberation movement. Nor could they agree with *Vekhi*'s demand that they call into question not only the ideas of the movement, but also the sacrifices its members had made over the years and the goals to which they had dedicated their lives. They therefore felt obliged to attack *Vekhi*, even when they actually agreed with much of its message, and to reaffirm traditional intelligentsia assumptions.[22] The socialist parties, on the other hand, targeted by *Vekhi* for failing in their mission to educate the people, and therefore responsible for the failure of the revolution, were even less likely to sympathize with *Vekhi*'s arguments. The ensuing debate indicates that most of the intelligentsia's spokesmen not only failed to agree with *Vekhi*'s answers, which was hardly unexpected, but refused even to acknowledge the relevance of the questions.

Not all the criticism of *Vekhi* was hostile, however, nor did all the praise come from conservatives. The artistic avant garde produced a defender in the person of Andrei Belyi, one of the outstanding symbolist poets and novelists.[23] Perhaps the most incisive favorable response was an article by Prince Evgenii Trubetskoi, a philosopher who had also contributed to the 1903 *Problems of Idealism*. Trubetskoi wrote from a position close to *Vekhi*; he published a magazine, *The Moscow Weekly* [Moskovskii ezhenedel'nik], with Struve and Berdiaev among its contributors, that attempted to further a Christian, gradualist liberalism. His sympathetic discussion of *Vekhi* was one of the few commentaries that actually explicated the issues raised by the book.[24] The daily newspaper *The Word* [Slovo] also shared some of the concerns and positions of the *Vekhi* authors and opened its columns to them. In other words, *Vekhi* did speak for a certain segment of Russia's educated, politically conscious class, albeit, as the book's reception demonstrated, a very small one.

* * *

After a year or so the *Vekhi* controversy died down, although the book remained well known and was frequently cited. The authors went their separate ways, and the revolution of 1917 found them divided by ideology, career, and geography. Struve and Kistiakovskii had quarreled during World War I, when Kistiakovskii's advocacy of Ukrainian autonomy clashed with Struve's Great Russian nationalism. After the revolution, Kistiakovskii went to Kiev and threw in his lot with the independent Ukraine. Struve briefly joined the White armies in the south of Russia, but in mid-1918 he returned to Moscow. Struve's prewar visibility as an increasingly conservative political journalist, coupled with his attachment to the White forces, made him more subject to repression by the Bolshevik government than the other *Vekhi* authors, and so he was forced to remain in hiding. Also in Moscow at the time were Berdiaev, Bulgakov, and Gershenzon. Berdiaev was teaching the godlessness of the Bolshevik revolution at the Free Academy of Spiritual Culture, which he had founded. Bulgakov, relieved by the separation of the Orthodox Church from the despotic state, had fulfilled his long-cherished dream to become a priest. Gershenzon made his peace with the Bolshevik regime because, in Berdiaev's words, "he sincerely believed that the devastating revolutionary storm would free the modern soul from the oppressive scales of excessive culture and knowledge."[25] Frank was in Saratov teaching at the university there.

The revolution and the turbulence of civil war revived interest in *Vekhi*. To authors and readers alike, the volume now appeared as a prophetic and tragically accurate warning of Russia's social, political, and cultural collapse. Struve felt the catastrophe called for new commentary, and in 1918 he organized all the original authors except Gershenzon and Kistiakovskii, along with six newcomers, in a new symposium entitled *Out of the Depths* [Iz glubiny]. Like the original authors, the newcomers were intellectuals who combined scholarship, journalism, and social engagement. Among them were Pavel Novgorodtsev, who had edited *Problems of Idealism* and had been one of the first to disseminate idealist views at the turn of the century, and the symbolist poet Viacheslav Ivanov. The book was apparently printed in the early autumn of 1918, but for political reasons was not distributed until 1921. It was then immediately confiscated by the authorities, and no more than two copies appear to have reached the West.[26] Only in the 1960s was it reprinted and made readily available.[27]

Out of the Depths was a very different book from *Vekhi*. The title came from the opening of Psalm 130, "Out of the depths have I cried unto thee, O Lord," and this set the tone for the entire volume. Every page reflected the authors' feeling that their familiar world was crashing down around them. Although it restated many of *Vekhi*'s major themes, it tended to be more bitter and personal. Above all, the religious element was much stronger. *Vekhi* had expressed, or implied, belief in some kind of objective order governing the universe, but the articles had concentrated their attention on specific aspects of the intelligentsia's political and cultural outlook. In *Out of the Depths* the Christian cycle of sin, repentance, and redemption recurred frequently, not merely as a metaphor for the revolution but as an explanation and solace for it. It is a poignant book, in which a group of cultivated, sensitive, and politically moderate intellectuals attempted to come to terms with a historical cataclysm. As a reaffirmation of some of *Vekhi*'s principles in the drastically changed circumstances of 1918, it provides an interesting philosophical and historical commentary on its more celebrated predecessor. But on the whole it lacks *Vekhi*'s substance and its insight into the condition of Russia.

Given the circumstances in which it was written, it was natural that the authors should regard the events of 1917–18 as a vindication of *Vekhi*. "The historian will note," Struve wrote in his preface, "that the majority of Russian educated society did not heed the warning it was given, not recognizing the great danger approaching the culture and the state."[28] But now, in this period of turmoil, the circle of people sympathetic to *Vekhi*'s themes widened, and others shared the authors' dismay at the nihilism of the Russian revolution. Maksim Gor'kii, for example, later a faithful adherent of the Bolshevik regime, was expressing very similar sentiments in his newspaper articles at this time. He complained that the revolution had awakened in the Russian people the basest instincts of lawlessness, anarchism, and lack of respect for human life, and that the Bolsheviks were encouraging these instincts. In terms strongly reminiscent of *Vekhi*, he called on the intelligentsia to educate the people to an appreciation of the value of human life, self-discipline, and love of labor—that is, to build the kind of civic culture that existed in the West.[29]

Gor'kii, like other writers distressed by the vandalism of the revolution, emigrated temporarily in 1921. The *Vekhi* debate also shifted to the emigration. In 1921 and 1922 controversy flared up again with the emergence of a short-lived school of thought among the Paris and Berlin exiles called "Change of Landmarks" [Smena vekh]. A collection of articles, and then a newspaper, by that name tried to use some of *Vekhi*'s ideas to justify reconciliation with the Soviet regime. In urging the intelligentsia to soften its opposition to Soviet rule, the adherents of this trend attempted to use the criticism *Vekhi* had voiced of the intelligentsia's revolutionism. Just as *Vekhi* had called on the intelligentsia to overcome its "dissociation" from the Russian state, national tradition, and cultural heritage, the "change of landmarks" writers urged it to reconcile itself to the Bolsheviks as the new guardians of the Russian state and culture.[30]

Within Russia, in what seemed almost a reprise of the *Vekhi* controversy, the *Change of Landmarks* [Smena vekh] collection elicited a counter-collection called *On Change of Landmarks* [O smene vekh], with A.S. Izgoev as one of its contributors. Outside Russia, Struve, who had emigrated by now, spoke out against *Change of Landmarks*. Both Izgoev and Struve used the occasion to reaffirm the principles of *Vekhi* and to denounce their exploitation and distortion. They rejected the notion that *Vekhi* could serve as an ideological bridge to Bolshevism, which they still regarded as incapable of providing the framework for the creative, self-disciplined society and culture that *Vekhi* had envisioned. With its atheism, its scorn for national tradition, and its commitment to international revolution, Bolshevism remained in their eyes an embodiment of the "nihilism" whose catastrophic consequences *Vekhi* had foretold.[31]

The "change of landmarks" debate was the last occasion on which the *Vekhi* symposium figured prominently in the Russian intelligentsia's discussions, although many of the book's themes continued to be expressed and developed in émigré literature. Despite their occasional collaborative efforts, each of the *Vekhi* authors had always pursued an independent political and philosophical course; now, more than ever, each followed his individual path in adjusting his life and thought to the circumstances created by the advent of Soviet rule. Kistiakovskii had died in 1920, during the civil war. Of the surviving six, only Gershenzon remained in Russia. He continued to write and teach until his death in Moscow in 1925.

The other five spent the rest of their lives in emigration in Western Europe. Struve, the first to leave Russia, remained the most political of the group. After going abroad in 1918 he maintained close contacts with anti-Bolshevik émigré groups, a policy that was to alienate him from his former *Vekhi* colleagues. Toward the end of 1922 the Soviet authorities expelled a large group of prominent scholars and writers, among whom were Izgoev, Frank, and Berdiaev; Bulgakov was expelled at the beginning of 1923. For the most part the later arrivals repudiated the White movement. They felt that Russia's salvation lay not in armed intervention but in some form of inner renewal of the Russian people.[32] Each now went his separate way. Struve devoted himself primarily to journalism and edited a series of Russian-language newspapers. He died in Paris in 1944. Izgoev also continued his journalistic career, contributing articles on current political and economic questions to various émigré publications. After spending several years in Prague he settled in Haapsalu, Estonia, where he died in 1935.

Bulgakov, Berdiaev, and Frank pursued their religious and philosophical careers. Bulgakov remained a prolific writer on theological subjects, and in 1925 he became the head of the newly created Orthodox Theological Institute in Paris. He taught there until his death in 1944. Berdiaev, to most Westerners the best known of the *Vekhi* authors, also eventually settled in Paris, as editor-in-chief of the YMCA Press. He continued to develop his religious philosophy, and also provided philosophical interpretations of the Russian and Bolshevik experience for Western readers. He died in Paris in 1948. Semen Frank lived in Germany, France, and finally England, where he died in 1950. In his nearly three decades of emigration he published a number of philosophical works and lectured throughout Europe.

* * *

Vekhi's historical visibility stems from the scope and intensity of the debate it touched off. Because the authors couched their arguments in general philosophical and cultural terms, assuming a stance above party politics, they produced a useful critique of the "positivist" outlook that dominated the pre-revolutionary Russian intelligentsia. Since that outlook was officially enshrined in the Marxist-Leninist ideology of the Soviet regime, *Vekhi* continued to play a role in Russian intellectual life. Official Soviet historiography carried on the somewhat off-target attack launched by Lenin in 1909. For some Soviet dissidents, on the other hand, *Vekhi* was a most useful part of their cultural heritage. It provided telling criticism of the regime's positions from a distinctively Russian, yet not illiberal, point of view. The absence of a genuine Russian liberal intellectual tradition made *Vekhi*'s assertion of liberal principles particularly important to Soviet dissent.

In a general sense, the revival of religious interest that marked the post-Stalin era showed affinities with *Vekhi*. On the one hand, this revival took the form of a search for "the meaning of life," which the official ideology was incapable of satisfying; on the other, it was one response to the moral disorientation that followed the disclosures of the atrocities of the Stalin years. Forms of worship were less important to it, on the whole, than religious thought as a source of moral and philosophical guidance. This revival awakened considerable interest in the Russian religious philosophers of the late nineteenth and early twentieth centuries, such as Vladimir Solov'ev, Berdiaev, and Bulgakov. Thus, the metaphysical, idealist, and religious motifs that marked *Vekhi* emerged once again in response to the cultural aridity and moral relativism of official Soviet ideology.[33]

Direct references to *Vekhi* could also be found in Soviet Russia's "underground" literature. A search for the roots of Stalinism led several writers to the volume and its analysis of the weakness and limitations of the intelligentsia's outlook. Nadezhda Mandel'shtam, widow of the great poet Osip Mandel'shtam, was one writer who used *Vekhi*. Her reminiscences of the thirties, *Hope Against Hope*, refer to the book specifically and embody a number of its themes, particularly the problem of moral relativism. She saw the origin of Stalinism in the transformation of Marxism into a new religion which invested man with a godlike authority over the future; the substitution of a relative "class truth" for absolute values; and a childlike fear of individual moral responsibility expressed in the desire to identify oneself totally with the revolution and the forces of history. Like the *Vekhi* authors, she concluded that the social and cultural values that make civilized life possible cannot be based on rationalism alone.[34]

Nadezhda Mandel'shtam and her husband were adults at the time of the revolution, and official doctrines never monopolized their viewpoint. Aleksandr Solzhenitsyn is a generation younger, and his search for the answers to the harsh moral questions raised by Stalinism led him to a rediscovery of the intellectual ferment of the decade preceding the revolution. Gor'kii's *Untimely Thoughts*, cited above, apparently first familiarized him with the type of cultural criticism found in *Vekhi*,[35] and *Vekhi* itself helped make him aware of Russian religious thought. The quest for the meaning of the present in the problems of the prerevolutionary period is manifested in his novel *August 1914*. One of the central characters is a sensitive student who is buffeted by the conflicting intellectual currents of the time. Among these influences is *Vekhi*, and upon reading it he finds it "the complete reverse of all he had read before, yet true, piercingly true!"[36] Later he is educated through contact with a number of unusual characters—a mysterious intellectual, a female university instructor, and a Jewish revolutionary-turned-capitalist—each of whom criticizes prevailing intellectual attitudes in terms very reminiscent of *Vekhi*.

The most striking evidence of *Vekhi*'s influence on dissident circles was the appearance in 1974 of *From Under the Rubble* [Iz-pod glyb], a collection of essays by the now exiled Solzhenitsyn and several intellectuals still in the Soviet Union. The book was in many respects modeled on *Vekhi* and, even more, on *Out of the Depths*, whose title it echoes. The new collection cited both of the earlier works and used a number of their motifs to examine Soviet life and the premises of Marxism-Leninism. In one of his essays, for example, Solzhenitsyn took *Vekhi*'s criticism of the prerevolutionary intelligentsia as a starting point for criticism of the Soviet educated elite of his own day, which he accused of moral and spiritual hypocrisy.[37] Although there were differences among the authors, as there were in *Vekhi* and *Out of the Depths*, many of them turned to religious thought as the only way out of the spiritual impasse they felt the prevailing ideology had created.

In some respects these critics diverged fundamentally from *Vekhi* itself, for they used the book merely as a point of departure, from which they reached quite different conclusions.[38] As a source of inspiration, however, *Vekhi*'s contribution to Soviet intellectual ferment was unmistakable. In reasserting the general ethical, cultural, and religious orientation that *Vekhi* upheld against the dogmatic rationalism, materialism, and moral relativism of Soviet Marxism-Leninism, these dissidents revived the debate that began more than seventy years earlier. In Solzhenitsyn's words, "the ulcers we are shown [in *Vekhi*] seem to belong not just to a past historical era, but in many respects to our own times as well."[39]

* * *

If *Vekhi* experienced a "second youth" in the sixties and seventies, as one dissident put it,[40] in more recent years it has undergone a veritable rebirth. With the advent of *glasnost'* in the late eighties and then the collapse of the Soviet Union it became possible for *Vekhi* to re-emerge into public view and become a prominent element in Russia's search for a "usable past." Familiarity with the book is no longer confined to a narrow stratum of intellectuals and academics. In the summer of 1990 the weekly newspaper *Moscow News* [Moskovskie novosti] hailed the first reprinting in Russia of this book "of legendary significance."[41] Three other editions have subsequently appeared, bringing the total number of copies to an astonishing 215,000.[42] (By comparison, the five editions of *Vekhi* issued in 1909–10 totaled 15,000 copies.)

One example of the open discussion of *Vekhi* in the period of *perestroika* was a book titled *Is Stalinism Really Dead?* by the philosopher Aleksandr Tsipko.[43] While continuing to express a commitment to socialism, and cautiously shielding Lenin from the criticism leveled against other Bolshevik leaders, Tsipko traced the roots of Stalinism to the leftist extremism and "apocalyptic view of history" which the prerevolutionary intelligentsia harbored. In criticizing this view he included a number of citations to *Vekhi*. For the most part, however, he did not go beyond the position of the dissidents of the sixties and seventies. At a time when Khrushchev's revelations about Stalin had undermined confidence in Soviet principles, but there still seemed little immediate hope of achieving fundamental change in the system, the dissidents had regarded *Vekhi* primarily as a warning against the ethical relativism of a "class morality." Similarly, Tsipko used *Vekhi* to issue a call for firm moral values as the basis for reform.

As *perestroika* and then the post-Soviet rebuilding of Russian institutions proceeded, however, the most recent commentators have looked to *Vekhi* for more concrete inspiration in the task of renewal. Like the authors of *Out of the Depths* in 1918, they agree that the intelligentsia's revolutionary mentality led Russia into a catastrophic "blind alley," just as *Vekhi* had predicted it would. They view the now-repudiated ideology of Marxism-Leninism as the embodiment of that mentality, and *Vekhi* has become part of their arsenal of weapons against it.[44] As a result, *Vekhi* has come to be viewed both in a broadly cultural light and in a more specifically political one.

On the one hand, *Vekhi* represents a channel to the intellectual and philosophical ferment of the Silver Age, a link to the time "before Russian history stopped."[45] There has been a considerable revival of interest in Russia's prerevolutionary philosophers: almost every issue of Russia's leading philosophical journal, *Problems of Philosophy* [Voprosy filosofii], published by the Academy of Sciences, contains articles about or selections from the writings of prominent philosophers of the Silver Age, and among them the *Vekhi* authors are well represented. Publication of archival materials is enabling scholars to understand the creation of the volume more clearly and accurately.[46] Given the resurgence of traditional values in present-day Russia, as well as the danger that those values may take a reactionary turn, *Vekhi* represents a moderate and responsible treatment of religious and metaphysical motifs that can serve as a springboard for contemporary discussion.

At the same time, as post-Soviet Russia seeks to build new, more democratic institutions, *Vekhi* serves as a link with the liberalism of the prerevolutionary era. Freed from Lenin's summary judgment of *Vekhi* as "an encyclopedia of liberal renegadism," Russian scholars are now able to investigate the effort of the *Vekhi* authors to find a liberal, reformist path between the maximalism of the radical intelligentsia and the policies of the tsarist government. As P.P. Gaidenko, writing in *Problems of Philosophy*, put it, *Vekhi* represented a centrist position, "which as a rule is stronger than the extreme poles but in Russia, alas, was weaker, and was subjected to withering criticism both by the right and by the left."[47]

Thus, a number of themes in *Vekhi* have prompted the "rediscovery" of the book in post-Soviet Russia and made it once again a vital part of Russian intellectual life. The most original and valuable of those themes is the broad vision of social life that informed its criticism of the intelligentsia. *Vekhi* argued that the true purpose of human life is to master natural and social forces through conscious, disciplined creativity. "Wealth," "productivity," "abundance," "enrichment" in every sense—spiritual, intellectual, and cultural, as well as material—are words that recurred throughout the articles and, in various forms, in the authors' other works as well. (Gershenzon, with his Tolstoian view of culture, is something of an exception here, but even he urged the intelligentsia to cultivate and enrich its personal life.) This is the conception they opposed to the intelligentsia's ideology of radicalism, with its woefully oversimplified view of human happiness and fulfillment. They called on the intelligentsia to repudiate its "nihilism" and to lay the positive intellectual and moral foundations for building a viable civil society, a meaningful national identity, and a rich and creative culture. The urgency of this task in post-Soviet Russia has given this voice from the past not only a remarkable new birth but a new, broad, and perhaps more receptive audience.

Notes

1. For Gershenzon's biography and views, see Arthur A. Levin, "The Life and Work of Mikhail Osipovich Gershenzon (1869–1925): A Study in the History of the Russian Silver Age" (Doctoral Dissertation, University of California, Berkeley, 1968); and *idem*, "The Making of a Russian Scholar: The Apprenticeship of M.O. Gershenzon," *California Slavic Studies*, 7 (1974), 99–120. A summary of his career can be found in the introduction to James P. Scanlan's translation of Gershenzon's *A History of Young Russia* [Istoriia molodoi Rossii] (Irvine, Calif.: Charles Schlacks Jr., Publisher, 1986). Donald Davies, "Mikhail Gershenzon's 'Secret Voice': The Making of a Cultural Nihilist," in Charles Timberlake, ed., *Religious and Secular Forces in Late Tsarist Russia: Essays in Honor of Donald W. Treadgold* (Seattle and London: University of Washington Press, 1992), pp. 168–84, provides insight into the views Gershenzon expressed in his *Vekhi* article.

2. Nicolas Berdyaev, *Dream and Reality: An Essay in Autobiography*, trans. Katherine Lampert (New York: Collier, 1963) remains the best source for Berdiaev's life, though it is far from accurate in detail and the translation is faulty.

3. It is quite probable that the "new religious consciousness" was influenced by the nineteenth-century rediscovery and interpretation of the works of Joachim of Flora. See Marjorie Reeves, *Joachim of Fiore and the Myth of the Eternal Evangel in the Nineteenth Century* (Oxford: Clarendon Press, 1987).

4. Although episodic and primarily concerned with his religious development, Bulgakov's *Avtobiograficheskie zametki (Posmertnoe izdanie)* (Paris: YMCA-Press, 1946) contains some biographical information. A brief character sketch of Bulgakov as a teacher appears in Nikolay Valentinov, *Encounters with Lenin*, trans. Paul Rosta and Brian Pearce (London: Oxford University Press, 1968), pp. 155–59.

5. Information on Izgoev is meager. Some details about his life appeared in two obituary articles published in *Segodnia* (Riga), 12 July 1935, p. 1, and 13 July 1935, p. 2.

6. For biographical information on Kistiakovskii, see Susan Eva Heuman, "Bogdan Kistiakovskii and the Problem of Human Rights in the Russian Empire, 1899–1917" (Ph.D. Dissertation, Columbia University, 1977) and Heuman's biography of Kistiakovskii, forthcoming from the Harvard Ukrainian Research Institute Press.

7. For Struve's biography, see Richard Pipes, *Struve*, 2 vols. (Cambridge, Mass.: Harvard University Press, 1970, 1980).

8. Biographical information on Frank can be found in S.L. Frank, *Biografiia P.B. Struve* (New York: Chekhov, 1956), and Vasilii Zenkovskii, ed., *Sbornik pamiati Semena Liudvigovicha Franka* (Munich, 1954).

9. Gershenzon to his brother, A.O. Gershenzon, 15 November 1908, cited in B. Proskurinaia and V. Alloi, "K istorii sozidaniia 'Vekh,' " *Minuvshee: Istoricheskii al'manakh*, vol. 11 (Moscow–St. Petersburg: Atheneum Feniks, 1992), p. 282.

10. Berdiaev, according to Frank, was "one of the few writers who has spoken boldly and freely against the intelligentsia." Frank to Gershenzon, 19 October 1908, *ibid.*, p. 252. Bulgakov's Orthodoxy would provide an important rebuttal to the religious radicalism of Merezhkovskii. Frank to Gershenzon, 16 November 1908, *ibid.*, p. 283.

11. Gershenzon to A.O. Gershenzon, 15 November 1908, *ibid.*, p. 282.

12. General treatments of the Silver Age include: Nicolas Zernov, *The Russian Religious Renaissance of the Twentieth Century* (New York: Harper & Row, 1963); and George Frederick Putnam, *Russian Alternatives to Marxism: Christian Socialism and Idealistic Liberalism in Twentieth-Century Russia* (Knoxville: University of Tennessee Press, 1977). Several articles dealing with cultural matters appear in Theofanis George Stavrou, ed., *Russia Under the Last Tsar* (Minneapolis: University of Minnesota Press, 1969); and George Katkov et al., eds., *Russia Enters the Twentieth Century, 1894–1917* (London: Temple Smith, 1971). On the specific case of Nietzsche's influence, see Edith W. Clowes, *The Revolution of Moral Consciousness: Nietzsche in Russian Literature, 1890–1914* (DeKalb: Northern Illinois University Press, 1988). Berdiaev's *Dream and Reality* is an important source for this period. Other source material can be found in Carl Proffer and Ellendea Proffer, eds., *The Silver Age of Russian Culture* (Ann Arbor: Ardis, 1975) and Martha Bohachevsky-Chomiak and Bernice Glatzer Rosenthal, eds., *A Revolution of the Spirit: Crisis of Value in Russia, 1890–1918* (Newtonville, Mass.: Oriental Research Partners, 1982). On changing sexual attitudes, see Laura Engelstein, *The Keys to Happiness: Sex and the Search for Modernity in Fin-de-siècle Russia* (Ithaca: Cornell University Press, 1992).

13. On the early thought of the *Vekhi* authors, see Richard Kindersley, *The First Russian Revisionists: A Study of 'Legal Marxism' in Russia* (Oxford: Clarendon Press, 1962); and Arthur P. Mendel, *Dilemmas of Progress in Tsarist Russia: Legal Marxism and Legal Populism* (Cambridge, Mass.: Harvard University Press, 1961).

14. P.N. Novgorodtsev, ed., *Problemy idealizma: Sbornik statei* (Moscow: Izdanie Moskovskogo psikhologicheskogo obshchestva, 1903).

15. Judith Zimmerman, "Russian Liberal Theory, 1900–1917," *Canadian-American Slavic Studies,* 14, no. 1 (Spring 1980), 16.

16. S. Spiro, "L.N. Tolstoi o 'Vekhakh,'" *Russkoe slovo,* 21 May 1909, p. 2; for the text of Tolstoi's unpublished article, see L.N. Tolstoi, "[O 'Vekhakh']," *Polnoe sobranie sochinenii,* Jubilee ed., 90 vols. (Moscow: Gosudarstvennoe izdatel'stvo khudozhestvennoi literatury, 1928–1985), 38: 285–90, 571–73.

17. V.I. Lenin, "O 'Vekhakh,'" *Sochineniia,* 4th ed., 45 vols. (Moscow: Gosudarstvennoe izdatel'stvo politicheskoi literatury, 1941–67), 16: 106–14.

18. A.I. Stolypin, "Intelligenty ob intelligentakh," *Novoe vremia,* 23 April 1909, p. 4; and "Eshche o 'Vekhakh,'" *ibid.,* 28 April 1909, pp. 3–4. For an analysis of the various parties' responses, see Gisela Oberländer, "Die Vechi-Diskussion (1909–1912)" (Ph.D. Dissertation, Cologne, 1965). Two other accounts of the debate, the first sympathetic to *Vekhi* and the second sympathetic to its critics, are Leonard Schapiro, "The *Vekhi* Group and the Mystique of Revolution," *The Slavonic and East European Review,* 34, no. 1 (December 1955), 56–76; and Jeffrey Brooks, "*Vekhi* and the *Vekhi* Dispute," *Survey,* 19, no. 1 (86) (Winter 1973), 21–50. See also Christopher Read, *Religion, Revolution and the Russian Intelligentsia, 1900–1912: The Vekhi Debate and Its Intellectual Background* (Totowa, N.J.: Barnes and Noble, 1979).

19. P. Struve, "Razmyshleniia," *Slovo,* 25 April 1909, p. 2. Gershenzon subsequently published a collection of his articles, *Istoricheskie zapiski o russkom obshchestve* (Moscow, 1910), which reprinted his *Vekhi* article in somewhat altered form and omitted the offending sentence. Struve, in his review of the collection, commented, "Better late than never." "Na raznye temy," *Russkaia mysl'* (December 1909), p. 188. Berdiaev, on the other hand, felt the statement should remain as it was. Berdiaev to Gershenzon, 14 May 1909, Proskurinaia and Alloi, "K istorii sozidaniia 'Vekh,'" p. 279.

20. Frank, *Struve,* pp. 87–88.

21. The *Vekhi* authors were by no means opposed to social welfare programs or state involvement in economic life. They believed that the Russian socialist parties' all-out rejection of the existing state was incompatible with any positive approach to social organization, even after the tsarist state had been transformed.

22. See, for example, the rebuttal by the leader of the Kadet Party, Pavel Miliukov, "Intelligentsiia i istoricheskaia traditsiia," *Intelligentsiia v Rossii: Sbornik statei* (St. Petersburg: Zemlia, 1910), pp. 89–192.

23. Andrei Belyi, "Pravda o russkoi intelligentsii: Po povodu sbornika *'Vekhi,'*" *Vesy* (May 1909), pp. 65–68.

24. Kn. Evgenii Trubetskoi, "*'Vekhi'* i ikh kritiki," *Moskovskii ezhenedel'nik*, 12 June 1909, pp. 1–18.

25. Berdyaev, *Dream and Reality*, p. 230.

26. Frank, *Struve*, pp. 120–21.

27. *Iz glubiny: Sbornik statei o russkoi revoliutsii*, 2nd ed. (Paris: YMCA-Press, 1967), p. 25. There is also an English translation by William F. Woehrlin, *Out of the Depths: A Collection of Articles on the Russian Revolution* (Irvine, Calif.: Charles Schlacks, Jr., Publisher, 1986).

28. Woehrlin, trans., *Out of the Depths*, p. xxxix.

29. Maxim Gorky, *Untimely Thoughts: Essays on Revolution, Culture and the Bolshevivks, 1917–1918*, trans. Herman Ermolaev (New York: Paul S. Ericksson, 1968).

30. The first edition of *Smena vekh: Sbornik statei* was printed in Prague in 1921, and a second edition in 1922. Twenty issues of the weekly newspaper *Smena vekh* were printed in Paris from October 1921 to March 1922. On the "change of landmarks" controversy, see Erwin Oberländer, "Nationalbolschewistische Tendenzen in der russischen Intelligenz: Die 'Smena Vech'—Diskussion 1921–1922," *Jahrbücher für Geschichte Osteuropas*, 16, no. 2 (June 1968), 194–211; Robert C. Williams, "Changing Landmarks in Russian Berlin, 1922–1924," *Slavic Review*, 27, no. 4 (December 1968), 581–93; and Mikhail Agurskii, *Ideologiia natsional-bol'shevizma* (Paris: YMCA-Press, 1980). A full-length study is Hilde Hardeman, *Coming to Terms with the Soviet Regime: The "Changing Signposts" Movement Among Russian Émigrés in the Early 1920s* (DeKalb: Northern Illinois University Press, 1994).

31. A.S. Izgoev, "*'Vekhi'* i 'Smena vekh,'" in *O smene vekh* (Petrograd: "Logos," 1922), pp. 7–24; Petr Struve, "Proshloe, nastoiashchee, budushchee: Mysli o natsional'nom vozrozhdenii Rossii," *Russkaia mysl'* (Prague) (January–February 1922), pp. 222–31.

32. Frank, *Struve*, pp. 128–33.

33. See, for example, James H. Billington, *The Icon and the Axe: An Interpretive History of Russian Culture* (New York: Alfred A. Knopf, 1966), pp. 579–83; and Peter Reddaway, "Freedom of Worship and the Law," in Abraham Brumberg, ed., *In Quest of Justice: Protest and Dissent in the Soviet Union Today* (New York: Frederick A. Praeger, 1970), pp. 62–75. A collection of articles devoted to this subject is W.C. Fletcher and A.J. Strover, eds., *Religion and the Search for New Ideals in the USSR* (New York: Frederick A. Praeger, 1967).

34. Nadezhda Mandelstam, *Hope Against Hope: A Memoir*, trans. Max Hayward (New York: Atheneum, 1970), pp. 64, 162–69, 329.

35. Aleksandr I. Solzhenitsyn, *The Gulag Archipelago*, I, trans. Thomas P. Whitney (New York: Harper & Row, 1974), p. 194.

36. Alexander Solzhenitsyn, *August 1914*, trans. Michael Glenny (New York: Farrar, Straus & Giroux, 1972), p. 20.

37. A. Solzhenitsyn, "Obrazovanshchina," *Iz-pod glyb: Sbornik statei* (Paris:

YMCA-Press, 1974), pp. 217–59. See also the translation by A.M. Brock et al., *From Under the Rubble* (Boston: Little, Brown, 1975).

38. See Marshall S. Shatz, *"From Under the Rubble* and its Predecessors," *Canadian-American Slavic Studies*, 10, no. 1 (Spring 1976), 111–17.

39. Solzhenitsyn, "Obrazovanshchina," p. 217.

40. M. Meerson-Aksenov, "Rozhdenie novoi intelligentsii," in P. Litvinov et al., eds., *Samosoznanie: sbornik statei* (New York: "Khronika," 1976), p. 89.

41. *Moskovskie novosti*, No. 31, 5 August 1990, p. 2. The edition of *Vekhi* was published in Moscow by Novosti, 1990.

42. These editions are as follows: Sverdlovsk: Izdatel'stvo Ural'skogo universiteta, 1991; Moscow: Izdatel'stvo "Pravda," 1991, an edition which also contains a reprinting of *Iz glubiny*; and Moscow: "Molodaia gvardiia," 1991, which also contains a reprinting of *Intelligentsiia v Rossii*.

43. Alexander S. Tsipko, *Is Stalinism Really Dead?* trans. E.A. Tichina and S.V. Nikheev (San Francisco: HarperSanFrancisco, 1990). See also Professor V. Sirotkin, " 'Vekhi': K 80-letiiu 'Sbornika statei o russkoi intelligentsii,' " which appeared in *Uchitel'skaia gazeta* [The Teachers' Newspaper], 25 November 1989, p. 4. This curious article, which appeared in a publication of the Central Committee of the Soviet Communist Party, used *Vekhi* to argue for a moderate, nonradical course of reform in the era of *perestroika*, citing *Vekhi*'s criticism of "worship of the people" and its fear of popular anarchy.

44. For a Western example of this type of use of *Vekhi*, see Gary Saul Morson, "What is the Intelligentsia? Once More, an Old Russian Question," *Academic Questions* (Summer 1993), 20–38. Morson links *Vekhi* with an entire counter-intelligentsia tradition in his "Prosaic Bakhtin: *Landmarks*, Anti-Intelligentsialism, and the Russian Counter-Tradition," *Common Knowledge*, 2, no. 1 (Spring 1993), 35–74.

45. Aleksandr Tsipko, "Neobkhodimo potriasenie mysl'iu," *Moskovskie novosti*, no. 26, 1 July 1990, p. 3. This brief article was originally intended as a preface to the 1990 edition of *Vekhi*, but was not printed in the volume.

46. See, for example, the editorial notes to the 1991 "Pravda" edition, pp. 500–507, as well as the letters from *Vekhi* authors to Gershenzon in Proskurinaia and Alloi, "K istorii sozidaniia 'Vekh,' " cited in note 9 above.

47. P.P. Gaidenko, " '*Vekhi*': neuslyshannoe predosterezhenie," *Voprosy filosofii*, no. 2, 1992, p. 106. For an English translation, see *Russian Studies in Philosophy*, 32, no. 1 (Summer 1993), 16–46.

A Note on the Text

The present translation of *Vekhi* (Landmarks) is a reworking of the version which appeared in the journal *Canadian Slavic Studies* (Montreal) in eight issues between 1968 and 1971, which is no longer available. The footnotes and annotations almost all come from this earlier edition, with only minor changes. The text, however, has been substantially modified in an effort to achieve greater accuracy and fluency.

The translation has been made from the second edition of *Vekhi*, which followed the first by about two months and contained some of the authors' replies to their critics. There were no other significant changes. The three subsequent editions were unchanged, except for the bibliography appended to the fifth edition, which is included in this translation.

The seven articles that comprise the volume were printed in alphabetical order by author according to the Russian alphabet; that order has been retained in the translation. Explanatory notes by the editors are indicated by the signature "*eds.*"; all other notes belong to the original authors. Names and terms mentioned in the text are identified in the Guide to Names and Terms.

A simplified Library of Congress system has been used in transliterating Russian names, with pre-revolutionary orthography modernized. Throughout the book, dates have been given according to Russian usage prevailing at the time (i.e., Old Style before 1918, and New Style thereafter). Biblical quotations are according to the King James Version.

The editors would like to thank Mary Walsh for her patience and stamina in typing the entire manuscript.

Preface to the First Edition

The aim of the articles in this collection is not to pass a doctrinaire judgment on the Russian intelligentsia from the height of established truth; they were not written with contempt for the intelligentsia's past, but with anguish for it and with burning concern for our country's future. The revolution of 1905-06 and the events that followed it served as a nation-wide test of those values which our social thought had preserved for more than half a century as something of the utmost sanctity. Long before the revolution a few minds, working deductively, had clearly perceived the error of these spiritual principles; on the other hand, the practical failure of a social movement does not in itself, of course, testify to the inherent falseness of the ideas which gave rise to it. Thus, the intelligentsia's defeat did not reveal anything essentially new. But it had enormous significance in another sense. In the first place, the entire intelligentsia was deeply shaken by its defeat and felt the need for a conscious, fundamental re-examination of its traditional world-view, which hitherto it had blindly accepted on faith. Secondly, the details of the events, that is, the concrete forms which the revolution and its suppression took, enabled those who had recognized the erroneousness of this world-view in general terms to comprehend the sins of the past more clearly and to provide more evidence for their position.

And so, this book was born. Its contributors could not keep silent about those things which for them had become manifest truth. Furthermore, they were guided by the conviction that their critique of the intelligentsia's spiritual foundations would help meet the generally recognized need that these be re-examined.

The men who have joined forces here differ greatly among themselves both on basic questions of "faith" and in their practical preferences; but there are no disagreements on this joint enterprise. Their common platform is the recognition of the theoretical and practical primacy of spiritual life over the external forms of community. They mean by this that the individual's inner life is the sole creative force in human existence, and that this inner life, and not the self-sufficient principles of the political realm, constitutes the only solid basis on which a society can be built. Since they hold this view, the contributors see the Russian intelligentsia's ideology, which rests entirely on the opposite principle—recognition of the unconditional primacy of social forms—as inherently erroneous and futile in practice. That is, it both contradicts the nature of the human spirit and is incapable of achieving the goal which the intelligentsia has set for itself, the emancipation of the people.

Within the framework of this general idea the contributors have no disagreements. Proceeding from it, they investigate the intelligentsia's world-view
from various angles. If on occasion they seem to contradict one another, on
the question of the intelligentsia's "religious" nature, for example, this stems
not from a difference of opinion on fundamental premises but from the fact
that the different contributors are investigating the question on different levels.

We do not judge the past, because its historical inevitability is clear to us;
but we do point out that the path society has taken up to now has led it into
a blind alley. Our warnings are not new: all of our most profound thinkers,
from Chaadaev to Solov'ev and Tolstoi, said the same things again and again.
They were not heeded, the intelligentsia passed them by. Perhaps now, awakened by a great shock, it will listen to weaker voices.

Mikhail Gershenzon

VEKHI

PHILOSOPHICAL VERITY AND INTELLIGENTSIA TRUTH

Nikolai Berdiaev

Now that the intelligentsia is undergoing a crisis and becoming aware of its errors, and old ideologies are being re-evaluated, we must also consider our attitude to philosophy. The Russian intelligentsia's traditional attitude to philosophy is more complex than might appear at first glance, and analysis of it may reveal the basic spiritual features of the intelligentsia's world. I am using "intelligentsia" in the traditional Russian sense of the word, to mean our sectarian intellectuals who are artificially isolated from national life. This unique community has hitherto led a cloistered existence, oppressed by two kinds of rigid conformity: the external conformity imposed by a reactionary government and an internal conformity imposed by intellectual inertia and emotional conservatism. There is good reason for calling this group "*intelligenty*," as distinct from "intellectuals" in the broad national and historical sense of the word. Those Russian philosophers whom the intelligentsia chooses to ignore, whom it relegates to another, hostile world, are genuine intellectuals, but they are foreign to the spirit of the intelligentsia.

Just what has been the traditional attitude of our intellectual cliques to philosophy, an attitude that remained constant despite the rapid change in philosophical fashions? We have always combined an underlying conservatism and inertia with a penchant for novelties, for the latest European trends, which we have never fully assimilated. This was the case in regard to philosophy as well.

The first thing that strikes the observer is that our approach to philosophy was just as shallow as our approach to other spiritual values: we denied the autonomous significance of philosophy and instead subordinated it to utilitarian social goals. We were dominated, wholly and despotically, by a utilitarian moral standard, and also wholly and oppressively governed by love for the people and the proletariat. We worshipped "the people," their welfare and interests, and were spiritually depressed by political despotism. All this resulted in a very low level of philosophical culture, and our intelligentsia displayed little learning or accomplishment in this area. Only scattered individuals possessed a high philosophical culture, and this in itself set them apart from the world of the intelligentsia. It was not simply that we lacked philosophical learning—that could have been remedied—but our temperament and our whole standard of values served to block our comprehension of genuine philosophy and made philosophical creation seem a phenomenon from a different and mysterious world. Perhaps a few people did read philosophy books and to all

1

appearances understood what they read, but inwardly they communed as little with the world of philosophical creation as with the world of beauty.

The reason for this was not intellectual deficiency but an act of volition: we willed the creation of that traditional intelligentsia milieu which absorbed the Populist world-view and utilitarian ethic into its flesh and blood, and which stubbornly persists to this day. We long considered it almost immoral to devote oneself to philosophy, regarding this sort of occupation as a betrayal of the people and the people's cause. A person too deeply engrossed in philosophical questions was suspected of indifference to the peasants' and workers' interests. The intelligentsia took an ascetic view of philosophy; it demanded abstinence in the name of its god—the people—in order to conserve its strength for the struggle with the devil—absolutism. This Populist, utilitarian, ascetic attitude to philosophy persisted even in those intelligentsia groups which seemed to transcend Populism and reject crude utilitarianism, for it was an attitude embedded in the subconscious. The psychological principles underlying this attitude to philosophy and, indeed, to the creation of spiritual values in general, can be expressed as follows: *in the thought and feelings of the Russian intelligentsia, the claims of distribution and equalization always outweighed the claims of production and creation.* This applies equally to the material and the spiritual realms, for the Russian intelligentsia regarded philosophical creation in precisely the same way as it regarded economic production.

The intelligentsia was always eager to accept an ideology that gave primacy to the problems of distribution and equality while relegating creation to the background: then its trust was boundless. But an ideology that concentrated on creation and values aroused its suspicions and a preconceived determination to reject and expose it. This attitude ruined N. K. Mikhailovskii's philosophical talent, just as it destroyed the great artistic talent of Gleb Uspenskii. Many abstained from philosophical and artistic creation because they considered it immoral from the standpoint of furthering distribution and equality and saw it as a betrayal of the people's welfare. There was even a time, in the seventies, when reading books and increasing one's knowledge were not considered particularly valuable pursuits, and a thirst for education was morally condemned. This period of Populist obscurantism is long since over, but the bacillus has remained in our blood. Knowledge, creation, the higher life of the spirit were persecuted again during the revolution, and even today the infection persists. The same moral judgments prevail, whatever new terms may have been adopted on the surface. To this day our educated youth cannot admit the autonomous value of science, philosophy, education and universities; to this day it submits to the claims of politics, parties, trends and cliques. The defenders of unconditional and independent knowledge, knowledge as a principle that transcends everyday concerns, are still suspected of reaction. And always, the Ministry of Education made no small contribution to this disrespect for the sanctity of knowledge. In this sphere, too, political absolutism has so crippled the soul of the progressive intelligentsia that a new spirit is making its way into the consciousness of the young only with difficulty.[1]

But it cannot be said that philosophical themes and problems were foreign to the Russian intelligentsia. We can even say that our intelligentsia was always interested in questions of a philosophical nature, though not in their philosophical formulation. It managed to give even the most practical social concerns a philosophical character: it transformed the concrete and the particular into the abstract and the general; it saw the agrarian and labor problems as problems of universal salvation, and it gave sociological doctrines an almost theological color. Our journalism reflected this tendency, for it taught the meaning of life and tended to be abstract and philosophical rather than concrete and practical, even when examining economic issues. Westernism and Slavophilism were philosophical, and not merely journalistic, schools. Belinskii, one of the fathers of the Russian intelligentsia, knew little philosophy and never mastered philosophical method, but all his life he was tormented by the "cursed questions," universal and philosophical in nature. The same philosophical questions preoccupy the heroes of Tolstoi and Dostoevskii.

In the sixties philosophy was in a decline and was shunted aside. Iurkevich was scorned, although compared to Chernyshevskii he was at least a genuine philosopher. But even then the enthusiasm for materialism, the most primitive and elementary form of philosophizing, reflected an interest in philosophical and universal questions. The Russian intelligentsia wished to live and to determine its attitude to the most practical and prosaic aspects of social life on the basis of a materialist catechism and metaphysics.

In the seventies the intelligentsia was carried away by positivism; its mentor, N. K. Mikhailovskii, was a philosopher in terms of his intellectual interests and scope, but he lacked genuine training and erudition. For philosophical substantiation of its revolutionary social aspirations the intelligentsia turned to P. L. Lavrov, a man of great erudition and breadth of intellect, though devoid of creative talent. And Lavrov did give philosophical sanction to the aspirations of the young people—generally taking the creation of the universe as the point of departure for his argument.

The intelligentsia always had its own domestic philosophers and its own tendentious philosophy, cut off from world philosophical traditions. This home-grown, almost sect-like philosophy satisfied the profound need of our intelligentsia youth for a "world-view" that would provide answers to all the

---

1. *Note to the Second Edition.* The accuracy of my characterization of the intelligentsia's psychology has been strikingly confirmed by the character of the polemic that *Vekhi* has touched off. I did not anticipate, however, that the inability to criticize the essence of *Vekhi*'s work of spiritual reform would prove so universal.

fundamental questions of life and would unite theory with social practice. Our *intelligenty*'s need for an integrated social and philosophical world-view is vital when they are young, and they accepted as their mentors only those who, from a general theory, derived a sanction for their libertarian social aspirations, democratic instincts, and demand for justice at any price. In this respect, the classical "philosophers" of the intelligentsia were Chernyshevskii and Pisarev in the sixties, and Lavrov and Mikhailovskii in the seventies. These writers contributed almost nothing to philosophy or to the nation's spiritual culture, but they did answer the need of the educated youth for a world-view, and they provided the intelligentsia's vital aspirations with a theoretical basis. To this day they remain its teachers and are lovingly read in early youth.

In the nineties, with the emergence of Marxism, the intelligentsia's intellectual interests developed considerably. The young people became more European and began to read scholarly works, and the purely emotional Populist character-type began to change under the impact of this current of intellectualism. Dialectical materialism and then neo-Kantianism began to satisfy the need for a philosophical sanction for the intelligentsia's social aspirations, although the latter did not become very popular because of its philosophical complexity. Bel'tov-Plekhanov, who ousted Mikhailovskii from the hearts of the young people, became the "philosopher" of the day. Then Avenarius and Mach appeared on the scene, heralded as the philosophical saviors of the proletariat, and Messrs. Bogdanov and Lunacharskii became the "philosophers" of the Social-Democratic intelligentsia. (Idealist and mystical currents arose from another direction, but this was a totally different stream in Russian culture.) But the Marxists' victories over Populism did not lead to a fundamental crisis within the Russian intelligentsia—even in the European garb of Marxism it remained Populist, true to the old belief. By professing Social-Democratic theory the intelligentsia was denying its own existence, but in Russia this theory too became merely an ideology of the traditional cliques. The attitude toward philosophy remained unchanged, except for that critical tendency in Marxism which later turned into idealism, but which was never very popular with the intelligentsia.[2]

For most members of the intelligentsia, interest in philosophy was limited to their need for philosophical sanction of their social sentiments and aspirations. These were neither shaken nor re-evaluated as a result of philosophical reflection; they remained fixed, like dogmas. The intelligentsia does not care whether Mach's theory of knowledge, to take one example, is true or false; its only concern is whether or not this theory favors the idea of socialism, whether it serves the welfare and interests of the proletariat. It does not care if meta-

2. Berdiaev is referring here to himself and most of his *Vekhi* collaborators, who constituted almost the entirety of the "critical" (neo-Kantian) tendency in Marxism. *Eds.*

physics is possible, or if metaphysical truths exist; its only concern is whether metaphysics harms the people's interests by distracting attention from the struggle with autocracy and from service to the proletariat. The intelligentsia is prepared to accept on faith any philosophy that sanctions its social ideals, while it will reject uncritically even the truest and most profound one if it is suspected of being unfavorably disposed toward these traditional sentiments and ideals, or even merely critical of them. The hostility to both idealism and religious mysticism and the neglect of an original Russian philosophy that is full of creative promise are rooted in this "Catholic" psychology. The greater part of the intelligentsia still holds social utilitarianism in all value judgments and worship of "the people"—now defined as the peasantry, now as the proletariat—as moral dogmas. Even Kant began to find readers only because critical Marxism promised to base the socialist ideal on his thought. Then we set to work on the quite indigestible Avenarius, for his extremely abstract and "pure" philosophy, unbeknown to him and through no fault of his own, suddenly presented itself as the philosophy of the Social-Democratic Bolsheviks.

This peculiar approach to philosophy of course revealed our thorough cultural shallowness, our primitive lack of discrimination, our feeble awareness of the unconditional value of truth, and our mistaken moral judgment. Independent speculative interests have always been weak in Russia. But our intellectual traditions also revealed the promise of positive and valuable qualities: a thirst for an integral world-view that would fuse theory and life, and a thirst for faith. The intelligentsia is justifiably suspicious of and hostile toward abstract academicism, the dissection of living truth, and in its demand for an integral view of the world and of life one can discern a streak of unconscious religiosity.

We must, however, sharply distinguish the "right hand" from the "left hand" in the intelligentsia's traditional psychology. We should not idealize the weakness of its theoretical philosophical interests, its low level of philosophical culture, the absence of serious philosophical learning, and the incapacity for serious philosophical reflection. Nor should we idealize the almost insane tendency to judge philosophical doctrines and truths according to political and utilitarian criteria, and the inability to examine philosophical and cultural achievements in their essence, from the point of view of their absolute value. Right now the intelligentsia needs self-criticism, not self-adulation. We can come to a new consciousness only by way of repentance and self-indictment. In the reactionary eighties there were some who praised our conservative, truly Russian virtues, and Vladimir Solov'ev performed an important task when he censured this part of society and called for self-criticism and repentance, for the revelation of our ills.[3] Then came a time when people began to

3. In the 1880s Solov'ev conducted a lengthy critique of Slavophilism, in the course

speak of our radical, but still truly Russian, virtues. Now this other part of society must be exhorted to self-criticism, repentance, and exposure of ills. Improvement is impossible for one enraptured by his own virtues, for such rapture dims even truly shining qualities.

Its historical situation brought this misfortune upon the Russian intelligentsia: *love for egalitarian justice, for social good, for the people's welfare, paralyzed love for the truth and almost destroyed any interest in truth.* But philosophy is a school of love for the truth, for the truth above all. The intelligentsia could not take a disinterested approach to philosophy because it did not have a disinterested approach to truth itself. It demanded instead that truth become an instrument of social upheaval, of the people's prosperity, and of human happiness. It succumbed to the temptation of the Grand Inquisitor, who demanded the renunciation of truth in the name of man's happiness.[4] The intelligentsia's basic moral premise is summed up in the formula: let truth perish, if its death will enable the people to live better and will make men happier; down with truth, if it stands in the way of the sacred cry, "down with autocracy."

This falsely directed love of man, it turned out, destroyed love of God, because love for the truth, like love for beauty or for any absolute value, is an expression of love for the Deity. This was a false love because it was not based on true respect for men as equals and kinsmen by their One Father. On the one hand, it was compassion and pity for the man of "the people," and on the other it turned into worship of man and worship of the people. Genuine love for people is not love against truth and against God, but in truth and in God; it is not pity, which denies a person's dignity, but recognition of God's own image in every human being. In the name of this false love of man and of the people we developed police-search methods for judging philosophical endeavors and movements. Essentially, no one entered the field of philosophy; the Populists were prevented by a false love for the peasantry, the Marxists by a false love for the proletariat. But this attitude toward the peasantry and proletariat implied a lack of respect for the absolute significance of man, for this absolute significance is based on the divine and not on the human, on truth and not on interest.

Avenarius was "better" than Kant or Hegel not because his philosophy caught a glimpse of the truth but because he was imagined to be more favorable to socialism. This means that interest was placed above truth, the human above

---

of which he denounced Russian chauvinism and national self-satisfaction. His articles on the subject were republished in a two-volume collection, *The National Question in Russia* [Natsional'nyi vopros v Rossii] (St. Petersburg: M. M. Stasiulevich, 1888-91). *Eds.*

4. A reference to the "Grand Inquisitor" passage in Book V of Dostoevskii's *The Brothers Karamazov*. Berdiaev believed this figure epitomized the demonic potential of positivism. *Eds.*

the divine. To refute philosophical theories on the ground that they do not favor Populism or Social Democracy is to scorn truth. No one will listen to a philosopher suspected of being "reactionary" (and what don't we call "reactionary"!), for no one is really interested in philosophy and truth *per se*. Mr. Bogdanov's crude sectarian apologetics will always be preferred to the work of the remarkable and original Russian philosopher Lopatin. Lopatin's philosophy demands serious intellectual effort, and no programmatic slogans follow from it, while one can react to Bogdanov's work on a purely emotional level and it all fits into a five-kopeck pamphlet.

The Russian intelligentsia combined a rational consciousness with extreme emotionalism and with a weak appreciation of intellectual life as an autonomous value. Our prevailing attitude toward philosophy, as toward other spheres of life, was demagogic; demagogy characterized the controversies between philosophical schools carried on in the intelligentsia's circles, and these were accompanied by unworthy, furtive glances at who liked what, and why. Demagogy of this sort is spiritually demoralizing and creates an oppressive atmosphere. Moral cowardice develops, while love of truth and intellectual daring are extinguished. The thirst for justice on earth that is rooted in the soul of the Russian intelligentsia, a thirst which is fundamentally holy, is corrupted. Moral pathos degenerates into monomania. Among the Marxists, "class" explanations of various ideologies and philosophical doctrines turn into a kind of pathological obsession. This monomania has infected the greater part of our "leftists." We see symptoms of intellectual, moral, and cultural decadence in the division of philosophy into "proletarian" and "bourgeois," "left" and "right," in the assertion of two truths, one useful and the other harmful. This road leads to the disintegration of the universal consciousness, binding on all, with which the dignity of man and the growth of his culture are necessarily associated.

Russian history created an intelligentsia with a spiritual temper averse to objectivism and universalism, and this cast of mind made genuine love for objective, ecumenical truth and value impossible. The Russian intelligentsia distrusted objective ideas and universal norms on the assumption that they hampered the struggle with autocracy and service to "the people," whose well-being was considered more important than ecumenical truth and good. This fatal characteristic was a consequence of the intelligentsia's sad history; the responsibility lies with the regime, which crippled Russian life and fatally goaded the intelligentsia into an exclusive concern with the struggle against political and economic oppression. As a result, the Russian intelligentsia apprehended European philosophical doctrines in distorted form, adapting them to its own particular interests, and completely ignored the most significant products of philosophical thought. Scientific positivism, and economic materialism, and empirio-criticism, and neo-Kantianism, and Nietzscheism were all distorted and adapted to domestic conditions.

The Russian intelligentsia construed scientific positivism in a totally false and unscientific manner, so that it played a completely different role here than in Western Europe. Our intelligentsia approached "science" and the "scientific spirit" with respect and even idolatry, but it understood science as a special materialist dogma and the scientific spirit as a special faith: a dogma that exposed the evil of autocracy and the falsehood of the bourgeois world, and a faith that would deliver the people or the proletariat. Scientific positivism, like everything Western, was taken over in its most extreme form, and it became not only a primitive metaphysics but a special religion that replaced all earlier ones. But science itself and the scientific spirit did not take root; they were absorbed only by a few individuals and not by broad segments of the intelligentsia. Scholars never enjoyed much respect or popularity, and if they were indifferent to politics even their science was considered suspect. The educated youth began its study of science with Pisarev, Mikhailovskii or Bel'tov—its own domestic, sectarian "scholars" and "thinkers." Many had never even heard of real scholars.

The spirit of scientific positivism is in itself neither progressive nor reactionary; it is simply concerned with the investigation of truth. But we always interpreted it to mean political progressivism and social radicalism. The spirit of scientific positivism in itself excludes no metaphysics nor religious faith, but neither does it support any metaphysics or faith.[5] But we always interpreted scientific positivism to mean the radical negation of every metaphysical system and religious faith, or, to be more precise, for us scientific positivism was identical with a materialist metaphysics and a social-revolutionary faith. Not one mystic, not one religious believer, can deny *scientific* positivism and science. No antagonism can exist between the most mystical religion and the most positivist science, since they have completely different spheres of competence. The religious and metaphysical consciousness does indeed deny an exclusive position for science and the supremacy of scientific cognition in spiritual life, but science itself can only profit from such a limitation of its scope.

We had difficulty grasping the objective and scientific elements of positivism, but we accepted all the more passionately those elements that turned it into a faith, a definitive interpretation of the universe. What attracted the Russian intelligentsia was not the objectivity of positivism but its subjectivity, which idolized mankind. In the seventies Lavrov and Mikhailovskii transformed positivism into the "subjective sociology" that became the home-grown, sec-

---

5. I mean not *philosophical* but *scientific* positivism. The West created a scientific spirit which there too became a weapon against religion and metaphysics. But Slavic extremism is foreign to the West; the West also created *science*, which is neutral toward religion and metaphysics.

tarian philosophy of the Russian intelligentsia. Vladimir Solov'ev very wittily observed that the Russian intelligentsia always reasons according to a strange syllogism: man is descended from the apes, therefore we ought to love one another. The intelligentsia perceived scientific positivism wholly in terms of this syllogism; positivism was merely an instrument for affirming the reign of social justice and for utterly destroying those metaphysical and religious ideas which, the intelligentsia dogmatically assumed, support the reign of evil. Chicherin was much more of a scholar than Mikhailovskii, and much more of a positivist, in the sense of being scientifically objective, but that did not prevent him from being a metaphysical idealist and even a believing Christian. But the Russian intelligentsia found Chicherin's scholarship remote and repugnant, while Mikhailovskii's was near and dear.

We must finally acknowledge that it is "bourgeois" science that is real, objective science, while the "subjective" science of our Populists and the "class" science of our Marxists are more like a form of faith than science. The entire history of our intelligentsia ideologies confirms this: the materialism of the sixties, the subjective sociology of the seventies, and the Russian version of economic materialism.

In Russia, economic materialism was subjected to the same misinterpretations and distortions as scientific positivism in general. Economic materialism is preeminently an objective doctrine, in that it assigns central importance in the social life of the community to the objective principle of production, not the subjective principle of distribution. It sees the essence of human history in the creative process of conquering nature, in the economic creation and organization of productive forces. The entire social structure, with the modes of distributive justice inherent in it, and all the subjective feelings of social groups, are subordinate to this objective principle of production. It must be said that the objective and scientific side of Marxism contained a healthy kernel, which was maintained and developed by our most cultivated and scholarly Marxist, P. B. Struve. But on the whole we misunderstood economic materialism and Marxism; we construed them "subjectively" and adapted them to the intelligentsia's traditional psychology. Economic materialism lost its objective character: production and creation were reduced to secondary importance, while the *subjective, class* side of Social Democracy came to the fore. Marxism underwent a Populist rebirth, and economic materialism was turned into a new form of "subjective sociology." The Russian Marxists were possessed by an extreme love for equality, combined with extreme faith in the nearness of the socialist consummation and in the possibility of achieving this consummation in Russia even sooner, perhaps, than in the West. The element of objective truth was completely submerged in the subjective element, in a "class" point of view and a class psychology. In Russia the philosophy of economic materialism was wholly transformed into "class subjectivism" and even a class mystique of the proletariat. With such a philosophy, no thought could be given to the objective conditions for Russia's development; attention was necessarily concentrated on attaining an abstract maximum for the proletariat — a maximum, that is, from the intelligentsia's sectarian point of view, which refuses to recognize any objective truths. The conditions of Russian life made it impossible for objective social philosophy and science to flourish. The intelligentsia understood philosophy and science in its own subjective fashion.

Neo-Kantianism suffered less distortion, for it was not as popular and widespread. But even so, there was a period when we were too exclusively concerned with making use of neo-Kantian criticism to refine Marxism and substantiate socialism in a new way. In his first book,[6] even the objective and scholarly Struve erred in interpreting Riehl's theory of knowledge in an overly sociological manner and in giving his epistemology a construction favorable to economic materialism. And at one time we considered Simmel almost a Marxist, although he has little in common with Marxism. Later, the neo-Kantian and neo-Fichtean spirit became a means of liberating ourselves from Marxism and positivism, and a way of expressing the idealist sentiments that had matured. But no creative neo-Kantian traditions developed here; authentic Russian philosophy followed another path, which we shall discuss later. Justice demands, however, that we acknowledge that the interest in Kant, Fichte, and German idealism raised our philosophical level and served as a bridge to higher forms of philosophical consciousness.

Empirio-criticism suffered immeasurably greater distortion. This highly abstract and refined form of positivism, which grew out of the traditions of German criticism, was interpreted almost as a new philosophy of the proletariat, and Messrs. Bogdanov, Lunacharskii, *et al.* felt they could treat it familiarly, as their own property. Avenarius's epistemology is sufficiently general, formal and abstract that it does not prejudge any metaphysical questions. Avenarius even resorted to using letters as symbols so that he might not be bound to any ontological propositions. He is terribly afraid of any remnants of materialism, spiritualism, etc. Biological materialism is just as unacceptable to him as any form of ontologism. One should not be misled by the apparent biologism of his system; it is purely formal and so general that any "mystic" could accept it. One of the most intelligent empirio-critics, Cornelius, even considered it possible to include a deity among the *given*.

But our Marxist intelligentsia interpreted Avenarius's empirio-criticism purely in the spirit of biological materialism, for this helped justify the materialist view of history. Empirio-criticism became the philosophy not merely of the Social Democrats, but of their Bolshevik faction.[7] Poor Avenarius, he

---

6. Petr Struve, *Critical Remarks on the Problem of the Economic Development of Russia* [Kriticheskie zametki k voprosu ob ekonomicheskom razvitii Rossii] (St. Petersburg: I. N. Skorokhodov, 1894). *Eds.*

7. By the time *Vekhi* appeared, the theories of Bogdanov and Lunacharskii could no longer

never suspected that his name, innocent and remote from worldly strife, would figure in the quarrels of the Russian Bolshevik and Menshevik *intelligenty*. *The Critique of Pure Experience* suddenly proved to be a virtual "book of symbols" of the revolutionary Social-Democratic religion. The rank-and-file Marxist intelligentsia scarcely read Avenarius at all, for he is not easy reading, and many probably believed in all sincerity that he was an extremely intelligent Bolshevik. In reality, Avenarius bore as little relation to Social Democracy as any other German philosopher, and the liberal bourgeoisie, for example, could have used his philosophy with no less success, and even justified their leaning "to the right" with it.

The main point is that if Avenarius were as simple as he seems to Messrs. Bogdanov, Lunacharskii, *et al.*, if his philosophy consisted of biological materialism with central importance assigned to the brain, he would not have had to devise various "S systems" free of all preconceptions, and he would not be recognized today as a powerful and rigorously logical intellect, even by his opponents.[8] To be sure, the empirio-critical Marxists no longer call themselves materialists, leaving materialism to such backward Mensheviks as Plekhanov *et al.*, but they give empirio-criticism itself a materialist and metaphysical overtone. Mr. Bogdanov zealously preaches a primitive metaphysical concoction, taking in vain the names of Avenarius, Mach and other authorities, while Mr. Lunacharskii has even thought up a new religion of the proletariat, using this same Avenarius. Most European philosophers are abstract and too cut off from life; they do not suspect the role they play in our intelligentsia's quibbles and quarrels, and would be astonished to learn how their ponderous thoughts are turned into flimsy pamphlets.

Nietzsche's fate here was especially sad. We subjected this solitary enemy of any kind of democracy to the most shameless democratization. We pulled him asunder, and everyone managed to use him for his own personal ends. It suddenly turned out that Nietzsche, who died thinking he was unneeded and would remain alone on his mountain top, was very much needed, even to refresh and revitalize Marxism. On the one hand, whole droves of Nietzschean individualists came to life, while on the other Lunacharskii mixed a sauce from Marx, Avenarius and Nietzsche—it proved piquant, and many found it to their

be considered representative of Bolshevism; in fact, Lenin had always disagreed with them, but had maintained a strictly political alliance with the empirio-critics against Plekhanov and the Mensheviks. Political differences, however, came to a head in 1908, and Lenin broke with the two men, signalizing the rupture with an attack on their philosophical novelties in *Marxism and Empirio-Criticism*. Bogdanov and Lunacharskii then formed a separate ultra-left faction around the journal *Forward* [Vpered]. *Eds.*

8. Avenarius did not succeed in freeing himself of "preconceptions." His epistemological point of view is very inconsistent, it smacks of "materialism," "spiritualism," and what have you—but it is not simple.

taste. Poor Nietzsche, and poor Russian thought! The hungry Russian intelligentsia takes whatever it is fed and thrives on it, in the hope that the evil of autocracy will be vanquished and the people freed. I fear that even the most metaphysical and mystical doctrines will be similarly adapted for domestic use. But the evils of Russian life, despotism and slavery, will not be vanquished in this way, since evil is not to be vanquished by the distorted assimilation of all kinds of extreme doctrines. Neither Avenarius nor Nietzsche, nor even Marx himself, are of much help to us in the struggle with the age-old evils that have deformed our nature and made us so unreceptive to objective truth. We belittled theoretical speculation, yet even the most practical struggle with evil always assumed the character of the profession of abstract theoretical doctrines. We called true that philosophy which furthered the struggle with autocracy in the name of socialism, and we made the obligatory profession of such a "true" philosophy an essential part of the struggle itself.

These psychological peculiarities led the intelligentsia to overlook original Russian philosophy as well as the philosophical content of Russia's great literature. A thinker of the caliber of Chaadaev was totally ignored and was not understood even by those who did mention him. There seemed every reason to acknowledge Vladimir Solov'ev as our national philosopher and to create a national philosophical tradition around him. Surely such a tradition could not be created around Cohen, Windelband, or any other German, foreign to the Russian soul. The philosophy of any European country could take pride in a Solov'ev. But the Russian intelligentsia neither read nor knew him and did not regard him as one of its own. Solov'ev's philosophy is profound and original, but it does not substantiate socialism. It is alien to both Populism and Marxism and cannot conveniently be turned into a weapon for the struggle against autocracy. Therefore, he did not furnish the intelligentsia with a suitable "world-view," and he seemed even more alien than the "Marxist" Avenarius, the "Populist" Auguste Comte, and other foreigners.

The greatest Russian metaphysician was, of course, Dostoevskii, but his metaphysics was quite beyond the powers of most of the intelligentsia. He was suspected of all kinds of "reactionary tendencies," and with good reason. Sad to say, the intelligentsia, with its positivist bias, felt no affinity with the metaphysical spirit of the great Russian writers. But it remains an open question who is more national, these writers or the intelligentsia community with its prevailing consciousness. The intelligentsia did not genuinely accept even Lev Tolstoi, but it came to terms with him because of his Populism, and for a time it submitted to the spiritual influence of his doctrines. Tolstoyism, too, was hostile to higher philosophy and creation, finding them a sinful luxury.

I find it particularly sad that the intelligentsia has persistently refused to become familiar with the seeds of Russian philosophy. For Russian philosophy is not exhausted by the single brilliant phenomenon of Vladimir Solov'ev. As early as Khomiakov one can find the rudiments of a new philosophy that transcends European rationalism by means of a higher consciousness. To one side stands the quite substantial figure of Chicherin, from whom one might learn a great deal. Then there are Kozlov, Prince Sergei Trubetskoi, Lopatin, Nikolai Losskii, and, finally, the little-known V. I. Nesmelov, the most profound product of the ecclesiastical academies—a milieu far from the intelligentsia's heart. There are, of course, many different strains in Russian philosophy, but there is also something common to them all, something original, forming a new philosophical tradition distinct from those reigning in contemporary European philosophy. In its basic tendency, Russian philosophy carries on the great Greek and German philosophical traditions of the past; the spirit of Plato and of classical German idealism lives on in it. But German idealism never went beyond the stage of extreme abstraction and rationalism that culminated with Hegel. Beginning with Khomiakov, Russian philosophers sharply criticized Hegel's abstract idealism and rationalism, and they moved on not to empiricism, nor to neo-criticism, but to *concrete idealism*, to ontological realism, to a mystical corrective to European philosophy's reason, which had lost its vital essence. One cannot fail to see the creative promise of a new path for philosophy in this development. Russian philosophy is greatly concerned with religion, and it reconciles reason with faith.

Thus far, Russian philosophy has not provided a "world-view" in the sectarian sense of the word, the only sense that interests the intelligentsia. It has no direct relation to socialism, although Prince Sergei Trubetskoi did call his doctrine on the communality of consciousness *metaphysical socialism*. It is not concerned with politics in the literal sense, although in its best representatives there lay hidden a religious yearning for the kingdom of God on earth. But Russian philosophy does have one feature that reveals its kinship to the Russian intelligentsia—the thirst for an integral world-view, for an organic fusion of truth and goodness, of knowledge and faith. Even the academically-minded Russian philosophers tend to be hostile to abstract rationalism. I believe that concrete idealism, combined with a realistic attitude to life, could become the foundation of our national philosophy and could establish the national philosophical tradition[9] we need so much. Tradition must be counterposed to our fickle enthusiasm for fashionable European doctrines, but the tradition must be both universal and national—only then will it be culturally fruitful.

An ecumenical tradition, European and universal, lives in the philosophy of Vladimir Solov'ev and other Russian philosophers of kindred spirit, but

---

9. Truth cannot be national—truth is always universal. But different nationalities may be called upon to illuminate particular facets of the truth. The qualities of the Russian national spirit indicate that we are called upon to work in the area of religious philosophy.

some elements of this philosophy could create a national tradition as well. This would lead neither to the neglect nor to the distortion of all the significant products of European thought, as they have been neglected and distorted by our cosmopolitan-minded intelligentsia, but to a deeper and more critical penetration into their essence. What we need is not a sectarian concoction but a serious philosophical culture, universal and at the same time national. Indeed, Vladimir Solov'ev and Prince Sergei Trubetskoi were better Europeans than Messrs. Bogdanov and Lunacharskii; they were bearers of the world philosophical spirit, and at the same time they were national philosophers, since they laid the foundations for a philosophy of concrete idealism.

Historically conditioned prejudices prevented the intelligentsia from recognizing in Russian philosophy the substantiation of its own quest for truth. Indeed, our intelligentsia cherished *freedom* and professed a philosophy in which there is no place for freedom; it cherished the *individual* and professed a philosophy in which there is no place for the individual; it cherished the *idea of progress* and professed a philosophy in which there is no place for the idea of progress; it cherished the *brotherhood of man* and professed a philosophy in which there is no place for the brotherhood of man; it cherished *justice* and everything noble, and professed a philosophy in which there is no place for justice or for anything howsoever noble. This has been an almost continuous aberration of consciousness, a product of our entire history. The best members of the intelligentsia were fanatically prepared for self-sacrifice, and with the same fanaticism they professed materialism, which denies all self-sacrifice. The atheistic philosophy that always captivated the revolutionary intelligentsia could not sanction anything holy, but the intelligentsia lent this very philosophy a sacred character and cherished its own materialism and atheism in a fanatical, almost "Catholic" manner. Creative philosophical thought must eliminate this aberration and lead the intelligentsia's consciousness out of its impasse. Who knows what philosophy will be fashionable with us tomorrow—perhaps the pragmatic philosophy of James and Bergson, who will be exploited like Avenarius and the others, or perhaps some other novelty. But this will not advance our philosophical development by a single step.

The intelligentsia's traditional hostility to philosophical endeavor finds expression even in modern Russian mysticism. *The New Way*, a journal of religious searchings and mystical sentiments, suffered primarily from the absence of a clear philosophical consciousness, and it treated philosophy almost with contempt. Our most outstanding mystics—Rozanov, Merezhkovskii, Viacheslav Ivanov—do furnish rich material for a new statement of philosophical themes, but they themselves are distinguished by an anti-philosophical spirit, an anarchistic denial of philosophical reason. Vladimir Solov'ev, who united mysticism with philosophy in his own person, remarked that disparagement of the rational principle is characteristic of Russians. I might add that dislike for objective reason can be found in equal measure in both our "right" and our "left" camps. Meanwhile, Russian mysticism, which is essentially very valuable, needs philosophical objectivization and norms if it is to serve the interests of Russian culture. I would put it this way: the dionysian principle of mysticism must be combined with the apollonian principle of philosophy. Love for the philosophical investigation of truth must be imparted both to the Russian mystics and to the atheist *intelligenty*. Philosophy is one of the ways of *objectifying* mysticism, and only positive religion can be a higher and more complete form of objectivization. In the past the intelligentsia regarded Russian mysticism with suspicion and hostility, but lately a reaction has set in; now there is a danger that they will reinforce each other in their hostility to objective reason, and that mysticism will be inclined to place itself at the disposal of the traditional social objectives.[10]

The intelligentsia's consciousness needs radical reform, and the purifying fire of philosophy will have no small role to play in this important task. All the historical and psychological facts indicate that the Russian intelligentsia can pass to a new consciousness only by means of a synthesis of knowledge and faith, a synthesis which will satisfy its valuable demand for an organic union of theory and practice, of "just truth" and "true justice."[11] But right now we have a spiritual need to recognize truth as a value in itself, to show humility before the truth, and to be prepared to make sacrifices for its sake.[12]

This regard for the truth would revitalize our cultural life. For philosophy is an organ of self-consciousness of the human spirit, one that is not individual but communal and supra-individual. But the communality of philosophical consciousness can be realized only within a universal and national tradition. Consolidation of such a tradition would further Russia's cultural renaissance. This long desired and joyous renaissance, the awakening of dormant spirits, requires not only political liberation but liberation from the oppressive power of politics, an emancipation of thought which hitherto has been hard to find among our political liberationists.[13]

The Russian intelligentsia was what Russian history made it, and its psychological tenor reflected the sins of our painful past, our system of government, and our eternal reaction. An obsolete despotism deformed the intelligentsia's soul, enslaving it not just externally but internally as well, by setting a negative standard for all its spiritual values. But it is unworthy of free be-

10. Berdiaev is here referring to the views of Merezhkovskii and his follower D. M. Filosofov, who exalted revolution as an apocalyptic event. *Eds.*

11. *Pravda-istina* and *pravda-spravedlivost'* in the Russian, i.e., *pravda* in its dual meaning of truth and justice. *Eds.*

12. Humility before the truth has great moral significance, but it must not lead to a cult of lifeless, abstract truth.

13. *Note to the Second Edition.* Political liberation is possible only in conjunction with and on the basis of a spiritual and cultural renaissance.

ings always to blame everything on external forces and thus justify their own failings. The intelligentsia too is guilty; its atheism is the fault of its will, for it freely chose the path of worshipping man and thereby crippled its soul and deadened within itself the instinct for truth. We must realize that our will, which is influenced by our reason, is guilty; only this realization can lead us to a new life. We will be freed from external oppression only when we are freed from internal bondage, i.e., when we accept responsibility and cease blaming everything on external forces. Then the new soul of the intelligentsia will be born.

HEROISM AND ASCETICISM

Reflections on the Religious Nature of the Russian Intelligentsia

Sergei Bulgakov

I

Russia has experienced a revolution, and it did not bring the expected results. Many people feel that so far the achievements of the liberation movement are problematical, to say the least. Russian society, exhausted by its recent strain and failures, is in a state of torpor, apathy, spiritual malaise, and despondency. Our state life still shows no signs of the renewal and consolidation it needs so much, and, as though in a dream world, every part of it has come to a standstill once again, overcome by an irresistible drowsiness. Civic life, clouded by many executions, an extraordinary increase in crime, and a general coarsening of manners, has positively regressed. Literature has been engulfed by a muddy wave of pornography and sensationalism. There is good cause for despair and for grave doubt as to the future of Russia. In any case, now, after all we have been through, neither the naive, rather starry-eyed Slavophile faith nor the pretty utopias of the old Westernism are still tenable. The revolution has brought into question the very viability of Russian state and civic life. Unless we take into account this historical experience, the historical lessons of the revolution, we can make no positive statement about Russia; nor can we fall back on the clichés of either the Slavophiles or the Westernizers.

The political crisis was followed by a spiritual crisis which demands deep, concentrated reflection, introspection, self-examination, and self-criticism. If Russian society really is still living and viable, if it contains seeds of the future, this must be manifested first and foremost in a readiness and ability to learn from history. For history is not mere chronology, relating the sequence of events; it is life experience, the experience of good and evil which makes spiritual growth possible. Nothing is so dangerous as a deathly immobility of minds and hearts, an inert conservatism in which we content ourselves with repeating clichés or simply brushing aside the lessons of the past, in the secret hope of a new "emotional upsurge," spontaneous, accidental, and irrational.

Reflecting upon our experiences of recent years, we cannot regard it all as an historical accident or simply the play of spontaneous forces. History pronounced a verdict here; the various players in the historical drama were judged, and the balance sheet was drawn up for an entire historical period. The "liberation movement" did not produce the results it should have; it did not bring reconciliation and renewal, and it has not yet brought improvement in the system of government (although it left a green shoot for the future, the State Duma), nor an upsurge in the economy. This is not simply because it proved too weak for the struggle with the dark forces of history. No, the liberation movement could not prevail because it was not equal to its task and was itself weakened by internal contradictions. The Russian revolution developed enormous destructive energy, like a gigantic earthquake, but its creative forces proved far weaker than the destructive ones. For many, the net result of their experiences was this bitter realization in their hearts. Should it be silenced? Isn't it better to give voice to it, in order to ask, "Why is this so?"

I have already publicly expressed the view that the Russian revolution was an intelligentsia revolution.[1] It was our intelligentsia, with its world-view, habits, tastes, and social mores, that provided the revolution's spiritual leadership. The *intelligenty* do not admit it, of course, thereby showing that they are indeed *intelligenty*, and, each according to his own catechism, they name one or another social class as the sole motive force of the revolution. We do not dispute the fact that it took a whole complex of historical circumstances (with the unfortunate war, of course, foremost among them) and very serious vital interests to arouse the various social classes and groups and throw them into a state of unrest. Nonetheless, we insist that the intelligentsia gave the revolution all its ideological baggage and its whole spiritual arsenal, along with its front-line fighters, skirmishers, agitators, and propagandists. It gave spiritual expression to the instinctive desires of the masses and fired them with its own enthusiasm—in short, it was the nerves and brain of the gigantic body of the revolution. In this sense the revolution is the intelligentsia's spiritual offspring, and, consequently, the history of the revolution is history's verdict on the intelligentsia.

The soul of the intelligentsia, this creation of Peter the Great, is the key to the future destiny of Russia's state and society. For good or ill, the fate of Petrine Russia is in the hands of the intelligentsia, however oppressed and persecuted, however weak and even impotent it may seem at the moment. It is the window that Peter cut open to Europe, and through it we receive Western air, at once life-giving and poisonous. This handful of people holds the Russian monopoly on European education and enlightenment, and they are the chief agents for its transmission to a nation of a hundred million people. If Russia cannot do without this enlightenment on pain of political and national death, then how exalted and important the intelligentsia's mission becomes, how awesome its historical responsibility for our country's immediate as well as distant future! That is why a patriot who loves his nation and grieves over the

---

1. In my essay, "The Intelligentsia and Religion" [Intelligentsiia i religiia], *Russian Thought* [Russkaia mysl'], No. 3 (1908), pp. 72-103; also published separately (Moscow: A. I. Snegirova, 1908).

needs of the Russian state can find no more compelling subject for reflection than the nature of the Russian intelligentsia. Nor can he have any more agonizing and anxious concern than whether it will rise to its task and give Russia the educated class she needs so badly, one with a Russian soul, enlightened reason, and a firm will. For otherwise the intelligentsia, in league with the Tatar barbarism still so prevalent in our state and society, will destroy Russia.

After witnessing the revolution, many people were keenly disappointed in the intelligentsia and questioned its fitness for its historical role; in the revolution's singular failures they saw the bankruptcy of the intelligentsia as well. The revolution exposed, underscored, and intensified certain of the intelligentsia's spiritual features that only a few individuals (Dostoevskii especially) had previously divined in all their real significance. It was like a spiritual mirror for all of Russia, and for her intelligentsia in particular. To be silent about these traits now would be not merely improper but downright criminal. For now our one hope is that the years of social collapse will also be years of salutary repentance, in which spiritual forces will revive and new people, new toilers in the Russian vineyard, will be trained. But Russia cannot be renovated without first renovating her intelligentsia (along with much else). And it is the duty of conviction and patriotism to speak of this loudly and openly. A critical attitude toward some of the intelligentsia's spiritual features is not necessarily the product of any one world-view that is especially alien to the intelligentsia. People of varied and widely divergent views can agree in this attitude, and that is the best sign that the time really has come for self-criticism, and that it answers a vital need of at least a part of the intelligentsia itself.

The Russian intelligentsia's character was shaped by two basic factors, one external and the other internal, to speak in general terms. The first was the merciless and unremitting pressure applied by the police, which could have crushed and completely destroyed a group with a weaker spirit. The fact that the intelligentsia remained alive and vigorous even under this pressure bears witness at least to its extraordinary courage and viability. The intelligentsia's isolation from real life, imposed upon it by the whole atmosphere of the old regime, intensified that "underground" mentality which was part of its innate character in any case. Isolation numbed its spirit, supporting and to a certain extent justifying its political obsession (the "Hannibal's vow" of struggle against autocracy), and hampering normal spiritual development. Only now are the objective conditions for that development becoming more favorable, and here, at least, we can see an undeniable spiritual achievement of the liberation movement.

The second, subjective factor that determined the character of our intelligentsia is its special world-view and the spiritual outlook that accompanies it. This essay will be wholly devoted to a characterization and critique of that world-view.

I cannot help seeing the intelligentsia's attitude toward religion as its most

fundamental characteristic. Nor can we understand the fundamental characteristics of the Russian revolution unless we focus our attention on this attitude. Furthermore, Russia's historical future, too, is involved in the question
of what position the intelligentsia will adopt in regard to religion: will it remain in the same moribund condition, or does an upheaval await us in this
sphere, too, a real revolution of minds and hearts?

II

Following Dostoevskii, it has frequently been noted that the Russian intelligentsia's spiritual make-up contains elements of religiosity which sometimes
even approximate Christianity. The intelligentsia's historical predicament was
primarily responsible for fostering these traits: on the one hand, government
persecution gave it a feeling of martyrdom and confessorship, while forcible
isolation from life, on the other, produced dreaminess, occasional starry-eyed
idealism, utopianism, and, in general, an inadequate sense of reality.

Another trait is connected with this apparent religiosity: the intelligentsia
is psychologically alien, although perhaps only temporarily, to the solid bourgeois tenor of life of Western Europe, with its everyday virtues and its economy
based on hard work, but with its barrenness and limitations as well. In the
works of Herzen we have the classic expression of the Russian *intelligent*'s
spiritual collision with European "bourgeois philistinism."[2] Similar reactions
have appeared on a number of occasions in recent Russian literature, too. This
constricted and spiritually earthbound way of life sickens the Russian *intelligent*, though we all know how imperative it is for him to learn at least the
technology of life and labor from Western man. In return, these vagabond men
of Rus', these émigré freebooters still feeding on the inspiration of Sten'ka
Razin and Emel'ka Pugachev, though translated into contemporary revolutionary jargon, are repulsive and incomprehensible to the Western bourgeoisie.
In recent years this spiritual antagonism seems to have reached a fever pitch.

If we attempt to analyze the "anti-bourgeoisness" of the Russian intelligentsia, it turns out to be a *mixtum compositum* of highly diverse elements.
There is some hereditary lordliness, the product of generations of freedom from
the cares of earning a living and from the humdrum, "philistine" side of life
in general. There is a considerable dose of plain slovenliness, of failure to develop persistent, disciplined work habits and a measured pace of life. But
doubtless there is also some smaller dose of an unconsciously religious aver-

---

2. On this point, see the essay "Herzen's Spiritual Drama" [Dushevnaia drama Gert-
sena] in my *From Marxism to Idealism: A Collection of Articles, 1896-1903* [Ot marks-
izma k idealizmu. Sbornik statei, 1896-1903] (St. Petersburg: "Obshchestvennaia pol'za,"
1903). Also published separately (Kiev: S. I. Ivanov, 1905).

sion to spiritual philistinism, to "the kingdom of this world," with its placid self-satisfaction.

A certain otherworldliness, an eschatological dream of the City of God and the future reign of justice (under various socialist pseudonyms), and a striving for the salvation of mankind—if not from sin, then from suffering—are, as we know, the immutable and distinctive peculiarities of the Russian intelligentsia. Anguish at the disharmony of life and a yearning to overcome it distinguish the foremost *intelligent* writers (Gleb Uspenskii, Garshin). It may be that in this striving for the Future City, beside which earthly reality pales, the intelligentsia has preserved in their most recognizable form some features of its lost life in the church. While I listened to the stormy speeches of the atheistic· left bloc in the Second State Duma,[3] how often I heard—remarkably—echoes of the psychology of Orthodoxy, as the effects of the members' spiritual indoctrination by it were suddenly revealed.

In general, the spiritual habits instilled by the church explain a number of the Russian intelligentsia's best qualities, but it loses them the more it departs from the church. Among them are a certain puritanism, rigorous morals, a distinctive asceticism, and a general strictness of personal life. Such leaders of the Russian intelligentsia as Dobroliubov and Chernyshevskii (both seminarians, brought up in religious clerical families) preserve their earlier moral nature almost intact, but their historical children and grandchildren gradually lose it. In the spiritual make-up of the most outstanding figures of the Russian revolution we can discern Christian traits which they absorbed, sometimes without knowledge or desire, from their surroundings, from family and nurse, from a spiritual atmosphere steeped in church life. But since this merely obscures the real opposition between the Christian temperament and that of the *intelligent*, it is important to point out that these traits are superficial, borrowed, and in a certain sense atavistic. They disappear with the weakening of former Christian habits, revealing the full-blown image of the *intelligent*. That image made its most forceful appearance during the revolution, when it sloughed off the very last vestiges of Christianity.

The Russian intelligentsia, especially in earlier generations, was also distinguished by a feeling of guilt toward the people, a kind of "social repentance," not before God, of course, but before the "people" or the "proletariat." Although there is a touch of lordliness in the historical origins of these sentiments of the "repentant nobleman" or the "classless *intelligent*," they do leave a mark of special profundity and suffering on the intelligentsia's countenance. Another apparently religious trait is the intelligentsia's self-sacrifice, the constant readiness of its best representatives to make any sacrifices

---

3. Bulgakov sat in the Second Duma (1907), where he was affiliated with the Kadets (liberals), although he described himself as a Christian Socialist. *Eds.*

and even to seek them. Whatever its psychological motivation, the readiness for sacrifice reinforces that otherworldliness which makes the intelligentsia's outlook so foreign to bourgeois philistinism and gives it distinctive religious features.

And yet, despite all these qualities, it is common knowledge that there is no intelligentsia more atheistic than the Russian. Atheism is the common faith into which all who enter the bosom of the humanistic intelligentsia church are baptized, not only those who come from the educated class but those who come from the people as well. Such was the custom from the very beginning, starting with Belinskii, the spiritual father of the Russian intelligentsia. Just as every social group elaborates its own customs and special creeds, the Russian intelligentsia's traditional atheism has come to be taken for granted —it is considered a mark of bad taste even to talk about it. In the eyes of our intelligentsia a certain level of education and enlightenment is synonymous with indifference to religion or rejection of it. The different groups, parties and "orientations" do not argue about this; it unites them all. It pervades the intelligentsia's meager culture from top to bottom, through its newspapers, magazines, orientations, programs, morals, and prejudices, just as the blood, oxygenated by respiration, diffuses through the whole organism. There is no fact in the history of Russian enlightenment more important than this one.

At the same time, we must realize that Russian atheism is by no means a conscious rejection, the fruit of a complex, agonizing and prolonged effort of the mind, the heart and the will, the product of personal experience. No, most often it is taken on faith and preserves the characteristics of a naive religious belief, only inside out. The fact that it takes militant, dogmatic, pseudo-scientific forms makes no difference. This faith rests on a series of uncritical, unverified and, in their dogmatic form, of course, incorrect assertions: that science is competent to provide final answers even to religious questions, and, moreover, that these answers are negative. In addition, there is a suspicious attitude toward philosophy, especially metaphysics, which also is rejected and condemned without investigation.

Learned and ignorant, old and young, all share this faith. It is absorbed in adolescence, which of course comes earlier in life for some, later for others. At that age it is usually easy and even natural to reject religion and immediately replace it with faith in science and progress. Those who have adopted this faith feel these questions have been adequately explained once and for all, and they are hypnotized by the unanimous acceptance of this opinion. The adolescents become mature men. Some of them acquire sound scientific knowledge and become eminent specialists. Then they place the weight of their authority as learned men on the scales in favor of the atheism which they embraced dogmatically as adolescents on the school bench, although in this field they are not a bit more authoritative than any thinking and feeling person. This creates the spiritual atmosphere in our universities and professional schools, where the younger generation of the intelligentsia is molded. It is remarkable how slight an impact people of profound education, intellect, and genius made on the Russian intelligentsia when they summoned it to look more deeply into religion and to awaken from its dogmatic stupor. Our religious thinkers and Slavophile writers, Vladimir Solov'ev, Bukharev, Prince Sergei Trubetskoi, and others, went almost unnoticed, and the intelligentsia remained deaf to the religious message of Dostoevskii and even of Lev Tolstoi, despite the superficial cult of the latter.

The most striking feature of Russian atheism is its dogmatism, the religious frivolity, one might say, with which it is accepted. Until recently, Russian "educated" society simply ignored the problem of religion and did not understand its vital and exceptional importance. For the most part it was interested in religion only insofar as the religious problem involved politics or the propagation of atheism. In matters of religion our intelligentsia is conspicuously ignorant. This is not an indictment, for there is, perhaps, sufficient historical justification for this ignorance, but a diagnosis of the intelligentsia's spiritual condition. As far as religion is concerned, our intelligentsia simply has not emerged from adolescence. It has not yet thought seriously about religion and has not consciously determined its attitude toward it. It has not yet experienced religious thought and therefore, strictly speaking, it is not above religion, as it likes to think, but outside it.

The best proof of this contention is the historical origin of Russian atheism. We assimilated it from the West, and not without reason it became the first article in the creed of our "Westernism." We accepted it as the last word in Western civilization, first in the form of Voltairianism and the French Encyclopedists' materialism, then as atheistic socialism (Belinskii), later as the materialism of the sixties, as positivism or Feuerbachian humanism, more recently as economic materialism, and, in the last few years, as neo-Kantian critical philosophy. Western civilization is a tree deeply rooted in history, with many branches; we chose only one, without knowing or wishing to know any of the others, fully confident that we were grafting onto ourselves the most authentic European civilization. But European civilization has not only a variety of fruits and a number of branches, but also roots which feed the tree and with their healthy sap to some extent render harmless the many poisonous fruits. Therefore even negative doctrines, in their native land and amid the other powerful spiritual tendencies contending with them, have a psychological and historical significance which alters radically when they appear in a cultural desert and claim to be the sole foundation of Russian enlightenment and civilization. *Si duo idem dicunt, non est idem.*[4] No culture has yet been built upon such a foundation.

---

4. "If two people say the same thing, it is not the same thing." *Eds.*

Nowadays we tend to lose sight of the fact that Western European culture has religious roots and is at least half built on the religious foundations laid down by the Middle Ages and the Reformation. Whatever our view of Reformation dogma and of Protestantism in general, we cannot deny that the Reformation stimulated a tremendous religious upsurge throughout the Western world, even in the areas that remained true to Catholicism but were forced to renew themselves in order to combat their enemies. In this sense, a new European personality was born in the Reformation, and this origin left its mark. Political freedom, freedom of conscience, and the rights of man and the citizen were also proclaimed by the Reformation (in England). Recent investigations are shedding light on the significance of Protestantism, especially in the Reformed Church, Calvinism, and Puritanism, for economic development, for it molded individuals fit to become the leaders of a developing national economy.[5] Modern learning, and especially philosophy, also developed primarily in Protestant areas. And all these advances proceeded with strict historical continuity and gradualness, without chasms or avalanches. The cultural history of the Western European world is a coherent whole, in which both the Middle Ages and the Reformation are still alive and occupy their necessary place alongside the trends of modern times.

The spiritual current which proved decisive for the Russian intelligentsia emerged at the same time. Alongside the Reformation, the humanistic Renaissance revived classical antiquity, and with it some elements of paganism. Parallel with the religious individualism of the Reformation, a neo-pagan individualism that extolled natural, unregenerated man grew up. It viewed man as inherently good and beautiful, human nature being corrupted only by external circumstances. All that needs to be done is to restore man's natural condition, and this will accomplish everything. Here is the root of the various natural law theories, of modern doctrines of progress and the power of external reforms alone to resolve the human tragedy, and, consequently, of all modern humanism and socialism. The apparent, external similarity of religious and pagan individualism does not eliminate their profound internal difference, and so we see in modern history not only parallel development but also mutual conflict between these two tendencies.

The so-called "Enlightenment" of the seventeenth, eighteenth, and part of the nineteenth centuries is characterized in intellectual history by an intensification of the motifs of humanistic individualism. The Enlightenment drew the most radical negative conclusions from the premises of humanism: in the field of religion, by way of deism, it came to skepticism and atheism; in phi-

---

5. This is almost certainly a reference to Max Weber, *The Protestant Ethic and the Spirit of Capitalism*. Bulgakov showed familiarity with Weber's work from the very beginning of the latter's career. *Eds.*

losophy, through rationalism and empiricism, to positivism and materialism; in ethics, through "natural" morality, to utilitarianism and hedonism. Materialist socialism, too, can be viewed as the latest and ripest fruit of the Enlightenment.

This orientation, in part a product of the dissolution of the Reformation but itself one of the forces of disintegration in the spiritual life of the West, has been highly influential in modern history. It inspired the great French Revolution and most of the nineteenth-century revolutions. On the other hand, it provides the spiritual foundation for European bourgeois philistinism, which has temporarily become dominant, superseding the heroic age of the Enlightenment. Although the face of Europe is steadily being disfigured, its features stiffening in the chill of philistinism as the popular philosophy of the Enlightenment permeates the masses, we must not forget that in the history of culture the Enlightenment has never played, nor does it now play, an exclusive or even dominant role. Unseen, the tree of European culture still feeds on the spiritual sap of its old religious roots. These roots, this healthy historical conservatism, keep the tree sound, although it too is beginning to wither and decay as the Enlightenment penetrates the roots and trunk. Therefore, Western European civilization cannot be considered irreligious in its historical foundations, although it is indeed becoming ever more so in the consciousness of recent generations.

Our intelligentsia's Westernism was restricted to the superficial assimilation of the latest political and social ideas. Moreover, they were adopted in conjunction with the most extreme and caustic forms of Enlightenment philosophy. The intelligentsia made this choice itself, and Western civilization as an organic whole is essentially not responsible for it. When the Russian *intelligent* surveys Western civilization, the role of the "gloomy" Middle Ages and of the Reformation era, with its enormous spiritual achievements, disappears completely, along with the entire development of scientific and philosophical thought other than that of the extreme Enlightenment. In the beginning was barbarism, then civilization shone forth, i.e., the Enlightenment, materialism, atheism, socialism—that is the average *intelligent*'s uncomplicated philosophy of history. One of our objectives in the struggle to create a Russian culture, consequently, must be a more profound, historically conscious Westernism.

Why was it the dogmas of the Enlightenment that our intelligentsia adopted so easily? Many historical reasons could be given, but to a certain extent the choice was a free act of the intelligentsia itself, one for which it must answer to its country and to history.

In any event, this broke the continuity of Russia's intellectual development, and the breach has made our country sick in spirit.

III

The intelligentsia rejects Christianity and its standards and appears to accept atheism. In fact, instead of atheism it adopts the dogmas of the religion of man-Godhood, in one or another of the variants produced by the Western European Enlightenment, and then turns this religion into idolatry. The basic tenet common to all the variants is belief in the natural perfection of man and in infinite progress. The latter is to be effected by human forces, but at the same time it is viewed in mechanistic terms. Since all evil is explained by the external defects of human society, and consequently there is neither personal guilt nor personal responsibility, it follows that the whole problem of social reorganization is to overcome these external defects—by means of external reforms, of course. Denying the existence of Providence and of any pre-eternal plan working itself out in history, man puts himself in place of Providence and sees himself as his own savior. A mechanistic, sometimes crudely materialistic conception of the historical process, which reduces it to the play of spontaneous forces (as in economic materialism), manifestly contradicts this image of man, but it develops nonetheless; man remains the sole rational, conscious agent, his own Providence.

In the West, this frame of mind arose at a time when culture flourished and man's power was clearly felt, and it was psychologically colored by a feeling of cultural self-satisfaction on the part of the newly rich bourgeois. It is true that measured by religious standards European philistinism's deification of itself—in socialism and individualism alike—is nothing but repulsive complacency and spiritual rapine, a temporary dulling of consciousness. But in the West this man-Godhood, its *Sturm und Drang* over, long ago grew tame and peaceful (though no one will say for how long), as has European socialism. For the time being, in any event, it will be unable to undermine the labor principles of European culture and the spiritual health of the European peoples (although it is doing so slowly but surely). In practice, age-old tradition and historic labor discipline still prevail over the corrupting influence of self-worship.

This is not the case in Russia, where historical continuity has been broken. Here the religion of man-Godhood and its essence, self-worship, were adopted not only with youthful ardor but with adolescent ignorance of life and its forces, and they assumed almost frenzied forms. Thus inspired, our intelligentsia felt called upon to play the role of Providence to its own country. It was conscious of its position as the sole bearer of light and European education in this land where everything, it felt, was lost in impenetrable darkness and seemed so barbaric and alien. The intelligentsia saw itself as Russia's spiritual guardian and determined to save her, as best it could and as best it knew how.

Relying on this estimate of itself, the intelligentsia heroically challenged and fought the Russian past and present. *Heroism*—for me, this word expresses the fundamental essence of the intelligentsia's world-view and ideal, and it is the heroism of self-worship. The intelligentsia's entire spiritual economy is based on it.

The *intelligent*'s isolation and rootlessness, the grim historical background, and his lack of solid learning and historical experience all stimulated the mentality of heroism. The *intelligent* would periodically fall into an heroic ecstasy, with a patently hysterical[6] overtone. Russia must be saved, and her savior can and must be the intelligentsia in general, and even the aforesaid *intelligent* in particular; aside from him there is no savior and no salvation. Nothing reinforces the mentality of heroism so much as persecution, victimization, reversals of fortune, danger, and even death. And, as we know, Russian history has not been grudging in these respects. The Russian intelligentsia developed in an atmosphere of continual martyrdom, and the holiness of its sufferings demands our admiration. But the tribute we pay to these sufferings, limitless in the past and grievous in the present, and to this "cross," voluntary or involuntary, does not compel us to silence the truth. We must not silence it, not even out of pious regard for the intelligentsia's martyrology.

Thus, suffering and oppression do most to canonize the hero, both in his own and his neighbor's eyes. Since the melancholy peculiarities of Russian life frequently subject him to this fate as a youth, a heroic self-consciousness also appears at an early age; then the rest of his life is simply a logical extension of an established pattern. Both in literature and from our own observations we can all easily find examples of the police regime's dual effect on its victims: on the one hand, it cripples them by depriving them of the possibility of useful work, while on the other it helps cultivate in them a special spiritual hauteur, a certified heroism, so to speak. The extent of the influence of the police regime on the Russian intelligentsia's mentality of heroism, its impact not merely on the course of people's lives but on their souls, their total outlook, is food for bitter reflection. In any case, the influence of the Western Enlightenment and its religion of man-Godhood and self-worship found an unexpected but powerful ally in Russian conditions. If a young *intelligent*—a university student or college girl, for example—still has any doubts whether he is mature enough for the historical mission of saving the fatherland, these usually disappear when he finds that his maturity is acknowledged by the Ministry of Internal Affairs. As far as inner exertion is concerned, the transformation of a Russian youth or yesterday's average citizen into a heroic figure is an uncomplicated and generally brief process. Once he masters a few dogmas of the religion of man-Godhood and the quasi-scientific "program" of some party, there is a corresponding change in his self-image, and the buskins

6. The text reads *istoricheskii* ("historical") in all editions. The sense of the passage, however, clearly indicates that *istericheskii* ("hysterical") was meant. *Eds.*

of heroism sprout of their own accord. Later on, sufferings, resentment at the cruelty of the authorities, grievous sacrifices and losses complete his evolution; he may then display a variety of character traits, but doubt as to his mission will no longer be one of them.

The heroic *intelligent*, therefore, is not content with the role of modest worker (even if he is forced to limit himself to this). His dream is to be the savior of mankind, or, at least, of the Russian people. He demands (in his dreams, of course) not the secure minimum but the heroic maximum. Maximalism is an integral feature of intelligentsia heroism, and one that revealed itself with such striking clarity during the Russian revolution. It is not the property of any one party—no, it is the very soul of heroism, for in general the hero will not settle for just a little. Even if he sees no possibility of realizing the maximum right now, and never will, it alone occupies his thoughts. In his imagination he makes an historical leap, and, with little interest in the road he has hurdled, he fixes his gaze on the bright spot at the very edge of the historical horizon. Such maximalism shows symptoms of monomania or auto-hypnosis; it fetters thought and produces a fanaticism deaf to the voice of life. This answers the historical question of why the most extreme orientations triumphed in the revolution, those which defined the tasks of the moment in ever more maximal terms (right up to the realization of a social republic or anarchy). It explains why the more extreme and patently senseless orientations grew stronger and stronger and, with the general movement to the left by our timorous, passive, easily intimidated public, drove out anything more moderate. (We need only recall the "left bloc's" hatred for the Kadets.)

Every hero has his own method for saving humanity and must work out his own program for doing so. Usually he accepts one of the programs of the existing political parties or groups, which differ in their procedures and methods but not in their goals (these are usually based on the ideals of materialist socialism or, lately, even anarchism). It would be an error to imagine that these party programs correspond psychologically to those of most parliamentary parties in Western Europe. They are much more: they are religious credos, infallible methods of saving mankind, ideological monoliths which can only be accepted or rejected *in toto*. The best representatives of the intelligentsia sacrifice their lives, health, freedom and happiness for the sake of their faith in the program. Although these programs usually claim to be "scientific" as well, thereby enhancing their charm, we had best not even speak of how genuinely scientific they are; and, in any case, the level of development and education of their most ardent adherents might make them bad judges of this question.

All feel that they are heroes, and all are called to be Providence and savior, but they do not agree on the ways and methods of achieving salvation. And since programmatic disagreements actually do touch the soul's most vital chords, party strife becomes unavoidable. Infected with "Jacobinism" and striving for a "seizure of power," a "dictatorship" in the name of the people's salvation, the intelligentsia inevitably breaks up and disintegrates into mutually hostile factions, and the higher the temperature of heroism, the more acute this fragmentation. Intolerance and discord are such familiar characteristics of our party intellectuals that we need only mention them. The intelligentsia movement seems to poison itself. The very essence of heroism presupposes a passive object of activity, the nation or humanity that is being saved, while the hero, individual or collective, is always thought of in the singular. Should there be several heroes and heroic methods, rivalry and discord are inevitable, for there cannot be several "dictatorships" at once. Heroism as a prevailing outlook is not a unifying but a divisive principle; it creates not colleagues but competitors.[7]

Our intelligentsia is almost unanimous in striving for collectivism, for the closest possible communality of human life, but its own temperament renders the intelligentsia itself an anti-communal, anti-collective force, since it bears within itself the divisive principle of heroic self-affirmation. The hero is to some extent a superman, confronting his neighbors in the proud and defiant pose of a savior; and for all its striving for democracy, the intelligentsia is only a special kind of aristocratic class, arrogantly contrasting itself to "common people." Anyone who has lived in intelligentsia circles is well aware of their arrogance and conceit, their sense of their own infallibility, their scorn for those who think differently, and the abstract dogmatism into which they fit all doctrines.

Because of its maximalism the intelligentsia is impervious to arguments based on either historical realism or scientific knowledge. It regards socialism itself not as a cumulative concept signifying a gradual socio-economic transformation made up of a series of partial and thoroughly concrete reforms, not as an "historical movement," but as a supra-historical "final goal" (to use the terminology of the famous quarrel with Bernstein) which must be reached in one historical leap by means of an act of intelligentsia heroism. This accounts for the intelligentsia's inadequate sense of historical reality, the geometric logic of its judgments and evaluations, and its notorious preoccupation with "principles." No other word seems to fly so often from the *intelligent's* lips: he judges everything first "in principle," which in fact means abstractly, without trying to grasp the complexity of reality, and thereby he often frees himself from the difficulty of evaluating a situation properly. Anyone who has ever worked with *intelligenty* knows the high cost of this "principled" impracticality, which sometimes leads to "straining at a gnat and swallowing a camel."[8]

7. Of course, dissension can also be observed in the history of Christian and other religious sects and confessions. Here, too, to a certain extent, we have the mentality of heroism, but these discords also have their own special causes unrelated to heroism.

8. Matthew 23:24. *Eds.*

The intelligentsia's maximalism is also the greatest obstacle to raising its educational level in precisely those areas it considers its specialty, social and political problems. For if you convince yourself that the goal and the methods of a movement have already been established, and "scientifically" at that, then of course you lose interest in studying the intermediary links that connect them. Consciously or unconsciously, the intelligentsia lives in an atmosphere of expectation, awaiting the social miracle, the universal cataclysm—it lives in an eschatological frame of mind.[9]

Heroism strives for the salvation of mankind by its *own* forces and by *external* means; hence the exceptional value it places on heroic acts which embody the program of maximalism to a maximal degree. Heroism commands that one set something in motion, accomplish something beyond one's strength, and in so doing give up what is most dear, one's own life. One can become a hero and, at the same time, a savior of mankind by an heroic act that goes far beyond the ordinary call of duty. Although only a few individuals can fulfill this dream that dwells in the intelligentsia's heart, it serves as the general standard of judgment, the criterion for vital assessments. To perform such an act is both exceptionally difficult, for the strongest instincts of fear and attachment to life have to be overcome, and exceptionally simple, for it demands only a comparatively brief exertion of will power, while the implied or expected results of the act are deemed to be so very great. Sometimes a desire to take leave of life because of failure to adjust to it and inability to bear its burden merges imperceptibly with heroic self-renunciation, so that you cannot help asking yourself: "Is this heroism, or is it suicide?" Of course, the calendar of intelligentsia saints names many heroes who made their whole lives a feat of suffering and prolonged exertion of the will, but the general atmosphere is not altered by distinctions that depend on the strength of particular individuals.

Obviously such an attitude is much better suited to the storms of history than to its calms, which debilitate heroes. The most fertile soil for heroism is composed of a maximum opportunity for heroic acts, an irrational "emotional upsurge," exaltation, and an intoxication with struggle that creates an atmosphere of heroic adventurism. This explains the great power of revolutionary romanticism, the notorious "revolutionism" of our intelligentsia. It should not be forgotten that revolution is a negative concept; it has no independent content and is characterized solely as the negation of what it destroys. The impulse of revolution consequently is hatred and destruction. Yet one of the foremost Russian *intelligenty*, Bakunin, formulated the notion that the spirit of destruction is also a creative spirit, and this belief is central to the mentality

---

9. There is no need to point out the extent to which this atheistic eschatology differs from Christian eschatology.

of heroism. It simplifies the task of historical reconstruction, since it implies that the primary requirements are strong muscles and nerves, mettle, and boldness. This simplified notion frequently comes to mind upon surveying the chronicle of the Russian revolution. . . .

By virtue of their place in society and their objective circumstances, certain groups are most naturally drawn to heroism and the inflexible logic of its maximalism, and they are the ones that make the greatest impression on the intelligentsia's own heroic mentality. In Russia, the most favorable combination of these attributes is to be found in the students. The physiology and psychology of youth, the substitution of zeal and self-confidence for life experience and scientific knowledge, and a privileged social position (which, however, does not go as far as the bourgeois exclusiveness of Western students), make our young people archetypes of heroic maximalism.

If Christianity regards age as the natural embodiment of spiritual experience and leadership, it was natural that the students assumed this role in regard to our intelligentsia. *Spiritual pedocracy*[10] is both the greatest evil of our society and a symptomatic manifestation of intelligentsia heroism, displaying its basic features but in heightened and exaggerated form. This abnormal relationship, in which elders are guided by the value judgments and opinions of the "student youth," turns the natural order of things head over heels, and it is equally pernicious for both sides. The students' spiritual hegemony is linked historically to the fact that by their outbursts they actually have played the role of vanguard in Russian history; but psychologically, the explanation for it lies in the spiritual outlook of the intelligentsia, whose most vivid and striking representatives never outgrow the world-view they held as students. Hence we watch with habitual and most deplorable indifference and, far worse, with tacit or even open approval, while our young people undertake serious social experiments equipped only with an abundance of intelligentsia heroism, but lacking either knowledge or experience. These experiments have dangerous consequences and, of course, succeed only in strengthening reaction. The extreme youthfulness of the groups that display the greatest maximalism in their actions and programs has not been sufficiently noted and appreciated. And, far worse, many find this situation perfectly normal; during the revolution "student" became the generic term for *intelligent*.

Each of life's stages has its advantages, and youth, with its latent forces, is especially rich in them. Anyone concerned with the future is most anxious about the younger generation. But to be spiritually dependent on it, to flatter it, to truckle to its opinions and take it as a standard, testifies to a society's spiritual weakness. In any case, an entire historical period and the whole spiritual tenor of intelligentsia heroism are symbolized by the fact that the ideal of the Christian saint, the ascetic, has been replaced here by the image of the revolutionary student.

10. Pedocracy: rule by children.

IV

Maximalist goals lead to the maximalist means which have so regrettably appeared in recent years. The lack of scruple in methods, the heroic "all is allowed," was foreshadowed in Dostoevskii's *Crime and Punishment* and *The Devils*. It is the supreme expression of the man-deifying nature of intelligentsia heroism, its inherent self-worship and its substitution of itself for God and Providence, in regard not only to goals and plans but also to the ways and means of realizing them. I am realizing my own idea, and for its sake I free myself from the bonds of ordinary morality; I give myself the right not only to the property of others, but to their life and death, should this be needed for my idea. Inside each maximalist there is a little Napoleon of socialism or anarchism. Amorality or, to use the old expression, nihilism, is the necessary consequence of self-worship. The danger of corruption lurks here, and downfall is inevitable. Those bitter disappointments which many suffered during the revolution, that unforgettable picture of wilfulness, "expropriations" and mass terror—none of this was accidental. It was, rather, a disclosure of the spiritual potentialities which are necessarily latent in the mentality of self-worship.[11]

In reality, only chosen natures can rise to heroism, and even then only at exceptional historical moments. But life is an everyday affair, and the intelligentsia does not consist solely of heroes. In the absence of genuine heroic acts or the opportunity to perform them, heroism becomes pretension, a defiant pose. Ultimately, we find a special atmosphere of heroic hypocrisy, irresponsible fault-finding, and eternal opposition "on principle," along with an exaggerated sense of one's rights and a weakened consciousness of one's duties and of personal responsibility in general. The most ordinary citizen, though he is in no way better than his neighbors and sometimes is even worse, no sooner dons the uniform of the *intelligent* than he begins to treat them with disdain. This evil is especially prevalent in the provinces. Self-worship on credit does not always make a man a hero, but it can make him arrogant. It deprives him of absolute norms and firm principles of personal and social conduct, and replaces them with wilfulness or a home-made code.

Nihilism, then, is a terrible scourge, a horrible spiritual ulcer eating away at our society. The heroic "all is allowed" imperceptibly cheapens into mere lack of principle in anything that concerns personal life and day-to-day personal conduct. It is one of the main reasons why, for all our abundance of heroes, we have so few people who are just orderly, disciplined, and hard-working;

11. The disclosures of the Azev affair revealed that with heroic maximalism the lack of scruple can go so far that you can no longer tell where the revolutionary ends and the police agent or provocateur begins.

and why those heroic youths, in whose wake the older generation follows, in later life so easily and imperceptibly turn into "superfluous men" or into Chekhovian and Gogolian types, ending up with wine or cards, if not worse. With the honesty of genius, Pushkin allows us a glimpse of the possible future of Lenskii, whose death is so tragic and untimely, and reveals a thoroughly prosaic picture.[12] Try to perform the same operation mentally on some other youth who is now surrounded by a hero's aureole, and imagine him as an ordinary worker when the affectation of heroism has burned itself out and left the the emptiness of nihilism in his soul. The *intelligent*-poet Nekrasov, author of "Knight for an Hour," had a point in feeling that an early death was the best apotheosis of intelligentsia heroism:

> Do not sob so wildly over him:
> It is good to die young!
> Relentless banality had no time
> To cast a shadow over him.[13]

This heroic affectation, superficial and unstable, explains the striking fickleness of the intelligentsia's tastes, creeds and moods, which change at the whim of fashion. The change in mood over the last few years, from heroic revolutionism to nihilism and pornography, is shocking to many, as is the epidemic of suicides, which they mistakenly try to explain solely on the grounds of political reaction and the grievous impressions of Russian life.

But even this hysterical succession of moods is natural for the intelligentsia. The alternation of historical holidays and workdays has not changed the intelligentsia's essence, but only disclosed it more fully; pseudo-heroism does not go unpunished. The intelligentsia's spiritual condition cannot fail to arouse grave anxiety. But the greatest cause for anxiety is the young generation now growing up, and especially the intelligentsia's children. The intelligentsia, rootless and cut off from an organic mode of life, without solid foundations of its own, with its atheism, inflexible rationalism, and general enervation and lack of principle in everyday life, passes these qualities on to its children, with just one difference: even in childhood the latter are deprived of that healthy sap which their parents absorbed from living among the people. I fear that degenerate traits are bound to appear with growing rapidity.

The concepts of *personal* morality, *personal* self-perfection, development

---

12. *Eugene Onegin*, Chapter vi, stanzas 37-39. *Eds.*

13. Bulgakov's quote is exact, but he has ascribed it to the wrong poem. He is quoting a short, untitled lyric that begins with these lines. It can be found in N. A. Nekrasov, *Collected Works* [Sobranie sochinenii], 8 vols. (Moscow: Khudozhestvennaia literatura, 1965-67), II, 252. "Knight for an Hour" [Rytsar' na chas] is another Nekrasov poem, which appears in the same volume of this edition. *Eds.*

of the *personality*, are extremely unpopular with the intelligentsia (while the word *social*, in contrast, has a special, sacramental quality). Although the intelligentsia's outlook is itself a case of extreme self-affirmation of the personality, its self-deification, ideologically the intelligentsia relentlessly persecutes the personality, sometimes reducing it without a trace to the influence of the environment and the spontaneous forces of history (in accord with the general doctrine of the Enlightenment). The intelligentsia will not grant that the personality holds living, creative energy, and it is deaf to everything that approaches the question: deaf not only to Christian doctrine but even to Tolstoi (whose doctrine does contain a healthy kernel of personal introspection), and to all philosophical doctrines that force consideration of the problem.

And yet, the absence of a correct doctrine of the personality is the intelligentsia's chief weakness. The root cause of its feebleness and inadequacy, its historical bankruptcy, is its distortion of the personality and the falseness of its very ideal of personal development. The intelligentsia must be corrected, not from without but from within; it alone can do this, through a free spiritual act, invisible but absolutely real.

V

The special character of intelligentsia heroism will become clearer if we contrast it with the opposite spiritual type, Christian heroism—or, more precisely, Christian asceticism,[14] for in Christianity the hero is the ascetic. The basic difference between them is not so much external as internal and religious. The hero puts himself in the role of Providence, and by this spiritual usurpation he assigns himself a responsibility greater than he can bear and tasks that are beyond the reach of men. The Christian ascetic believes in God the Provider, without Whose will not a hair falls from the head. In his eyes both history and a single human life are a realization of God's plan, and even though he does not comprehend it in its individual details he humbles himself before it in an act of faith. This frees him at once from heroic posturing and pretensions. He concentrates his attention on his true task, his real obligations, and their strict, absolute fulfillment. Of course, it may happen that both the definition and the fulfillment of these obligations will demand no less breadth of vision and knowledge than intelligentsia heroism claims to possess. But the ascetic focuses his attention on the recognition of personal duty and its fulfillment, and on self-control.

The shift of attention to oneself and one's obligations, the emancipation

---

14. In his *On Heroes, Hero-Worship and the Heroic in History*, [Thomas] Carlyle describes as the heroic a spiritual temperament which approximates what we have termed the ascetic type and which, in any case, is significantly different from atheistic heroism.

from a false image of oneself as the unacknowledged savior of the world and from the pride that inevitably goes with it, heals the soul and fills it with a sense of wholesome Christian humility. In his Pushkin speech, Dostoevskii called the Russian intelligentsia to this act of spiritual self-renunciation, to the sacrifice of its proud *intelligent*'s ego in the name of a higher sanctity. "Humble thyself, proud man, and first of all subdue thy pride. . . . If thou wilt conquer thyself, if thou wilt humble thyself, thou shalt become free as thou never imagined, and thou shalt begin a great work and make others free, and thou shalt see happiness, for thy life will be full. . . ."[15]

No word is more unpopular with *intelligenty* than *humility*, and few concepts have been more misunderstood and distorted, or fallen such easy prey to intelligentsia demagogy. Its hostility to this concept is perhaps the best testimony to the intelligentsia's spiritual nature and betrays its arrogant heroism resting on self-worship. And yet, in the unanimous witness of the Church, humility is the cardinal and fundamental Christian virtue; and even outside of Christianity it is an extremely valuable quality which, at the very least, attests to a high spiritual level. Even an *intelligent* has no trouble understanding that a genuine scholar, for example, only feels the depth of his ignorance more acutely as his knowledge deepens and broadens, so that the acquisition of knowledge brings with it increasing understanding of his ignorance and growing intellectual humility. The biographies of great scholars confirm this. And conversely, self-assured complacency or the hope of attaining complete, satisfying knowledge through one's own powers is a true and certain symptom of scholarly immaturity, or simply of youth.

The same sense of profound dissatisfaction with his own work, the feeling that it fails to correspond to the ideals of beauty and the purposes of art, distinguishes the genuine artist, too; his labor inevitably becomes a torment to him, although it is his whole life. No true artist lacks a feeling of perpetual dissatisfaction with his creations, and this may be termed humility before beauty.

The same feeling that his individual powers are inadequate in the face of broadening tasks seizes the philosopher, the statesman, the social reformer, etc.

But if it is relatively easy to understand that humility is natural and necessary in these limited spheres of human endeavor, why is it so hard to grasp in regard to the core of spiritual life—moral and religious self-examination?

---

15. F. M. Dostoevskii, *Complete Collected Works* [Polnoe sobranie sochinenii], Jubilee (6th) ed., with a biographical sketch by Professor S. N. Bulgakov, 14 vols. (St. Petersburg: P. F. Panteleev, 1904-06), XII, 425. The speech was delivered in 1880 and published in Dostoevskii's *Diary of a Writer* of the same year. Dostoevskii argued that Pushkin was Russia's prophetic poet in his delineation of denationalized "superfluous" men, his recognition of the Russian national genius, and his universal sympathy and understanding. *Eds.*

It is here that a higher standard, an ideal of personality, is of decisive importance. Is the standard for examining oneself the image of the perfect, Divine
personality, incarnate in Christ? Or is it self-deified man in one of his earthly,
limited guises (humanity, the people, the proletariat, or the superman)—a pro-
jection, in the last analysis, of one's own ego in an heroic pose? The ascetic's
sharpening spiritual vision constantly detects new imperfections in man, limited
and corrupted by sin and passions, and in himself first of all. His feeling of
remoteness from the ideal increases. In other words, the moral development
of his personality brings with it a growing awareness of his imperfections or,
in what amounts to the same thing, expresses itself in humility before God
and a "going before God" (as the patristic literature of the Church repeatedly
makes clear). The difference between heroic and Christian self-appraisal pervades all the recesses of a person's soul, his entire self-consciousness.

Because it lacks an ideal of the personality (or, more precisely, because it
has a distorted one), the intelligentsia totally neglects all that concerns the
religious cultivation of the personality, that is, its development and discipline.
It lacks the absolute norms and values which are required for this cultivation
and which only religion provides. And above all, it lacks the concept of sin
and the sense of sin, to the extent that the word "sin" sounds almost as barbaric and foreign to the *intelligent*'s ear as the word "humility." The power
of sin, its agonizing weight, its ubiquitous and profound influence on all human
life, in short, the whole tragedy of man's sinful condition which, in God's
preordained plan, only Golgotha could resolve—all this remains outside the
scope of the intelligentsia's consciousness. It has not outgrown religious childhood, so to speak; it is not above sin but below awareness of it. In common
with Rousseau and the whole Enlightenment, the intelligentsia came to believe that natural man is inherently good, and that the doctrine of original sin
and the innate depravity of human nature is a superstitious myth which in no
way corresponds to moral experience. This implies that special concern for
the cultivation of the personality (that much-derided "self-perfection") is
neither possible nor desirable; all one's energy should be expended instead on
the struggle to improve the environment. The intelligentsia asserts that the
personality is wholly a product of the environment, and at the same time suggests to it that it improve its surroundings, like Baron Münchausen pulling
himself out of the swamp by his own hair.[16]

The lack of a sense of sin or even of any timidity at the notion of sin explains many features of the intelligentsia's character and way of life, and—
alas!—many of the distressing aspects and events of our revolution and the

___

16. Baron Münchausen was the putative author of a book of tall stories of travel and
adventure, first published in Oxford in 1786 under the title *Baron Münchausen's Narrative of his Marvellous Travels and Campaigns in Russia*. The true author was a German
scientist and poet named Rudolf Eric Raspe. *Eds.*

spiritual decay that followed it. Our intelligentsia has been feasting on a number of savory dishes from the table of Western civilization, and the result is indigestion in a stomach that was ruined in any case. Isn't it time to remember our simple, coarse, but unquestionably wholesome and nourishing fare, the old Mosaic Commandments, and then go on to the New Testament! . . . .

Heroic maximalism is wholly projected outward, toward the attainment of external goals. In regard to personal life, exclusive of the heroic act and everything connected with it, it turns out to be minimalism, that is, personal life is simply disregarded. Hence, heroic maximalism is unsuited for the development of a stable, disciplined, hard-working individual standing on his own feet and not on a wave of public hysteria which soon collapses. The *intelligent's* character-type is defined by this combination of maximalism and minimalism, in which maximal pretensions can be advanced with minimal preparation of the personality, either in learning or in life-experience and self-discipline. The unnatural hegemony of the students, our spiritual pedocracy, reflects these qualities most vividly.

Christian asceticism perceives the world differently. I shall not dwell on what the atheistic and Christian faiths perceive as the goal of cosmic and historical development: for the former, it is the happiness of the last generations, who will triumph on the bones and blood of their forebears, though in their turn they will be no less subject to the inexorable fate of death (not to mention the possibility of natural calamities); for Christianity, it is faith in the universal resurrection, a new earth and a new heaven, when "God will be all in all."

Obviously, the faith of no positivistic, atheistic maximalism even remotely approaches Christian doctrine. At the moment, however, we are not interested in that side of the problem, but rather in how each doctrine is refracted in the life and psychology of the individual. Christian asceticism, in complete contrast to the pridefulness of intelligentsia heroism, is first of all maximalism in personal life, in the demands made on oneself; the tensions of external maximalism are, however, entirely eliminated. The Christian hero or ascetic (our terminology is somewhat inexact, of course) does not assign himself the tasks of Providence, and so does not link the fate of history or mankind to his own or anyone else's individual effort. He sees his activity primarily as the fulfillment of his duty to God, the carrying out of God's commandment as it is directed to him. He is obliged to fulfill it to the utmost, and equally to display the greatest possible energy and selflessness in determining his task and his obligations. In a way, he too must strive for maximalism in his actions, but maximalism of a totally different kind. One of the most common misconceptions in regard to humility (advanced, however, *mala* as well as *bona fide*) is that Christian humility—an inward and invisible act of struggle with egoism, wilfulness and self-worship—is persistently interpreted as outward passivity, reconciliation with evil, inertia and even servility,[17] or at least as inactivity in the objective sense. This is a confusion of Christian asceticism with one of its many forms (though a most important one), monasticism. But asceticism as an inner structuring of the personality is compatible with any outward activity that does not contradict its principles.

The contrast between Christian humility and the "revolutionary" temperament is quite a popular one. Without going into details, I shall show that revolution, meaning certain political actions, does not in itself predetermine the specific spirit and ideals that inspire it. When Dmitrii Donskoi set out against the Tatars with the blessing of St. Sergei, it was a revolutionary action in the political sense, for it was an uprising against the legal government. But at the same time, I feel that in the hearts of the participants it was an act of Christian asceticism indistinguishable from a supreme act of humility. Our recent revolution, on the contrary, based as it was on atheism, was spiritually very remote not only from Christian humility but from Christianity in general. Similarly, there is an enormous spiritual difference between the English Puritan Revolution and the atheistic French Revolution, just as there is between Cromwell and Marat or Robespierre, and between Ryleev, or any of the believers among the Decembrists, and the most recent revolutionaries.

In the proper historical circumstances, of course, individual "heroic" deeds are fully compatible with the mentality of Christian asceticism. They are performed not in their own name, however, but in God's name, not heroically but ascetically, and even though they bear an external resemblance to heroism their religious psychology is quite different. "The kingdom of heaven suffereth violence, and the violent take it by force." (Matthew 11:12.) "Violence," the maximum straining of one's powers for the realization of good, is demanded of every person. But this does not give him the right to a feeling of heroism, to spiritual pride, for it is only the fulfillment of duty: "when ye shall have done all those things which are commanded you, say, We are unprofitable servants: we have done that which was our duty to do." (Luke 17:10.)

Christian asceticism is unremitting self-control, struggle with the lower, sinful sides of one's character, spiritual *askesis*. If heroism is characterized by bursts of activity and a quest for great deeds, the norm here, on the contrary, is an even course, "measure," restraint, unflagging self-discipline, patience, and endurance—precisely those qualities the intelligentsia lacks. True asceticism

---

17. Of course, everything is open to falsification and distortion, and the term "humility" has been used to cover traits that in fact have nothing in common with it—in particular, cowardly and hypocritical servility (just as intelligentsia heroism and revolutionism frequently cover dissoluteness and hoodlum activity). The higher a virtue, the more vicious its caricature and distortion. But its essence should not be judged by its caricature.

consists in faithfully fulfilling one's duty, in bearing one's own cross in self-renunciation (not just outward, but, still more, inward) and leaving all the rest to Providence. In monastic usage there is an excellent expression for this religious and practical idea: *obedience*. That is the term for any occupation assigned to a monk, whether it be scholarly toil or the coarsest physical labor, as long as it is performed in the name of religious duty. This concept can be extended beyond the walls of the monastery and applied to any work whatsoever. In fulfilling their obligations the doctor and the engineer, the professor and the politician, the factory owner and his worker, can each bear obedience, guided not by personal interest (whether spiritual or material is not of concern) but by conscience, the call of duty. The discipline of obedience, "worldly asceticism" (from the German expression *"innerweltliche Askese"*[18]), had an enormous influence on the development of the personality in various fields of work in Western Europe, as can still be seen today.

The reverse side of intelligentsia maximalism is historical impatience, a lack of historical soberness, a desire to evoke social miracles, and the denial in practice of the evolutionism it professes in theory. By contrast, the discipline of "obedience" necessarily furthers the development of historical soberness, self-control and restraint. The yoke of historical obedience teaches one to bear the burden of history and instills a feeling of connection with and gratitude to the past, which is now so easily forgotten for the sake of the future; it restores the moral bond between fathers and children.

Humanistic progress, on the other hand, is scorn for the fathers, aversion to the past and complete condemnation of it, historical and sometimes even personal ingratitude; it legitimizes the spiritual discord between fathers and children. The hero creates history according to his own plan—he starts history off, as it were, and he regards everything around him as material or a passive object on which he can act. Hence, he inevitably loses either feeling or desire for historical continuity.

The foregoing parallel allows us to draw a general conclusion about the relationship between intelligentsia heroism and Christian asceticism. Despite a certain superficial similarity, there is no inner affinity between them, not a single point of contact beneath the surface. The mission of heroism is the external salvation of mankind (more precisely, its future portion) by one's own powers, according to one's own plan, "in one's own name." The hero is the man who most completely realizes his idea, even at the cost of his life; he is the man-God. The mission of Christian asceticism is to turn one's life into invisible self-renunciation and obedience, to perform one's toil with the utmost exertion, self-discipline and self-control, but to see it—and oneself—only as a tool of Providence. The Christian saint is the person who, by means of con-

18. See Max Weber, *The Protestant Ethic and the Spirit of Capitalism*, Chapter iv. *Eds*.

tinuous and unremitting effort, has most completely transformed his personal will and his empirical personality until they are permeated to the fullest possible measure with the will of God. The model of total permeation is the God-man, arriving "not to do his own will, but the will of His Father that sent him," and "coming in the name of the Lord."[19]

The tendency of the moment is to understate rather than overstate the difference between Christianity (or at least its ethical doctrine) and intelligentsia heroism, which historically appropriated some of its most fundamental dogmas from Christianity—above all, the idea of the equal value of all persons, the absolute dignity of the human personality, equality and brotherhood. The intelligentsia's failure to understand the real abyss between atheism and Christianity greatly encouraged this tendency, since it allowed the intelligentsia, with its usual self-assurance, frequently to "correct" the image of Christ, freeing it from "churchly distortions" and depicting Him as a Social Democrat or Socialist-Revolutionary. Belinskii, the father of the Russian intelligentsia, set the example.[20] This tasteless operation, which true religious feeling finds intolerable, has been performed a number of times. But the intelligentsia has no interest in this rapprochement in itself, and resorts to it primarily for political purposes or for "agitation."

Far more subtle and tempting is another, equally blasphemous falsehood, which in various forms has gained great currency lately: namely, the assertion that intelligentsia maximalism and revolutionism, which rest, as we have seen, on a spiritual basis of atheism, in essence differ from Christianity only in their lack of religious consciousness. Just substitute the name of Christ for Marx or Mikhailovskii, and the Gospels or, even better, the Apocalypse (it's more quotable) for *Capital*—or even change nothing at all, but simply heighten the intelligentsia's revolutionism and continue the intelligentsia revolution—and this

---

19. John 6:38, 5:43. *Eds.*

20. In his famous letter to Gogol', Belinskii wrote this ardent and classic expression of the intelligentsia's attitude: "What is there in common between Christ and any Church, and particularly the Orthodox Church? He was the first to teach men the ideals of liberty, equality, and fraternity, and He illustrated and proved the truth of His teaching by His martyrdom . . . But the true meaning of Christ's teaching was revealed by the philosophical movement of the last century." V. G. Belinskii, *Letter to Gogol'* [Pis'mo k Gogoliu], with an introduction by S. A. Vengerov (St. Petersburg: Svetoch, 1905).

[In 1847 Gogol', formerly considered a radical because of his merciless satires on Russian shortcomings, published *Selected Passages from Correspondence with Friends*, an apologia for submission to autocracy and the Orthodox Church. Belinskii responded with a letter to Gogol', which was published in Russia only in the twentieth century but had a wide circulation in manuscript. Its condemnation of injustice and oppression, and its insistence on the need for Western institutions in Russia, make it a classic statement of Westernism. The translation of the passages here and below is adapted from that of Valentine Snow in Marc Raeff, ed., *Russian Intellectual History: An Anthology* (New York: Harcourt, Brace & World, 1966), p. 256. *Eds.*]

is supposed to generate a new religious consciousness! (As if history had not already furnished an example of an intelligentsia revolution prolonged enough to manifest all its spiritual potentialities, namely, the great French Revolution.) If the suffering and persecuted *intelligent*, who bore on his shoulders the heroic struggle against bureaucratic absolutism, could still easily be confused with the Christian martyr before the revolution, this has become much more difficult since the revolution, in which the intelligentsia revealed its true spiritual qualities.

At present we can also observe the intelligentsia counterfeiting Christianity, adopting Christian words and ideas while preserving intact the whole spiritual outlook of intelligentsia heroism, and this is especially characteristic of our era. All we Christians who emerged from the intelligentsia have this spiritual flaw deep within us. Nothing is easier for intelligentsia heroism, newly garbed in Christian dress and sincerely taking its intelligentsia experiences and habitual heroic fervor for righteous Christian anger, than to step forth as church revolutionism and oppose its new sanctity and its new religious consciousness to the untruth of the "historical church." The christianizing *intelligent*, who in real life is sometimes incapable of satisfying the ordinary demands made of a member of the "historical church," has no trouble regarding himself as a Martin Luther, or even as the prophetic bearer of a new religious consciousness, called not only to renew church life but to create new forms of it, almost a new religion.

Similarly in secular politics, the most ordinary intelligentsia maximalism, the stuff of revolutionary programs, is simply seasoned with Christian terminology or texts and served up as true Christianity in politics. This intelligentsia Christianity leaves intact the most anti-religious element of intelligentsia heroism, its spiritual outlook; it is a compromise between antagonistic principles and has a temporary, transitory significance but no independent viability.[21] It is unnecessary for genuine intelligentsia heroism and impossible for Christianity. Like any religion, Christianity is jealous; it is strong in a person only when it seizes him entirely, soul, heart and will.

There is no reason to conceal or soften the contrast between genuine and intelligentsia Christianity. Just as there is no real similarity between the early Christian martyrs and those of the revolution, notwithstanding the external identity of their exploits, so there is an abyss which cannot be straddled between intelligentsia heroism and Christian asceticism, even though they resemble each other on the surface (a resemblance we can admit only partially and conditionally at that). One must die that the other may be born, and as the one dies the other grows and gathers strength. This is the true relationship

21. I am dealing here with the psychological aspect of all these problems, leaving aside any examination of their substance.

between the two outlooks. It is necessary to "repent," to review, rethink and censure one's former spiritual life to its depths and inner recesses, in order to be reborn for a new life. That is why the first word of the preaching of the Gospel is a call to repentance based on self-knowledge and self-appraisal. "Repent ye (μετανοεῖτε), for the kingdom of heaven is at hand." (Matthew 3:2, 4:17; Mark 1:15.) A new soul must be born, a new inner man who will grow, develop, and gain strength in the exploit of life. I am not talking about a change in political or party programs (the only way the intelligentsia usually conceives of renewal), nor even about programs at all, but about something much greater—the human personality itself; I am talking not about deeds but about the doer. This regeneration takes place unseen in the soul of man. If invisible agents are the strongest ones even in the physical world, then their power in the moral universe, too, cannot be denied simply because programs do not provide for them in special paragraphs.

The slow and arduous course of re-educating the personality lies before the Russian intelligentsia. There are no leaps, no cataclysms along the way, and only stubborn self-discipline can be victorious. Russia needs new workers in all walks of life: in politics, to institute "reforms"; in economics, to develop the national economy; in cultural affairs, to further Russia's enlightenment; in the church, to strengthen the forces of the teaching church, its clergy and hierarchy. The new people, if Russia finds them at last, will of course seek new practical avenues of service, quite apart from existing programs, and, I believe, these will be revealed to their selfless quest.[22]

VI

In its attitude toward the people, to whose service it has dedicated itself, the intelligentsia constantly and inevitably wavers between two extremes: worship of the people and spiritual hauteur. The very foundations of the intelligentsia's faith require worship of the people, be it in the form of the old

22. *Post-scriptum pro domo sua.* As regards my severe delineation of the intelligentsia's spiritual character (sections iii-v), the reproach might be made that I am pronouncing judgment on selfless, suffering, persecuted people. I myself have raised this question more than once. But however low an opinion I may have of myself, I feel an obligation (if only as a form of public "obedience") to tell everything that I see, everything that weighs on my heart as the sum total of all I have experienced, felt and thought in regard to the intelligentsia. My sense of responsibility and my agonizing concern, both for the intelligentsia and for Russia, enjoin me to do this. But when I criticize the spiritual character and ideals of the intelligentsia, I do not mean to judge particular individuals, just as, when I set forth my own ideals, which I am convinced are true, I in no way imply that I personally come closer to them than do others. And indeed, how can one feel that he is approaching an absolute ideal? But to urge it on others, to show it to those who do not see it, is not only permissible—it is obligatory.

Populism which originated with Herzen and was based on a belief in the socialist spirit of the Russian people, or in the latest form, Marxism, where the
same attribute is ascribed not to the whole people but to a single part of it,
the "proletariat." But this faith necessarily gives rise not only to worship of
the people but to the direct opposite as well: an arrogant view of the people
as an object of salvation, as a minor, unenlightened in the intelligentsia's
sense of the word and in need of a nursemaid to develop its "consciousness."

Our literature has repeatedly taken note of the intelligentsia's spiritual alienation from the people. Dostoevskii felt that it had been prophetically fore-
shown as early as Pushkin, first in the image of the eternal wanderer Aleko,
and then in Evgenii Onegin, who initiated a whole series of "superfluous
men."[23] And, indeed, the intelligentsia has remarkably little feeling for the
indissoluble bond of history; it has little sympathetic interest and love for its
history, or aesthetic appreciation of it. On its palette two colors predominate,
black for the past and rosy pink for the future. (The spiritual stature and acute
vision of our great writers, who plumbed the depths of Russian history and
drew from it *Boris Godunov, Song of the Merchant Kalashnikov*, and *War and
Peace*, appear all the more vividly by contrast.[24]) The intelligentsia generally
uses history as material for the application of the theoretical formulas which
hold sway at any given time (such as the theory of class struggle), or for journalistic or agitational purposes.

The Russian intelligentsia's cosmopolitanism is also well-known.[25] Brought
up on the abstract formulas of the Enlightenment, the *intelligent* finds it perfectly normal to assume the role of a Marquis de Posa and regard himself as
a *Weltbürger*.[26] This cosmopolitanism of the desert, the absence of healthy
national feeling, hinders the development of national self-consciousness and
is intimately connected with the intelligentsia's separation from the people.

The intelligentsia has not yet thought out the national problem, which pre-
occupied only the Slavophiles. From Chernyshevskii, who assiduously nullified
the independent significance of the national problem,[27] to the contemporary
Marxists, who dissolve it without a trace in the class struggle, the intelligentsia
has satisfied itself with "natural" explanations of the origins of nationality.

23. Dostoevskii made this statement in the Pushkin speech. Aleko is the hero of the
narrative poem "The Gypsies." *Eds.*
24. By Pushkin, Lermontov, and Tolstoi, and set in the Time of Troubles, the sixteenth
century, and the Napoleonic Wars, respectively. *Eds.*
25. Let us not even mention the unique and ominous form it took during the Russo-
Japanese War, lest we aggravate raw and painful memories.
[Bulgakov is evidently referring to the "defeatist" position espoused by some liberals
and revolutionaries during the Russo-Japanese War. The "defeatists" welcomed the pros-
pect of a Russian military defeat, on the grounds that it would weaken and discredit the
absolutist government and lead to internal reforms or revolution. *Eds.*]
26. See Schiller's *Don Carlos. Eds.*
27. In his notes to his translation of J. S. Mill's *Principles of Political Economy.*

The foundations of the national idea are not merely ethnographic and historical, they are primarily religious and cultural; it is based on religio-cultural messianism, into which all conscious national feeling is necessarily cast. So it was for the greatest bearer of the religio-messianic idea, ancient Israel, and so it remains for every great historical people. The desire for national autonomy, for the preservation and defense of nationality, is merely the negative expression of this idea and has value only by virtue of its implied positive content. The most outstanding spokesmen of our national self-consciousness, Dostoevskii, the Slavophiles, and Vladimir Solov'ev, understood the national idea in precisely this way, for they linked it with the world mission of the Russian church or Russian culture.

There is no reason why such a conception of the national idea must lead to nationalistic exclusiveness. On the contrary, it lays the only positive foundation for the idea of the brotherhood of peoples, rather than of nationless, atomized "citizens" or "proletarians of all countries" who have renounced their homeland. The idea of nationality, viewed in this way, is one of the necessary positive conditions for the progress of civilization. Our intelligentsia's cosmopolitanism does, of course, allow it to toss aside the many difficulties that inevitably arise when national problems are worked out in practice.[28] But this is purchased at the high price of deadening a whole side of the soul— the side that is turned directly toward the people. This enables the representatives of militant, chauvinistic nationalism to exploit the intelligentsia's cosmopolitanism very easily, for it gives them a monopoly on patriotism.

But this is not what creates the deepest gulf between the intelligentsia and the people, for it is really only a derivative distinction; the fundamental difference between them is their attitude to religion. The people's world-view and spiritual outlook are determined by the Christian faith. However great the distance between ideal and reality, however "dark" and unenlightened our people may be, their ideal is Christ and His teaching,[29] and their standard

28. Consequently, even the current "neoslavist" movement still lacks theoretical foundation.

29. "There may be brutality and sin in our people, but indisputably they do have one quality: as a whole, at least, they never take their sin for the truth and never wish to do so. . . . Sin is a transitory thing, but Christ is eternal. The people sin and defile themselves daily, but in their best moments, in Christ's moments, they are never mistaken about the truth. The important thing is what the people believe as their truth, wherein they think the truth resides, how they imagine the truth, what constitutes their best desires, what they have come to love, what they ask of God, what they weep for in prayer. And the people's ideal is Christ. And with Christ there is, of course, enlightenment, and in their highest, fateful moments our people always decide and always have decided their every general and national question in a Christian way." (Dostoevskii, *op. cit.*, p. 441.)

It is interesting to compare Dostoevskii's conception of the national soul, which he shares with the greatest Russian artists and thinkers, with that of the *intelligent* as expressed

is Christian asceticism. What has the whole history of our people been, if not asceticism: oppressed first by the Tatars and then by the Muscovite and Petersburg state, bearing the centuries-old historical burden of standing watch to safeguard Western civilization from the savage peoples and the sands of Asia, in this cruel climate, with its everlasting famines, cold, and sufferings. If our people have been able to bear all these afflictions while still preserving their spiritual forces, and come through alive though crippled, it is only because their faith and the ideals of Christian asceticism gave them a source of spiritual strength, a well-spring of national health and vitality.

Like the icon-lamps glimmering in the monastery cloisters[30] whither the people thronged through the centuries in search of moral support and instruction, these ideals, this light of Christ, illumined Rus'. Insofar as they possess this light our people—I say this without hesitation—for all their illiteracy, are more enlightened than our intelligentsia. But on just this crucial point, the intelligentsia has always regarded everything that concerns the people's faith with a total lack of understanding and even with contempt.

Contact between the intelligentsia and the people is, therefore, basically a clash of two faiths, two religions. The intelligentsia, by destroying the people's religion, corrupts their soul and dislodges it from its age-old, hitherto unshakable foundations. But what does the intelligentsia give in exchange? How does it view its mission of enlightening the people? It views it in the Enlightenment sense, as primarily the development of the mind and its enrichment with knowledge. However, because the enlighteners themselves lack time, opportunity, and, even more important, education, they replace this task with another: either the dogmatic exposition of the doctrines prevailing at a given time in a given party (all of them, of course, labeled "very strictly scientific"), or else the communication of a smattering of knowledge from various fields. This demonstrates most emphatically our general lack of culture, the inadequacy of our schools and textbooks, and, most of all, the absence of simple literacy. In any event, enlightenment in the intelligentsia's sense of the word receives priority over primary education, i.e., the communi-

in Belinskii's previously cited letter. "Take a closer look, and you will see that the Russian people are deeply atheistic by nature. They still have many superstitions, but not a trace of religious feeling [sic–S. B.]. . . . mystical exaltation is foreign to them; they have too much common sense, lucidity, and firmness of mind: therein may be the pledge of their future historical greatness." (*Letter to Gogol'*, p. 14.)

30. For an authoritative and masterly characterization of the moral significance of the monastery in Russian history, see Professor V. O. Kliuchevskii's speech, "A Beneficent Teacher of the Russian National Spirit (St. Sergei)" [Blagodatnyi vospitatel' russkogo narodnogo dukha (prep. Sergei)], *Trinity Flower* [Troitskii tsvetok], No. 9 [1892], pp. 1-32. See also V. A. Kozhevnikov, *The Past and Future of Christian Asceticism* [O znachenii khristianskogo podvizhnichestva v proshlom i v nastoiashchem], in preparation [actually published in Moscow: A. I. Snegirova, 1910. *Eds.*].

cation of elementary knowledge or simply reading and writing. For the intelligentsia enlighteners, the latter is inseparably connected with political and party goals, for which superficial education is only a necessary means.

We have all seen how the people's soul shuddered when it was given a heavy dose of the intelligentsia's kind of enlightenment, how deplorably it reacted to this spiritual devastation with an increase in crime, first under an ideological pretext and then even without one.[31] The intelligentsia mistakenly believes that it can build Russian enlightenment and culture on a spiritual foundation of atheism, while utterly neglecting the religious cultivation of the personality and substituting for it the mere communication of knowledge. The human personality is not just intellect; it is will and character above all, and disregard of these elements is cruelly avenged. Destruction of the age-old religious and moral foundations of the people's life frees in them the dark forces which have been so numerous in Russian history, deeply poisoned as it was by the affliction of Tatar barbarism and the instincts of the nomadic conquerors.

Throughout history a struggle has taken place within the soul of the Russian people between the precepts of St. Sergei's cloister and those of the Zaporozhian *sech'* or the freebooters who filled the regiments of the pretenders, Razin, and Pugachev.[32] The destructive nihilism of these menacing, unorganized, elemental forces gives them a superficial resemblance to the revolutionary intelligentsia, and the latter takes them for its own kind of revolutionism. In fact, these forces are very old, considerably older than the intelligentsia itself. The Russian state subdued them with difficulty; it set external limits on them and fettered them, but did not entirely defeat them. Among its other effects, intelligentsia enlightenment is arousing these dormant instincts and returning Russia to the chaotic state that rendered her powerless and that she overcame in the past only with great difficulties and sacrifices. Such are the lessons of recent years, the moral of fomenting popular revolution.

Hence, we can understand the underlying causes of the deep spiritual strife which is now tearing Russia apart, her schism, as it were, into two disconnected halves, a right and a left bloc, Black Hundreds and "Red Hundreds." Division into parties on the basis of different political opinions, social positions and property interests is a common and widespread occurrence in countries with popular representation, and in some sense it is a necessary evil. But nowhere does this division penetrate so deeply and destroy the spiritual and cultural unity of the nation to such an extent as in Russia. Even the socialist parties

31. I have already dealt with this subject in my essay, "The Intelligentsia and Religion." [See note 1. *Eds.*]

32. See Professor Kliuchevskii's characterization of the Cossacks and the *sech'. A Course in Russian History* [Kurs russkoi istorii], III (Moscow: G. Lissner i D. Sobko, 1908), lectures 45-46.

of Western Europe, which dissociate themselves the most from "bourgeois" society, in fact remain organic members of it and do not destroy the integrity of its culture. But our division into right and left is distinguished by the fact that it has as its source not just different political ideals but, in the overwhelming majority of cases, different world-views or faiths. A more exact parallel from the history of Western Europe would be the Reformation division between Catholics and Protestants with its consequent religious wars, rather than present-day political parties. We need only reduce the right and left blocs to their component spiritual elements to see this.

Russian enlightenment, which the Russian intelligentsia is called upon to serve, had to struggle with the age-old Tatar barbarism that had eaten deeply into various aspects of our life; with the arbitrariness of bureaucratic absolutism and its unfitness for government; in the past with serfdom and corporal punishment, and now with capital punishment and crudeness of manners; in general, it had to struggle for better conditions of life. The ideals of the so-called liberation movement can be reduced to these goals. The intelligentsia shouldered the burdens and difficulties of the movement, and in the struggle it won itself many a martyr's crown. But, unfortunately for Russian life, it bound the struggle inseparably to its own negative world-view. Therefore, those who cherished the treasure of the national faith and felt called upon to preserve it—primarily the men of the church—found it necessary to combat the intelligentsia's influence on the people for the sake of defending that faith. The rivalry of political and cultural ideals became entangled with religious strife, and our intelligentsia still does not fully appreciate how serious this conflict is, and how ominous for Russia's future.

The intelligentsia's almost unanimous departure from the church, and the cultural isolation in which the church found itself as a result, aggravated the historical situation still further. It goes without saying that for one who believes in the mystical life of the Church, its empirical shell at any given historical moment has no decisive importance; whatever that shell may be, it cannot and must not give rise to any doubt as to the ultimate triumph of the Church, when its light will be clear for all to see. But on an empirical plane, looking at the Russian national church as a factor of historical development, we cannot deem it unimportant that the Russian educated class almost to a man espoused atheism. Naturally, such a bloodletting could not fail to be reflected in the cultural and intellectual level of the remaining churchmen. The intelligentsia usually gloats over the numerous evils of church life, which we have no desire either to minimize or to deny (although the intelligentsia neither knows nor understands any of the positive sides of church life). But does the intelligentsia really have the right to criticize when it remains indifferent to religion or rejects it on principle, seeing in religion only darkness and idiocy?

A church intelligentsia combining true Christianity with a clear and enlightened understanding of cultural and historical tasks (which contemporary churchmen so often lack), were one to arise, would meet an urgent historical and national need. And even if it had to suffer in its turn the persecution and oppression which the intelligentsia endures for the sake of atheistic ideals, this would have enormous historical and religio-moral significance and would find a very special response in the people's soul.

But as long as the intelligentsia uses all the power of its education to undermine the people's faith, the defense of the faith, with sad inevitability, more and more assumes the character of a struggle not only against the intelligentsia but against enlightenment as well. Once the intelligentsia in fact becomes the sole disseminator of enlightenment, obscurantism becomes a means of defending religion. This predicament, unnatural for both sides and grown more acute in recent years, makes our present state especially tormenting. And to make matters worse, self-seeking reactionaries, frauds, and those who like to fish in troubled waters use the defense of the people's faith against the intelligentsia as a pretext. All of this gets intertwined into one historical and psychological knot: habitual patterns of thought and historical associations of ideas develop, and both their adherents and their opponents begin to see them as intrinsically binding and indissoluble. Opposite electrical charges build up steadily at both poles. People group themselves into camps according to this abnormal standard, and a corresponding psychological atmosphere forms, conservative and despotic. The nation splits in two, and its best forces are wasted in fruitless struggle.

This division is the product of our entire spiritual past, and the task of the time is to overcome and transcend it, once we have realized that it is based not on an inner, ideal necessity, but only on the force of historical fact. It is time to set about untying the Gordian knot of our history.

VII

Like all of Russian life, the soul of the Russian intelligentsia is woven of contradictions, and it arouses contradictory feelings. One cannot help both loving it and being repelled by it. Alongside the intelligentsia's negative features, which are symptoms of lack of culture and historical immaturity and must be overcome, elements of spiritual beauty shine from its tormented visage, causing it to resemble some very special, dear and tender flower nurtured by our severe history. It is as though the intelligentsia itself were that "red flower" nourished by tears and blood which appeared to one of its noblest representatives, the great-hearted Garshin.[33]

Alongside the anti-Christ element in the intelligentsia one can sense higher religious potentials as well, a new historical flesh waiting to be spiritualized.

33. See Garshin's short story, "The Red Flower." *Eds.*

Its intense search for the City of God, its yearning that God's will be done on earth as it is in Heaven, is profoundly different from bourgeois culture's desire for solid, earthly well-being. The intelligentsia's abnormal maximalism with its practical uselessness is the result of a religious perversion, but it can be overcome by religious healing.

The nature of the Russian intelligentsia is religious. In *The Devils*, Dostoevskii compared Russia, and particularly her intelligentsia, to the possessed man of the Gospels, who was cured by Christ alone and could find health and restoration of his powers only at the feet of the Savior.[34] This comparison still holds true. A legion of demons has invaded Russia's enormous body and is convulsing, tormenting, and crippling it. Only a religious feat, invisible but mighty, can cure Russia and free her from this legion.

The intelligentsia rejected Christ; it turned away from His countenance and cast His image from its heart; it deprived itself of the inner light of life, and together with its country it is paying for this betrayal, this religious suicide. But strangely, it does not have the strength to forget this wound to its heart, to restore its spiritual equilibrium, to rest after the devastation it has wrought on itself. Although it has renounced Christ, it bears His seal on its heart and burns with an unconscious longing for Him, not knowing how to slake its spiritual thirst. And this bewildering anxiety, this unearthly dream of unearthly justice, leaves its special mark on the intelligentsia and makes it strange, frenzied and unbalanced, as though possessed. It is like the beautiful Shulamite who had lost her lover: on her bed at night, in the streets and broad ways, she sought him whom her soul loved; she asked the watchmen that go about the city if they had seen her beloved, but instead of answering they only smote and wounded her. (Song of Songs, 3:1-3, 5:7.) And meanwhile, the Beloved, the One for Whom its soul yearns, is near. He stands and knocks at that heart, that proud, recalcitrant intelligentsia heart. . . . Will His knock someday be heard? . . .

34. Luke 8:27-33. *Eds.*

CREATIVE SELF-CONSCIOUSNESS

Mikhail Gershenzon

I

No, I will not tell the Russian *intelligent*, "believe," as do the preachers of the new Christianity; nor will I tell him, "love," as does Tolstoi. What is the use of sermons which will, at best, convince people of the need for love and faith? Before they can love or believe, those who neither love nor believe must be renewed inwardly—but here the consciousness can do almost nothing. The very fabric of a person's spiritual being must be regenerated; an organic process must take place in the sphere where spontaneous forces operate—in the will.

The one thing we can and must tell the Russian *intelligent* is: try to become a human being. Once he becomes human he will understand what he needs without our help—to love and to believe, and just how to do it.

For we are not people but cripples, all the Russian *intelligenty*, however many of us there are. And ours is not even a deformity of growth, such as frequently occurs, but an accidental and unnatural deformity. We are cripples because our personality is split and we have lost the capacity for natural development, when the consciousness grows as one with the will. Our consciousness, like a locomotive that has broken away from its train, vainly rushes off on its own, leaving our sensual and volitional life far behind. Above all, the Russian *intelligent* is a person who has literally lived *outside himself* since youth, recognizing as the only worthy object of his interest and sympathy something outside of his own personality: the people, society, or the state. Our public opinion is the most despotic in the world, and for three-quarters of a century now it has stubbornly adhered to the same overriding principle: it is egotistical and indecent to think about one's own personality, and the only real man is the one who thinks about public affairs, is interested in society's problems, and works for the common good. Even in Russia the number of *intelligenty* who put this program into practice was, of course, negligible, but everyone acknowledged the holiness of the banner. Even those who did nothing agreed platonically that this is the *only* activity that brings salvation, thereby completely freeing themselves from the need to do anything else. And so, while this principle did become the personal faith of those who really followed it, and thereby actually did redeem them, for the vast majority of *intelligenty* it became a source of great depravity by justifying to their minds the virtual absence of any idealistic action in their lives.

People have by now grown thoroughly accustomed to this state of affairs, and it occurs to no one that man cannot live perpetually "on the outside," and that this is the reason why subjectively we are ill and objectively, in our actions, impotent. We either channelled all the activity of our consciousness outward, toward the external world, or we gave the impression of doing so—in any case, we did not turn it inward and we have all become cripples, with a deep schism between our real selves and our consciousness.

Clouds continue to swirl within us, and blind, pent-up, chaotic forces move us convulsively, while our consciousness, torn from its soil, blossoms fruitlessly, a sterile flower. To be sure, even our everyday lives contain some faint light—we could not survive without it—but it glimmers on its own, without our active supervision, and everything in our lives is there by mere chance. With each generation the Russian *intelligent*'s sensual life changed, and new demands thrust themselves upon it with elemental force. Needless to say, these demands became manifest at once and asserted themselves most energetically. But the consciousness found it degrading to examine them, and all the labor for a truly creative, organic renewal of life took place purely spontaneously, beyond the control of consciousness, which merely registered the results retroactively. Hence, everything that happened was inevitable, and what happened was that the Russian *intelligent*'s life—personal, family, and public—grew misshapen and inconsistent, while his consciousness was deprived of substance and force.

II

In the unfathomable complexity of the human spirit there are no separate compartments. There are no mechanical transitions from lower movements to higher ones, from feeling to desire, from sensory perception to abstract thought; everything is merged and integrated. Nonetheless, immediate inner experience enables us to ascertain distinct spheres of our spirit and to discern their qualities. This pertains above all to the nature of our logical consciousness.

Two general laws can be formulated as self-evident, the doctrine of historical materialism notwithstanding. The first is that the *character* of the activity of our consciousness (its rhythm, intensity, and tone) depends wholly on the individual's innate psycho-physical structure. The second is that at a certain level the *direction* and *capacity* of the consciousness are largely autonomous. In other words, the *how* in the life of our consciousness is determined by the qualities of our central will, while the *what* and *how much* are comparatively independent of it. They are determined far more by the autonomous perfection of the mechanism and the material that education, environment, etc., bring to our consciousness for reworking.

This relative independence of the consciousness is the cardinal fact of our spiritual being. In the fullness of time, of course, consciousness too is subject to the universal plan, and in this sense is unfree; but each individual perceives it empirically as an autonomous force, and as such it comes to life. The consciousness can leave the personality far behind, roam freely along diverse paths, or soar up to heaven. It is that organ of the spirit which receives truth. Like a tall radio antenna, it picks up all the signals of the one and indivisible Divine truth. Out of the millennia of its life experience mankind is slowly assembling this truth by superimposing millions of analogous but individually distinct impressions. This truth represents an ideal only for each individual consciousness. In essence it is not a duty, but only a higher generalization of the experience of all mankind; it is the truly existent, the one reality, the norm that corresponds to the authentic and eternal essence of man. Because it springs from the very foundations of the human spirit, it strikes root with irresistible force in each human consciousness, so that the mind, once aware of it, comes to be dominated by it. There is no place to run from it, for it is God in man: man's conscious, cosmic self-definition.

Vast is the quantity of truth that the individual mind can absorb. We educated men all know so much Divine truth that a thousandth of what we know would be enough to make each of us a saint. But it is common knowledge that knowing the truth and living by the truth are different matters. Consciousness neither lives nor acts; it has no direct contact with the real world. Only a person's central will lives and acts, and consequently only through the will can the consciousness translate the truth it has learned into reality.

The autonomy of consciousness is both our greatest blessing and our greatest peril. A blessing, in that our consciousness, thanks to its considerable independence from our individual will, is able to perceive—and in huge quantities—that supra-individual truth we were just discussing. But clearly, the very weakness of these bonds constantly threatens man with a rift between his logical consciousness and his sensual personality. The peril is that the individual consciousness *may* separate itself from the personality, something we see all the time. Two consequences then follow. First, the consciousness ceases to guide the will, abandoning it, so to speak, to the arbitrary rule of its passions. Secondly, consciousness itself, when not controlled at every step of the way by that infallible practicality which is concentrated in our will, begins to wander aimlessly, loses perspective, becomes one-sided, and falls into the greatest errors. Mankind's universal consciousness does not err; but the individual consciousness in its private searchings never fails to err when it wilfully repudiates the personality.

Consciousness has its normal activity; this is difficult to formulate in words, but everyone senses it. This egocentricity (in the highest sense of the word) of consciousness is itself unconscious. It is a certain indescribable interaction of the consciousness and the sensual personality, their ceaseless struggle and moments of equilibrium. Deep within, it fosters the harmonious growth of the whole person, though on the surface it may produce a series of upheavals.

During this process, thought does not wander aimlessly. It avidly studies the depths of the personality—its own personality—and once it has disclosed the basic antinomies there it seeks with anguish and passion to resolve them in conformity with the truth it has learned. It does not absorb all truth indiscriminately, but takes only what it needs for this personal task. On the other hand, it uses all the truth it has taken, wasting nothing, so that it all goes into the organism's growth instead of remaining until death as unneeded wealth, like the supply of food a pelican stuffs into its pouch. What thought achieves on this level is not an individual resolution; it is a genuine transfiguration of universal flesh in an individual hypostasis, for this flesh is one in all, and any *essential* change in the atom is an irreversible cosmic act.

Are examples needed? Then here are two heroic models. John Bunyan, a poor, rude tinker who lived in the seventeenth century in a remote English village, in the middle of his obscure life was suddenly overcome by an extraordinary sorrow. From childhood he had known the simple evangelical truth known to all of us—but suddenly it came to life in him. Now a struggle began between supra-individual truth and an individual will. An inner voice asked persistently: do you wish to reject sin or to remain in it and destroy your soul? For two and a half years this torment continued.[1] "One day," Bunyan relates, "I walked to a neighbouring Town, and sate down upon a Settle in the Street, and fell into a very deep pause about the most fearful state my sin had brought me to; and after long musing, I lifted up my head, but me-thought I saw, as if the Sun . . . did grudge to give me light, and as if the very . . . tiles upon the houses did bend themselves against me; . . . I was abhorred of them, and unfit to dwell among them . . . because I had sinned against the Saviour. O, how happy now was every creature, over I was! . . . I [alone] was gone and lost."[2]

Bunyan triumphed and was resurrected to new life. Two hundred years later Carlyle engaged in the same struggle on a different plane. His spirit had long been paralyzed by the visceral terror so many know. In *Sartor Resartus* Carlyle tells how victory was won in him. "All at once, there rose a thought in me, and I asked myself 'What *art* thou afraid of? Wherefore, like a coward, dost thou forever pip and whimper, and go cowering and trembling? Despicable biped! what is the sum total of the worst that lies before thee? Death? Well, Death; and say the pangs of Tophet too, and all that the Devil and Man may, will or can do against thee. Hast thou not a heart; canst thou not suffer whatsoever it be; and, as a Child of Freedom, though outcast, trample Tophet itself under thy feet, while it consumes thee? Let it come then; I will meet and defy it!' and as I so thought, there rushed like a stream of fire over my

---

1. John Bunyan, *Grace Abounding to the Chief of Sinners*, edited by Roger Sharrock (Oxford: Clarendon Press, 1962), p. 10. *Eds.*

2. *Ibid.*, pp. 58-59. *Eds.*

whole soul; and I shook base Fear away from me forever. I was strong, of unknown strength; a spirit, almost a god. Ever from that time, the temper of my
misery was changed: not Fear or whining Sorrow was it, but Indignation and
grim fire-eyed Defiance."[3]

I have chosen these two vivid examples as graphic illustrations of how the
consciousness works *organically* when, instead of taking off to soar in boundless space, it turns inward to the personality and actually restructures the will.
For both Bunyan and Carlyle the spiritual struggle took a cataclysmic form,
and in this sense they are exceptional. Ordinarily, the work of consciousness is
incomparably less stormy, but it can be sound, i.e., organic, only when it is a
personal concern, a matter of the personality's self-consciousness, as was the
case in our two examples.

Every person is born fully fashioned and unique, with a definite psycho-
physical organization never to be duplicated in all the universe. Every living
thing has a sensual-volitional core, a central government, as it were, that trans-
mits its decisions from secret depths and acts with infallible expediency. Each
such core, that is, each individual will, is *unicum* in the world, regardless of
whether we are dealing with a man or a frog. Accordingly, nothing is more distinctive than the outlook of each living creature. All that lives lives individually, according to a perfectly complete plan specific for each being.

But human beings possess, in addition to this elemental will, an inherent
faculty of self-consciousness; becoming human implies, therefore, recognizing
the distinctiveness of one's own personality and rationally defining one's attitude to the world. As soon as the consciousness awakens, and multifarious life
begins to unroll before it, all the forces of the spirit, unless it is crippled, instinctively focus on an effort to interpret reality. They do this simply because
an unfolding consciousness cannot bear to contemplate chaos and *must* search
for unity in the world—a unity that is nothing other than the unity of its own
personality. In his observation of life, his experience, and his books a youth
seeks elements of *his own* consciousness, that is, he searches for those ideas
which will most fully and precisely accommodate the basic proclivities of his
nature. The search is by no means a one-sided, wholly intellectual process.
This is the age at which a person's sensual-volitional life attains its greatest
intensity, and his spirit's innate tendencies define themselves most clearly,
so that the quest proceeds in all areas until he finds his fully revealed self in
his consciousness.

Another process goes on simultaneously: the individual evaluates his personality on the basis of the supra-personal ideas his consciousness has gathered
and actively transforms it to conform to them. Experience shows that the

3. Thomas Carlyle, "Sartor Resartus," in *Sartor Resartus and On Hero Worship*,
edited by W. H. Hudson (London: J. M. Dent, 1954), p. 127. *Eds.*

personality can be molded in this manner. The consciousness can govern the will's separate movements and, by restraining or directing them, can instill habits that gradually train the will in accordance with the truth consciousness has learned. Consciousness plays the same role in public life as in the individual personality, for the laws and institutions of the state are nothing but objectified consciousness, which seek to re-educate wills by coercively regulating actions.

Inner concentration and freedom are the primary requisites for this normal spiritual life. The activity of the consciousness must be directed inward, to the personality itself, and must be free of any preconception or alien purpose imposed by the external demands of life. It is a mistake to think that this narrows the horizons of the consciousness. It is intrinsically *impossible* for an individual consciousness to be shut up within itself; it cannot withdraw from the universal life of reason. Therefore, any substantial movement of universal reason inevitably reverberates within each separate consciousness. In an integrated soul, however, none of reason's imaginary needs can find sustenance. Instead, eternal ideas fraught with all the profound seriousness of universal human truth flame into passion, as we saw in the cases of Bunyan and Carlyle. Only such an integrated person is able, first, to desire clearly and strongly, and then to apply his concentrated spiritual strength to the reconstruction of reality.

Of course, a person's identity in the highest sense, i.e., in terms of his religious, moral and political convictions, demands more than just this wholeness. But it is the first, *most elementary* condition for the creation of his identity, for it guarantees that he will assimilate a set of convictions because they correspond precisely and with instinctive force to the innate features of his will, and not for some ulterior, accidental or one-sided motive—to please accepted opinion or fashion, or because of the wit or charm of a book he has read. And it guarantees that the ideas assimilated in this deeply individual process of selection will not remain a sterile twinge of his consciousness, but will be the inner motive-force of his entire life; in contrast to purely speculative and essentially lifeless ideas, they will be what we may term idea-feelings or idea-passions. Although it does not predetermine the details of a person's worldview, this spiritual wholeness does categorically decide its general character, namely, its religiosity: a normal or spiritually whole person cannot help being religious because of the very nature of the human soul. But we will have more to say on this.

It would seem clear that the personality's self-consciousness and self-education is not a moral duty of any sort, but simply a law of human nature arising from the mere presence of consciousness in man. It is just as natural a process in a person's spiritual growth as cutting teeth or attaining puberty are in physical development. But a person's physical maturation is not subject to his own intervention, while in the spiritual process he is not only the object but also a free participant. Wisdom teeth will inevitably come through in their time, but normal spiritual development may be infinitely deformed by historical conditions, social prejudices, and people's individual errors. The Russian intelligentsia's spiritual life suffered just this sad deformity.

III

Our intelligentsia correctly traces its descent from Peter the Great's reforms. But like the people, the intelligentsia cannot remember them as good. The upper stratum of society had thrust upon it a tremendous number of ideas that were valuable in themselves but emotionally too remote, and this almost mechanically split its personality; it tore consciousness from the will and taught it to gourmandize on truth. The reforms taught people that if their consciousness had amassed a great wealth of truth they need not be ashamed that in reality life was dark and justice scant. By freeing consciousness from the everyday control of the will they condemned it to monstrous delusions. Today's Russian *intelligent* is the direct descendant and heir of the serf-owning Voltairean. *Divide et impera* worked even in this realm. Had there been even a handful of whole, fully conscious people in Russia, people whose high intellectual level was organically rooted in their personality, despotism would have been inconceivable. But where the most developed consciousnesses were disembodied, and the bodies lived without consciousness, despotism could not have had freer rein. This is an eternal law of history. If examples are necessary, we need only recall Cromwell's "saints" or the handful of youths who liberated Italy under the banner of *"Dio e popolo."*[4]

And the fruit became seed and yielded fruit an hundred fold. Inevitably, despotism provoked an exaggerated interest in social problems among the educated elements of society, a partial hyperesthesia of the sort produced in any living organism by excessive pressure on one spot. Public affairs dominated men's consciousness. The rift between the activity of consciousness and personal sensual-volitional life became the general norm and was even accepted as the criterion of sanctity and the only means of saving one's soul.

This disintegration of the personality proved fateful for the intelligentsia in three respects. Internally, it made the *intelligent* a cripple; externally, it tore him from the people; and, finally, the combination of these two factors doomed the intelligentsia to utter impotence in regard to the regime that oppressed it.

Truly, an historian would not be mistaken if he were to pursue the study of Russian society along two distinct lines, life and thought, for the two had almost nothing in common. Reason is not the only influence on people's volitional life. Obviously, there are other factors that act on it directly. In particular, there is artistic beauty—music, architecture and poetry. Art regulates

4. "God and the people": the slogan of Giuseppe Mazzini's Young Italy movement. *Eds.*

the rhythm of the will from without, as it were, and trains it in harmony. But consciousness, of course, holds pride of place. Its role is twofold. Thought is inherently rhythmic, and therefore the very process of thinking, mechanically, as it were, curbs the irregularity of the unconscious will. But it does not merely discipline the will formally, through its own operation; the *content* of thought— truth—provides the will with a goal and compels it to move not only in a regular rhythm but in a definite direction.

What has our intelligentsia's thought been doing for the last half-century? (I am referring, of course, to the intelligentsia rank-and-file.) A handful of revolutionaries has been going from house to house and knocking on every door: "Everyone into the street! It's shameful to stay at home!" And every consciousness, the halt, the blind and the armless, poured out into the square; not one stayed home. For half a century they have been milling about, wailing and quarreling. At home there is dirt, destitution, disorder, but the master doesn't care. He is out in public, saving the people—and that is easier and more entertaining than drudgery at home.

No one lived; everyone engaged in civic affairs (or pretended to do so). They did not even live egotistically, for they did not rejoice in life or freely delight in its pleasures. Instead, they snatched up scraps and gulped them down almost unchewed, ashamed but greedy, like a mischievous dog. It was a strange sort of asceticism, which renounced not personal sensual life itself, but merely all guidance over it. Sensual life proceeded on its own, in a slipshod way, gloomily and convulsively. Then suddenly consciousness would recollect—and somewhere there would be an outburst of savage fanaticism. Someone would begin to abuse a friend for drinking a bottle of champagne, and a group with some sort of ascetic purpose would spring up.

On the whole, the intelligentsia's way of life is horrible, a true "abomination of desolation." It lacks even the slightest, most superficial discipline or consistency. A day passes, and who knows why; today things are one way, and tomorrow a sudden fancy will turn everything upside down. In personal life there is idleness, slovenliness, and a homeric carelessness; in work, a naive lack of conscientiousness; and in public affairs an unbridled tendency toward despotism and total lack of respect for other people. The attitude to the regime vacillates between proud defiance and deference—not collective deference, I am not referring to that, but personal.[5]

---

5. *Note to the Second Edition.* This characterization of our intelligentsia rank-and-file has been termed slander and blasphemy. But here is what Chekhov wrote ten years ago: "I do not believe in our intelligentsia, which is hypocritical, false, hysterical, ill-bred, and lazy. I do not believe in it even when it suffers and complains, for its oppressors come from the same womb." (Letter to I. I. Orlov, 22 February 1899, in the collection of letters [*Pis'ma A. P. Chekhova*] edited by B. N. Bochkarev and just published [Moscow: I. D. Sytin, 1909], p. 54. Chekhov's last words are an apt remark in themselves: to a considerable extent the Russian bureaucracy is flesh of the flesh with the Russian intelligentsia.

Meanwhile, consciousness, torn from its natural function, led an unhealthy, phantasmal life. The less energy it expended on molding the personality, the more assiduously it filled itself up with truth—with every conceivable truth, both necessary and unnecessary. Once it had lost its sensitivity to the organic needs of the will, it had no course of its own. Isn't it striking that the history of our social thought is divided not into stages of internal development, but into periods dominated by one or another foreign doctrine? Schellingism, Hegelianism, Saint-Simonism, Fourierism, positivism, Marxism, Nietzscheism, neo-Kantianism, Mach, Avenarius, anarchism—whatever the stage, a foreign name. Our collective consciousness failed to work out its own life values and then gradually re-evaluate them, as was done in the West, and so we utterly lacked our own national evolution of thought. In our idle, though holy, thirst for truth we simply seized on what Western thought had created for itself, and we set great store by each gift until we received a new and better one. And conversely, we did not value the truth that *our* best minds—Chaadaev, the Slavophiles, Dostoevskii—had attained (through a personal effort of consciousness, of course). We failed to discern the element of national originality in it, and all because our consciousness was devoid of the substantiality which comes only from unceasing contact with the will.

Such disembodied thinking cannot remain sound. As soon as the vital circulation between consciousness and will ceases, thought grows sickly and is attacked by diseases, invariably the same ones for all people and at all times. First and most inevitably that general constitutional derangement of consciousness called positivism sets in. In the normal life of the spirit, *positivism as a world-view* is impossible. When consciousness is turned inward and is laboring on the personality, constantly in touch with the irrational elements of the spirit, it maintains steady contact with the world essence, for a single cosmic will circulates through all individual wills. Then it is necessarily mystical, i.e., religious, and no amount of learning can convince it to the contrary. It has direct knowledge of infinity, and this knowledge becomes second nature, the unvarying method of all its activity. But when consciousness is uprooted from its soil, its sense of the mystical dies at once, and God is gradually effaced from all its ideas. Its activity becomes a fantastic game and its every calculation untrue and unworkable, just as if an architect took it into his head to draw up his plans without regard for the laws of perspective or the properties of matter.

This is precisely what happened to the Russian intelligentsia. The history of our journalism, from Belinskii onward, is a sheer nightmare, as far as vital understanding is concerned. Absurd and alarming as it may be, the journalists made all their calculations on the assumption that the whole world, all things and all human souls, were created and are governed by the rules of human logic—only not consistently enough; hence, with our reason we can perfectly comprehend the laws of universal life, we can set provisional goals for the universe (there is no general goal, since our reason does not perceive one), we can truly change the nature of things, etc. It seems incomprehensible that entire generations could live under such a monstrous delusion. Indeed, they too had irrational feelings, they saw the miracle of life before them, saw death and expected it themselves. But they neither thought about their feelings nor looked at God's universe; and their thought lived a self-sufficient life playing with its anemic ideas.

A vicious circle was created. After all, the consciousness does need some material to work on, and the Russian intelligentsia found this material in public activity—the same activity that had done most to tear the consciousness from the personality. The focal point of its life shifted to a hypertrophied organ. From the first stirrings of his conscious thought, the *intelligent* became a slave to politics. He thought, read and argued only about politics; he looked for political meaning in everything, in the personality of others as well as in art; and he led the life of a virtual prisoner, not seeing the light of day.

Now the vicious circle was complete: the more people went into public affairs, the more their consciousness was crippled, and the more it was crippled, the more avidly it threw itself into public affairs. The youth was influenced· by the universal example, public opinion; but as the years passed, his thought became so accustomed to living away from home that it had no choice but to mill about in the square, though it might do nothing there but listen from behind other people's backs, or even not listen at all. One person did political work—he carried on propaganda among the workers; another enthusiastically read Lavrov—he at least listened. But the majority—Chekhovian people—simply whiled away the time, not daring to turn inward and, indeed, incapable of doing so or even of merely leading a normal life.

One might think that our great literature, which developed in this period, could have cured us, for it was not bound by our spiritual fetters. Inner autonomy is the primary characteristic of the true artist. You can prescribe neither a narrow area of interest nor an external point of view for him; he freely grasps the full range of phenomena and the full range of his own experience. Our great artists were free, and naturally, the more authentic their talent the more hateful they found the blinders of the intelligentsia's social-utilitarian morality. Thus, in Russia an almost infallible gauge of the strength of an artist's genius is the extent of his hatred for the intelligentsia. We need mention only the greatest of them: Lev Tolstoi and Dostoevskii, Tiutchev and Fet.

How shameful to know that our best people looked at us with disgust and refused to bless our cause! They called us to other roads, inviting us to leave our spiritual prison for the freedom of the wide world, the depths of our spirit, and the comprehension of eternal mysteries. What the intelligentsia lived by quite literally did not even exist for them; at the peak of the civic movement Tolstoi was glorifying the wise "stupidity" of Karataev and Kutuzov,[6] Dos-

6. See *War and Peace. Eds.*

toevskii was studying the "underground," Tiutchev was singing of primordial chaos, and Fet of love and eternity. But no one followed them. The intelligentsia applauded, for after all they did sing very well, but it was not swayed. Moreover, through its spiritual leaders, the critics and journalists, it set up a party tribunal to try the free truth of creativity, and it convicted Tiutchev of inattention and Fet of mockery, while Dostoevskii was pronounced reactionary and Chekhov indifferent. Its deeply prejudiced consciousness closed the intelligentsia's soul to artistic as well as living truth.

There were no individuals, only a homogeneous mass, for every individuality had been emasculated back in grade school. Where could vivid personalities come from, in the absence of that combination of freely revealed sensuality and self-consciousness which is the sole source of personal originality and strength? Formalism of consciousness is the best leveller in the world. Throughout the period when we were dominated by civic-mindedness, vivid figures could be found only among the revolutionaries, for active revolutionism was a form of asceticism. That is, it demanded of a person that his consciousness exert itself strenuously to form the personality by means of the inner renunciation of cherished ties, hopes for personal happiness, and life itself. It is not surprising that a person who had sustained such a great victory over himself was outwardly colorful and forceful. But most of the intelligentsia was impersonal, and its stupidly inert radicalism and fanatical intolerance gave it all the characteristics of a herd.

IV

Could this handful of crippled souls have remained close to the people? The people's thought, to the extent that it functions at all, undoubtedly addresses itself to essentials; everyone who has conscientiously studied the people, and Gleb Uspenskii above all, testifies to this. The people fail to understand us and hate us, but this is not the whole story. Can it be that they do not understand us because we are more educated than they are, and hate us because we do no physical labor and live in luxury? No, the main thing is that they do not regard us as human beings; to them we are man-like monsters, people without God in our souls. And they are right, for just as electricity appears at the point of contact of two oppositely charged bodies, so the Divine spark flares only at the point where the individual will meets the consciousness—and in us they do not meet. Hence the people do not sense that we are human, do not understand us, and hate us.

We never even suspected this. We were firmly convinced that the people differed from us only in the level of their education, and that if it were not for the obstacles imposed by the regime, we would long ago have given them a transfusion of our knowledge and become one flesh with them. It never even occurred to us that the people's soul is *qualitatively* different. We ignored the structure of the soul altogether, and tacitly agreed that "soul" meant simply the rationalistic consciousness, which was all we lived by. Our disregard was so total that we imagined that the people's psyches, too, are naked consciousnesses, only ignorant and still undeveloped.

This was an inevitable but appalling mistake. The Slavophiles tried to make us listen to reason, but their voice cried in the wilderness. Soulless ourselves, we could not understand that the people's soul is by no means a *tabula rasa*, where the characters of higher education may be inscribed without difficulty. Vainly the Slavophiles insisted that the people's spirit is already saturated with a content of its own, which keeps *our* education from penetrating it. Vainly they said that our people are not only children but old men as well: children in their formal knowledge, but old men in their life experience and the world-view they have drawn from it. Consequently, they have, and could not fail to have, a certain stock of unshakable ideas, beliefs and sympathies, and these ideas and beliefs are, in the first place, religious and metaphysical, the kind which, once formed, determine a person's entire mentality and activity.

The intelligentsia found this too preposterous even to dispute. It wore itself out trying to enlighten the people, flooding them with millions of copies of popular educational pamphlets, establishing libraries and reading rooms, and publishing cheap magazines for them. And all this was done in vain, because the intelligentsia never bothered to adapt this material to the people's existing concepts. Instead, it explained specific factual problems to the people without relating them to their central convictions, since the intelligentsia was entirely ignorant of not only the content but the very existence of such convictions, either in the people or in man in general.

Everyone who has observed our people with love and attention—and this includes individuals as different as S. Rachinskii and Gleb Uspenskii—agrees that the people seek only practical knowledge, and that of two varieties: lower, technical information, including literacy, and higher, metaphysical knowledge that clarifies the meaning of life and provides the strength to live. We gave the people none of this second type of knowledge—and have not even cultivated it for ourselves. Instead, we tried to give them massive doses of *our* knowledge, which, while abstract and devoid of moral elements, is permeated with a definite rationalistic spirit. The people cannot accept this knowledge because its general character clashes with their own instinctive understanding of the world. It is not surprising that all the intelligentsia's efforts were wasted. As Kireevskii said, "Substituting literary concepts for the people's native convictions is just as easy as substituting abstract thought for the bones of a mature organism."[7]

---

7. Ivan Vasil'evich Kireevskii, *Complete Collected Works* [Polnoe sobranie sochinenii], 2 vols. (Moscow: P. Bakhmetev, 1861), II, 35. Ivan Kireevskii was one of the leading theorists of the original Slavophile group. *Eds.*

A great dream inspired the Slavophiles. They started with the organic wholeness of the people's way of life, asserting that this must be the source of the country's higher culture, which must grow from it like fruit from the seed. All of national life, they said, must be bound together by a continuity that links the vague sentiments of the masses to the nation's highest artistic and intellectual creations. "Through literary activity unconscious thought, a product of history and of life's torments, obscured by its manifold relationships and diverse interests, rises along the scale of mental development from society's lowest strata to its highest circles, from instinctive tendencies to the ultimate stages of consciousness."[8] So understood, the concept of unconscious thought is neither a clever idea nor a dialectic game, but a profoundly serious matter of inner self-awareness. A radiant ideal! And we are farther from it than any other nation. It demands that the thought of the educated and the thought of the uneducated, notwithstanding all the differences in content and intensity, work in the same manner. In other words, the consciousness of the educated must live by the same principles as the consciousness of the toiling masses, who, amidst their physical labor and suffering, strain every spiritual nerve in the stubborn effort to comprehend this painful life through moral ideals and faith.

A crowd of sick men quarantined in their own country—that is the Russian intelligentsia. Both its inner qualities and its objective circumstances prevented it from conquering despotism; its defeat was preordained. It could not conquer through its own efforts, not because of numerical weakness but because of the duality, which meant impotence, of its psychic force. And the people could not support it, despite the temptation of common interest, because on the whole their unconscious hatred for the intelligentsia outweighed their greed—this is a general law of human psychology. There will be no freedom for us until we become spiritually healthy, for only strong hands joined in nation-wide cooperation can seize and consolidate freedom, and only the individual spirit, properly constituted, can achieve the conditions for freedom—personal firmness and solidarity with others.

In the West the attitude of the people toward the propertied, educated classes is radically different from what it is here. There too the people hate the lord and do not understand his language, but the misunderstanding and hatred are rooted in intelligible feelings. There they hate the lord because he grows fat without doing any physical labor, because he has used the labor of previous generations of the people to accumulate the great surplus that enables him to live in luxury, hold the people in perpetual bondage, and acquire the knowledge which helps exploit the people all over again. This is the slave's bitterness toward the master and the envy of the hungry for the sated. Fur-

8. *Ibid.*, p. 29. *Eds.*

thermore, both the volume and the abstractness of the masters' knowledge render it foreign to the masses; hence, the lack of understanding.

But our metaphysical discord does not exist in the West, or at least not to the same degree, because there is no profound *qualitative* difference in the spiritual constitution of the simple man and the lord. One reason for this is that some of the lord's knowledge has seeped down to the people over the centuries, and another is that the intelligentsia itself does not suffer from such a great schism between consciousness and life. Doubtless, the Western bourgeois is poorer in moral ideas than the Russian *intelligent*, but then his ideas do not greatly outstrip his emotional framework and, most important, he leads a comparatively integrated spiritual life. Hence, a peaceful outcome of the contest between the people and the masters is psychologically possible in the West. There the struggle takes place in the realm of positive interests and feelings, which naturally assume the form of ideas, and once this happens the individual consciousness becomes the major arena of struggle. In fact, the *ideas* of socialism are already playing a decisive role in the West. They are gradually transforming a mechanical collision into a chemical process, on the one hand solidifying the laboring masses and on the other slowly decomposing the bourgeoisie's ideology. In other words, they are inspiring the former with a sense of being right, and removing this feeling from the latter.

We are divided from our people by a different kind of discord. They do not see us as thieves, like their brother the village *kulak*, or even as outright foreigners, like the Turk or the Frenchman. They see our human and recognizably Russian features but do not sense a human soul in us, and therefore they hate us passionately, probably with an unconscious mystical terror. They hate us the more profoundly because we are their own. *Such as we are*, we not only cannot dream of merging with the people, but we must fear them more than all the government's executions, and we must bless this government which alone, with its bayonets and prisons, still protects us from the people's wrath.[9]

V

Such was our condition before the revolution, and such, at first glance, it still remains. But long before the revolution a profound change had begun in the intelligentsia's psyche.

9. *Note to the Second Edition.* The newspaper critics gleefully seized on this sentence as a public confession of my love for bayonets and prisons. I do not love bayonets and urge no one to bless them; on the contrary, I view them as a nemesis. The meaning of the sentence is that the intelligentsia's entire past has placed it in an unprecedented and horrible position: the people, for whom it has struggled, hate it, while the government, *against* whom it has struggled, turns out to be its defender, whether the intelligentsia likes it or not. "Must" in my sentence means "are fated to": with our own hands, without even realizing it, we wove this bond between ourselves and the government. This is what is so horrible, and this is what I am pointing out.

The inner disintegration of the personality was so unnatural; the disorder and slovenliness of a way of life not guided by consciousness was so oppressive; and the intellect itself was so exhausted by the constant chafing of abstract moral thought that a person could not remain healthy. And in fact, the average *intelligent*, one not intoxicated by active political involvement, felt more unwell with every passing year. He was already living very badly in the mid-eighties; in the long gallery of *intelligent* types drawn by so exact an observer as Chekhov there are barely five or six normal individuals. Nine-tenths of our *intelligenty* are neurasthenic. Scarcely any of them are healthy—they are all jaundiced, morose, anxious figures deformed by some secret dissatisfaction. Everyone is dissatisfied, some embittered and others aggrieved. Work is productive and satisfying only when one's profession conforms to his innate qualities, and this is impossible for us since it is achieved only when the personality is expressed in the consciousness. And so people stand at the most holy places, each cursing his hated post, and they work unwillingly and carelessly. We infect each other with jaundice, and we seem to have succeeded in saturating the very atmosphere with our neurasthenic attitude to life, so much so that a fresh person—someone who has lived abroad for a long time, for example—starts to suffocate on first falling in with us.

It went on like this, growing worse and worse, until the end of the nineties. Public opinion, which enjoyed such authority over the intelligentsia, maintained categorically that all life's woes have political causes; with the collapse of the police state, health and courage, as well as freedom, would at once prevail. No one suspected the real illness; everyone blindly believed this assertion, which removed all responsibility from the individual. This was one reason why the hopes for revolution assumed the character of religious chiliasm. In addition to its direct effects, a change in the political structure also had to justify the intelligentsia's past retroactively, give meaning to its tortured existence—and at the same time renew a personality that had become a burden to itself. The *intelligent* was suffocating, and thought he was suffocating *only* because he was in bondage. This was a cruel self-deception. A revolution really could have provided the people with everything they needed for a healthy life—freedom of self-determination and legal security. But what would political freedom have given us, the intelligentsia? Liberation is only the removal of fetters, nothing more; but removing the chains from a person consumed by an internal malady is not enough to restore him to health. For us, freedom would only have established conditions more conducive to recovery.

I believe, therefore, that the revolution's failure did the intelligentsia almost as much good as success would have done. This terrible blow rocked the intelligentsia's soul to its very foundations. While the journals argued over who was guilty, and the parties furiously exposed each other's errors, something unexpected was taking place behind their backs: little by little the audience went home, leaving the debaters alone. Not with its intellect, but with its whole being, the intelligentsia understood that the reasons for its failure lay in something other than programs and tactics.

Indeed, the intelligentsia gave little thought to the reasons. This was not just a material failure stemming from unequal strength or miscalculation; nor did the intelligentsia even feel the moral aspect of its defeat too keenly. Instead, panic fear for purely personal, almost physical, self-preservation came to the fore once it turned out that universal recovery had not taken place, and that each of us, therefore, would have to drag out his diseased existence for a still undetermined period. If hitherto, hypnotized by public opinion, people had endured their lives in the hope of a political panacea, now, when this hope had been betrayed, at least for the foreseeable future, they could not bear to wait any longer. In vain the journalists cried after the deserters that this was merely a temporary postponement, and recovery would surely come; the intelligentsia scattered in terror like a frightened herd. The sensation of personal illness was so acute that it dulled thought. The intelligentsia's disorder after the revolution was a psychological reaction of the *personality*, and not a transformation of social consciousness; the hypnotic power of civic activism which had dominated the intelligentsia for so many years suddenly disappeared, and the personality found itself at liberty.

VI

Our descendants will appreciate the importance of the crisis we are passing through, but those fated to bring about this historical change today with their own lives will have to suffer. Great confusion has seized the intelligentsia. Officially it still rallies around the old banner, but its former faith is gone now. The civic-minded fanatics are utterly amazed at the inertia and indifference the rank-and-file intelligentsia is displaying toward problems of politics and social organization in general. Reaction is triumphant, executions have not ceased, but society maintains the silence of the tomb. Political literature has disappeared from the market because of a total lack of buyers, and no one cares about the problems of the cooperative movement. Instead, heedless of politics, the intelligentsia's thought rushes about feverishly and avidly flings itself at each novelty. Yesterday's steadfast radical is unrecognizable; the doors are wide open for modernist poetry; people listen to the preaching of Christianity not just with tolerance but with obvious sympathy; the sex question was able to absorb the public's attention for a long time. Not one of these interests suggests the goal of the new searchings, but they all have a common implication.

The crisis of the intelligentsia is still just beginning. We can say in advance that it will be a crisis not of the collective spirit but of the individual consciousness. Instead of society shifting direction along the whole front, as has occurred more than once in the past, the personality *on its own* will begin to determine the direction of society.

The transformation under way in the *intelligent*'s soul consists of the fact that the tyranny of politics has come to an end. Hitherto, a single road to the good life was universally recognized—living for the people, for society. A few individuals did in fact follow this road, but the rest failed to follow not only this, but any other, for all other roads were deemed unworthy. For the majority the postulate of public service was at best self-deception, at worst intellectual prostitution, and in all cases self-justification for utter moral stagnation. Now the compulsory monopoly of civic activism has been overthrown. It was convenient, no question about it. A youth at the threshold of life was met by stern public opinion and immediately shown an exalted, simple and clear objective. The meaning of life was established beforehand, and it was the same for everyone, with no individual differences. Could its validity be doubted, when it was accepted by all progressive minds and consecrated by innumerable sacrifices? The very heroism of the martyrs who laid down their lives for this faith made doubt psychologically impossible. Only people with an exceptionally strong spirit could resist the hypnosis of a common faith and heroic deeds. Tolstoi resisted, and so did Dostoevskii, but the average person, even if he did not believe, dared not admit it.

Thus, a young man did not have to take the risk of defining the purpose of life for himself; he found it ready-made. For the crowd this was the first major convenience. Another was that it removed all moral responsibility from the individual. The political faith, like any other, by its nature demanded a heroic deed. But in every faith the same story is repeated: since only a few individuals are capable of heroic deeds, the crowd, which cannot perform them but wishes to be in communion with the faith, devises for itself some platonic confession that involves no practical commitment. And the priests and martyrs themselves tacitly legitimize this deception in order to keep the laymen at least formally within the church. In our political radicalism the rank-and-file *intelligenty* constituted the laymen. One had only to acknowledge oneself a true son of the church and occasionally participate in its symbolism in order to ease one's conscience and satisfy society. And the faith was of a sort to encourage the most unrestrained fatalism, a veritable Mohammedanism. All the dirt and disorder of personal and social life was blamed on the autocracy, and the individual was absolved of responsibility. It was a very convenient faith, responding fully to one of the ineradicable features of human nature: intellectual and moral sloth.

Now we are entering a new era fraught with many difficulties. It is an era when no ready-made ideal will greet a young man at the threshold of life. Instead, each one will have to determine the meaning and direction of his life for himself, and each will feel responsible for all he does and all he fails to do. There will be relapses into the general enthusiasm for politics, and individuals will still be moved by political concerns. In a country where political conditions distort the whole of life, suppress thought and speech, and cause millions to die in poverty and ignorance, it would be unnatural and inhuman to remain indifferent to political affairs. Life does not progress along a single straight line. At those moments when pain, shame and indignation again become very intense, or when external circumstances are favorable, there will be new outbreaks of the liberation struggle, and the old faith will flare up and fill the heart with enthusiasm. But after each of these outbursts society will disarm; only the older generation of today's intelligentsia will remain faithful unto death to politics-the-sole-salvation.

The tyranny of civic activism over young people will be shattered for a long time to come; it will not be restored until the personality, after plumbing its own depths, emerges with a new form of social idealism. The adolescent will hear nothing definite from his family, friends or schoolfellows. Like our fathers, we grew up in monotheism, in the atmosphere of Pisarev and Mikhailovskii. In the future a youth will find no ready-made, generally accepted dogma, but will encounter a variety of opinions, beliefs and tastes, which will merely guide him without removing his freedom of choice. He will have to choose for himself, and, moreover, he will have to do so regardless of any external objective, in accordance only with the demands and inclinations of his own spirit. And so, he will perforce become aware of himself and will have to think through his attitude to the world—and the world will lie open before him, not as it was for us, whom public opinion forbade to read Fet under pain of ridicule (at the very least). Then, once he matures, he will answer for his every step with his own personality, and throughout his entire life nothing will ever relieve him of this freely conscious responsibility. I am convinced that for a while the Russian intelligentsia's spiritual energy will turn inward, into the personality. But just as surely I know that only a regenerated personality can transform our social reality, and that it will surely do this (as part of its personal task), and will do it easily, without those agonizing strains and sacrifices that in the past brought society so little benefit.

This past has given the intelligentsia not just spiritual poverty and disordered nerves, but a positive legacy as well. The tyranny of civic activism crippled the personality but at the same time put it through a strict school. A whole series of generations was ruled by a law that regarded service to the common good, that is, to some supra-personal value, as the sole worthy object of life, and this fact is of enormous importance. Even though the majority did not actually satisfy this ideal of holiness, the very fact that they professed it had great educational force. Like people everywhere, they achieved personal success, tried to enhance it from day to day, and thus in practice trampled on all idealism. But they did so with their eyes averted, secretly aware of their dishonesty, so that however great our orgy of careerism and "business as usual," especially in the higher strata of the intelligentsia, it was never consecrated in theory. This is the cardinal difference between our intelligentsia and that of the West, where concern for personal prosperity is the accepted norm, something that goes without saying. Here it is regarded as cynicism, which we are forced to tolerate, but which no one would think of justifying on principle.

This ingrained idealism, the habit of demanding supra-personal justification for our individual lives, is the most valuable legacy bequeathed to us by the religion of civic activism. But in this, as in everything else, moderation is needed. The fanatical rejection of all egotism, whether personal or governmental, that was one of the chief dogmas of the intelligentsia's faith, brought us incalculable harm. Egotism, or self-assertion, is a powerful force; it is what makes the Western bourgeoisie a mighty, *unconscious* instrument of God's terrestrial purpose. Undoubtedly, the tendency now under way to concentrate on personal development will remove this fatal one-sidedness. One might even fear the opposite extreme, that at first this process may lead to unbridled egotism and to the personality's absorption in the creature comfort it scorned for so long. But this apprehension is misplaced in regard to the Russian intelligentsia. Its habit of seeing the meaning of personal life in ideal goods is too deeply ingrained, and it has amassed too many positive moral ideas to be in danger of wallowing in petty-bourgeois felicity. A person will realize that his goal was wrong and his path untrue, but he will continue to strive for ideal ends. He will find other supra-personal values within himself, and another ethic—one that will foster, not destroy, the present ethic of altruism and social commitment. He will no longer be torn between "I" and "we," for every objective good will become his personal need.

The aim of these pages was neither to refute the old doctrine nor to provide a new one. The movement I am describing—toward creative personal self-consciousness—has already begun: I am merely bearing witness to it. Sooner or later it had to begin, for the nature of the human spirit, so long repressed, demanded it. And because it is so natural this movement cannot stop, but will doubtless grow and intensify, continually reaching into new circles. One might say that it contains an immanent force, a kind of obligatory authority over people. But every social movement makes itself felt on two levels: in the society as a whole it is a spontaneous ferment of the collective spirit; in the individual it is a free moral act in which personal consciousness has the major role. Hence, we now have an urgent need to explain the meaning of the crisis society is undergoing, lest individual consciousnesses, through inertia or ignorance, remain paralyzed themselves and hold back others.

ON EDUCATED YOUTH

Notes on Its Life and Sentiments

A. S. Izgoev

In Paris I once was able to observe quite closely a very fine family of Russian revolutionaries. The husband had graduated from the *École de médecine*, and unlike the majority of his Russian colleagues, he was hard-working and conscientious, as French professors demand. The wife was a very energetic, educated woman, decisive and militant, one of those Russian women who are feared for their merciless, uncompromising tongue.

They were Socialist-Revolutionaries, and their actions did not diverge from their convictions, something they proved during the revolution. Even now both husband and wife are serving harsh administrative sentences.[1] When I knew them in Paris they had a lively and clever ten-year-old son whom they loved very much. They gave him whatever time they had left from their work and their civic activity in the Russian colony, where they rightfully held a prominent position. The parents worked hard on their son's education and brought him up in accord with their own rationalistic, revolutionary, and socialistic views. The boy was present at all the adults' discussions, and at the age of ten was remarkably well-informed about Russian tsarism, policemen, and revolutionaries. He would often join in the adults' conversations and amaze them with his shrewd opinions, to the obvious delight of his parents. He was brought up to be on a "comradely footing" with them. As far as God, religion, and priests were concerned, naturally he heard only the standard intelligentsia clichés.

And then one day the boy's father made a staggering discovery that upset all his ideas about his son. He saw him go up to a Catholic priest in the street, kiss his hand, and receive his blessing. The father began to watch his son. He soon noticed that when the boy received permission to go out and play with his French friends, he would run to the Catholic church and pray fervently. The father decided to have a talk with him. After some denials, the boy admitted everything. When asked why he did all this secretly, he confessed candidly that he had not wanted to hurt mama and papa. The parents were genuinely humane and reasonable people, and they did not try to eradicate their child's Catholic sympathies by force.

I do not know how this story ended. In Russia I was able to follow the

---

1. An administrative sentence was a penalty imposed by police officials, without trial and often on the basis of suspicion alone. *Eds.*

couple's activities only in the newspapers, which traced their involuntary itinary. I do not know what became of their son. I hardly think that the boy's naive Catholic faith could have long withstood the corrosive analysis of his rationalistic parents, and if not in Paris then later in Russia he probably entered the revolutionary faith of his fathers. But perhaps something else happened. . . .

I have told this story only as a vivid, though paradoxical, illustration of an almost universal feature of the Russian intelligentsia's life: parents have no influence on their children. Whether they concern themselves with their children's "development" or leave them to the servants and school; whether they acquaint them with their own outlook or conceal it; whether they treat the children in an authoritarian or a "comradely" manner; whether they resort to parental prerogative and shout at them, or exhaust the little ones with long, tedious scientific explanations, the result is always the same. No genuine bond develops between parents and children, and very often even a more or less covert hostility can be detected. The child's soul develops "contrariwise," by repudiating the soul of its parents. The Russian intelligentsia is unable to create its own family tradition; it is in no condition to build a family.

Our radical journalists regularly complained about our lack of "ideological continuity." Shelgunov and the writers for *The Cause* resented the fact that the "men of the seventies" ignored the precepts of the "men of the sixties." N. K. Mikhailovskii had more than a few bitter words for the men of the eighties and subsequent generations who "renounced the heritage of their fathers." But these "children who renounced their heritage" in their turn grew indignant at their own children for not wishing to acknowledge any ideological continuity.

In their bitter complaints the radical journalists were never able to get to the root of the problem: the family, the lack of family traditions, and the absence of any educational force in our intellectual families. Mikhailovskii, following the usual pattern, attributed the breach between fathers and children chiefly to the government repression that made the work of preceding generations inaccessible to the children. Does the superficiality of this explanation require comment?

Professor M. A. Chlenov's recently published *Sexual Census of the Moscow University Students*[2] contains some interesting material on our students' family relations. The majority of the students polled came from educated families (the fathers of 60 percent had received at least a secondary education). When questioned, at least half the students indicated that they felt no spiritual tie with their family. But on closer examination it turns out that even those stu-

---

2. M. A. Chlenov, *A Sexual Census of the Moscow Students and Its Social Significance* [Polovaia perepis' moskovskogo studenchestva i ee obshchestvennoe znachenie] (Moscow: A. Levenson, 1909). *Eds.*

dents who said they were on close terms with their parents were not significantly influenced by them. For example, only 1706 of the 2150 students
polled answered the question: did your family influence the development of
your ethical ideals, aesthetic tastes, set of friends, etc. Of these, 56 percent
denied any family influence, and only 44 percent acknowledged it. Of the
1794 students responding to the question: did your family influence you in
formulating a definite world-view, 58 percent replied in the negative and 42
percent in the affirmative. 2061 students answered when asked if the family
had influenced their choice of a field of study. Only 16 percent indicated that
they had been so influenced, while 84 percent denied it. Two-thirds of the
students denied family influence in the development of their attitude toward
women. Three-fourths of those responding indicated that their family had not
guided their reading at all. And of the one-quarter who acknowledged parental
guidance, 73 percent limited it to their childhood; only for the remaining
handful (172 students out of 2094) did it continue into adolescence.

The Russian intelligentsia has no family. Our children do not experience
the family's educational influence, and solid family traditions do not provide
that tremendous force which molds the ideological leaders of, for example,
the English people. Call to mind our most famous progressive civic leaders,
writers and scientists, especially those who are *raznochintsy*, and ask yourself
if many of them created solid families based on progressive traditions, where
the children carried on their fathers' work. It seems to me that only one answer is possible: with perhaps the rarest exceptions (and I cannot recall any),
there are no such families. I am an admirer neither of the Slavophiles nor of
the Russian nobility, a class whose role is ended and which is doomed to
rapid extinction. But there is no hiding the fact that in Russia solid ideological
families (the Aksakovs, Khomiakovs, and Samarins, for example) have hitherto existed only among the Slavophile nobility. Evidently these families possessed traditions, and they possessed as well the only thing that truly educates,
positive values, while this was not the case in progressive families; and the
children of our most talented progressive writers, satirists, and journalists
started out by rejecting their fathers.

The progressive family of rationalists, like the conservative family, is conspicuously sterile and cannot provide the nation with cultural leaders. But it
is guilty of a far graver sin as well. It cannot even preserve the children's
physical strength and protect them from premature corruption. And if it cannot do that, there is no point in even thinking about any kind of progress, the
radical reconstruction of society, or other exalted concerns.

The great majority of our children have already been corrupted by the
time they enter the university. Who among us is unaware of the fact that nowadays you rarely find a boy in the upper grades of gymnasium who is unacquainted with either the brothel or the chambermaid? We are so accustomed
to this that we no longer realize just how terrible it is when children do not

know childhood and not only dissipate their strength but destroy their souls, poison their imaginations, and distort their minds in early youth. I will not speak of England and Germany where, it is generally acknowledged, the sexual life of children of the educated classes proceeds normally, and where the corruption of children by a servant is exceptional and not the general rule, as it is here. Even in France, which we associate with all kinds of sexual excesses, even thère, in that land of southern sun and frivolous literature, sexual precocity in educated families is not so common as it is in northern, cold Russia.

In the questionnaire mentioned above, of the 967 students who specified the precise time of their first sexual relations, 61 percent began them by the age of seventeen, while 53 boys began them before the age of twelve and 152 before the age of fourteen. When a magazine recently published stories describing the "fall" of eight- and nine-year-old boys, our press let out a cry of indignation. This was justified insofar as the authors of the stories reveled in the details they provided about children being ruined and were merely pursuing sensation and exploiting a fashionable, titillating theme. But there was also an element of disgraceful hypocrisy in this indignation. Other critics asked: who were the models for these portraits? Who? Unfortunately, they were the children of Russian society and, even more unfortunately, the children of the progressive intelligentsia.

Another little book about the sex life of these same Moscow University students[3] indicates that there are some who began their sex life at the age of seven. The desire to conceal this truth and gloss over the fact that by the age of eight a dangerous sexual curiosity is aroused in the children of our educated families only attests to our faith in an ostrich policy for which our descendants and the whole nation will have to answer.

At this point we should mention another evil that endangers the race, masturbation. Three-quarters of the students answering this question (about 1600) had the courage to admit to this vice. The details they gave are as follows: 30 began to masturbate before the age of seven, and 440 before the age of twelve!

II

For the child from the educated class, the school is second in importance to the family. Little need be said about the educational influence of our secondary schools; there can be no disagreement on this point. If the reader is interested in the figures of the Moscow questionnaire, we can point out, for example, that of 2081 students polled, 1791, or 86 percent, stated that they

---

3. *A Page from the Sexual Confessions of the Moscow Students* [Stranitsa iz polovoi ispovedi moskovskogo studenchestva] (Moscow: "Osnova," 1908). *Eds.*

felt no spiritual attachment to any of the teaching staff in their secondary school.

The assertion that the secondary school has no influence on the development of the student's world-view is perhaps not entirely accurate. It has an influence, but it is purely negative. If the child is educated "contrariwise" even in his family, and repudiates both the actions and the ideas of his parents, this becomes the predominant pedagogical method in school. There the child feels himself to be in an enemy camp where they are plotting and scheming against him and preparing his ruin. To him, school is a great but, unfortunately, unavoidable evil. He has to get through it with as little damage to himself as possible; he must receive the best grades while giving the school as little work as possible, and while carefully concealing his own personality from it. Deceit, cunning, and false humility are all legitimate weapons of self-defense. The teacher attacks, and the pupil defends himself. To top it all off, he finds allies at home in the person of his parents, whose attitude to the school is not very different from his own. Indubitably, the primary blame for discrediting the schools lies with the educational administration, the Ministry of Education, which ever since 1871 has unreservedly aimed at turning the gymnasium into a political tool.[4] But by now everything is so confused in this area that it is very difficult to make heads or tails of it, and many serious observers feel that any attempt to restore the authority of the state secondary schools is doomed to failure.

Nevertheless, the cultured Russian youth does receive his education in secondary school, not, of course, from his teachers, but from his new circle of friends. This education continues at the university. Its positive aspects are undeniable. It gives a youth certain traditions and firm, definite views, trains him in civic affairs, forces him to take other people's opinions and desires into account, and exercises his will. The circle gives some positive intellectual interests to a youth who has emerged from his family and formal schooling a nihilist, a pure nay-sayer. The group begins as an offensive alliance against the teachers, for deceiving them and playing schoolboy pranks. But it continues, and not just for staging drinking bouts, visiting brothels, and telling dirty jokes. It also becomes a reading society, a self-education circle, and finally a circle for joint political activity. In the final analysis, this circle of friends is

---

4. In 1871, the so-called "classical system" of the reactionary Minister of Education (later Minister of the Interior) Dmitrii Tolstoi was introduced. It was a more or less overt attempt to isolate students from the modern world and independent thought. Tolstoi considered the natural sciences to be dangerous sources of materialism and atheism, and he dropped them from the gymnasium curriculum. He sharply reduced the number of hours devoted to history and literature, with the result that the students spent the bulk of their time in an almost purely grammatical study of the classical languages. Tolstoi also imposed rigid discipline on school administration and student life. *Eds.*

the sole cultural influence to which our children are exposed. Without it, the number of morally and mentally stupefied children wallowing in drunkenness and depravity would be much greater than it is now.

But in its Russian form, this "sole" cultural influence educating our youth also has many dangerous and harmful aspects. In his schoolboy circle the youth has already gone underground and become a renegade, and in the underground an individual's personality is gravely distorted. The youth dissociates himself from the entire world around him and becomes hostile to it. He scorns the scholarship of the gymnasium (and later of the university, too) and creates his own, which of course has nothing in common with the genuine article. The youth who joins a self-education circle is immediately filled with the greatest respect for himself and the greatest arrogance toward others. The "developed" gymnasium student not only scorns his teachers, parents, and the other mere mortals surrounding him, but overwhelms with his grandeur those of his classmates who are unfamiliar with illegal literature. My own gymnasium memories date back to the eighties, but judging by what I have occasion to see and hear now, the mentality of today's young people is basically unchanged. Only the subject of their arcane scholarship has changed here and there, and instead of the writings of the People's Will, the crown of knowledge now is *Sanin* and Weininger's book. This is scarcely cause for rejoicing!

In my day, as a rule the more democratic the ideas a boy professed, the greater his arrogance and contempt for others, both adults and students, who did not rise to his ideological level. Starting in the upper grades of gymnasium, this attitude intensifies during the university years and unquestionably turns into that spiritual arrogance and intellectual intolerance so characteristic of our intelligentsia in general. Almost all the bright, mature boys with good and honest intentions, but who lack any outstanding creative talent, inevitably pass through the youthful revolutionary circles, and it is only by plunging into them that they are preserved from moral ruin and intellectual stagnation. Somehow, the exceptionally gifted spirits—poets, artists, musicians, inventors, etc.—are not carried away by these circles. Quite often the average "developed" pupils have great contempt for those classmates who are destined to achieve wide renown in the near future. And this observation of mine is not limited to gymnasium and university circles. Prior to the recent revolutionary period, Russia's creative, gifted spirits seemed to avoid the revolutionary intelligentsia, unable to bear its arrogance and despotism.

III

The spiritual qualities that begin to emerge in the upper grades of gymnasium reach full development in the university. The students are the quintessence of the Russian intelligentsia. The highest praise you can give a Russian *intelligent* is to call him an old student. For the vast majority of educated Russians, intellectual (or, more precisely, "revolutionary") activity is confined to the university. Upon graduation they "go to seed," as they love to say of themselves with a drunken tear in pre-dawn penitential conversations with their intimate friends.

In progressive circles the Russian students may be discussed only in rapturous tones, and this flattery has always done us a great deal of harm. Without denying the students' good qualities, we must nonetheless firmly point out their negative traits, and these perhaps ultimately outnumber the positive ones. First of all, we must put an end to the legend, which no one dares question, that Russian students stand head and shoulders above those of other countries. This cannot be true, if only because Russian students study no more than half as much as foreign students. My calculations are based on objective figures; on days and hours of work, and not on a subjective estimate of the intensity of work, although there is no doubt that the Russian student does work much less intensively. His holidays are at least three times as long as vacations and holidays abroad. Furthermore, the foreign student is also much busier during the class day. In Russia the students in the Medical Faculty study hardest, but even there the number of compulsory lectures per day does not exceed six (it is four or five in the Law Faculty), while the French medical student is occupied for seven or eight hours.

In our Law Faculty, only a few students take lecture notes; they are regarded with amazement, and their colleagues make fun of them. Visit the Paris *École de droit*, and you will see that the vast majority of auditors are transcribing the professor's lecture—and how skillfully they do it! I still remember my surprise when I looked over the notes of an "average" French student, one whom we would have considered "undeveloped": they did not need recopying, so expertly had he grasped the professor's central ideas and invested them in literary form in his mind. Indeed, attending lectures is rather pointless if the students do not take notes. Every psychologist knows that it is impossible to sustain passive attention uninterruptedly for even one hour, much less for five. Only a rare oratorical talent can seize the student's attention and hold it undiminished for an entire lecture. In most cases, his attention is continually distracted, if only for a moment, and directed elsewhere. He loses the train of thought and essentially misses the whole lecture. And how do our students listen? Just like schoolboys, they read books and newspapers, carry on conversations, and so forth and so on. Even attendance at lectures is haphazard, and mostly for purposes of registration. Frankly, Russian classroom attendance cannot be counted as work, and the great majority of university students, aside from their practical training, do no work at all.

They "work," and feverishly, at home before examinations or recitations, cramming to the point of stupor from short textbooks adapted to the syllabus or from mimeographed digests. The short Gepner that my medical school colleagues at Tomsk University used for anatomy, and the many huge volumes of Farabeuf that the French students pored over—reducing the Russians at the Paris *École de médecine* to utter despair—will always symbolize in my mind the comparative amount of work done by our own students and the French. Things are no better in the Law Faculty. A French student cannot graduate without familiarizing himself with the classic works of French jurists and statesmen in their original form; but I will venture to state that 95 percent of our lawyers graduate without looking at anything but the official textbook—and that is a digest.

I am not personally familiar with the teaching arrangements in higher technical schools here and abroad, and can judge only on the basis of secondhand information. Undoubtedly, in these schools (as also, to some extent, in the Medical Faculty) practical training forces the students to work much harder than in the Law Faculty, the Historical and Philological Faculty, the economics division of the Polytechnicum, etc. But even here, the general consensus is that there is no comparison between the diligence of Russian and foreign students.

Russian young people study little and badly. Anyone who sincerely loves them is obliged to tell them so, constantly and to their faces, instead of singing them dithyrambs or assigning exalted socio-political motives to what quite often can be explained by weak development of the mind and will, moral slovenliness, and a habit of phrasemongering.

Those who flatter our youth argue that Russian students are superior to the English and Americans because English students concentrate on sport and on strengthening their muscles, and therefore develop into brawny animals who shun all spiritual interests. Once again, this is untrue. Naturally, there is a great deal about English student life that is traditionally English and will strike a Russian as strange and even unworthy of an educated man. Nonetheless, we should not lose sight of the fact that the English "brawny animal," so scorned by our *intelligenty*, is in many respects an unattainable ideal for them. Above all, the English student is healthy. In English universities you will not find that 75 percent of the students masturbate, as is the case with Russian revolutionary youth. The vast majority of English students are unacquainted with brothels; you cannot say the same of Russia's progressive students. The English "brawny animal" approaches a woman with elevated sentiments and gives her physically healthy children. In England the "intelligentsia" is, above all else, the physical bulwark of the race, producing sturdy, powerful human specimens. In Russia the physically strongest group in the nation, the clergy, deteriorates and degenerates as it passes through the intelligentsia, and begets puny, scrofulous, myopic progeny.

The progressive Russian student naturally feels nothing but contempt for the German students, the "*Burschen*," with their corporations and their stupid ceremonies, caps, buffoonery, *Kneiper*, *Mensur* duels, and so on.[5] And clearly there is nothing attractive in any of this. But here too we should not exaggerate. Personally, I saw carousing German corporation members only once. It was not a pleasant sight and on the whole corresponded to descriptions. But I must say that the stupid revelry of these young bull-calves was not as painful to me as the drinking bouts of progressive Russian students, which generally end in nocturnal visits to brothels. The most distressing thing about these parties is the impossible way they mix depravity and drunkenness with fine phrases about the people's misery, the struggle against tyranny, etc. The *Bursch* gets drunk, cracks stupid jokes, and behaves outrageously, but he does not array his drunken cavorting in the elegant garb of *Weltschmerz*. When he overturns signboards and smashes streetlights, he knows he is making a row and does not fancy that he is protesting against the system. But in Russia, even in taverns and worse places, the radical students are particularly fond of singing "The Oaken Cudgel" and "Show Me One Abode."[6]

Russian students apparently have little objective basis for the widespread view that European students are an inferior breed. In their diligence, the amount of genuine scholarly work they perform, and their moral purity, foreign students are, at any rate, no worse than our own. But this they do lack: our spirit of fellowship and our unique student culture built upon it. There is, of course, an element of truth in this contention. If anything makes us remember our university days for the rest of our lives, it is their spirit of youthful fellowship and their intensive communal life, which keeps the student in almost constant animation and does not allow him to become wrapped up in personal, selfishly professional interests. To a certain extent, I repeat, this is true. But at the same time it is almost universally acknowledged, and without embarrassment, that a fervent young idealist, full of the most exalted revolutionary impulses, no sooner receives his diploma than he is instantaneously transformed into a careerist bureaucrat or a self-seeking businessman. And this raises the question of whether there is not something false in our student idealism when it leads to such melancholy results, and if sometimes this exalted spiritual enthusiasm is no more than a hashish euphoria, temporarily exhilarating but ultimately debilitating.

In *Religion and Culture*, a collection of articles published about ten years ago, V. V. Rozanov devotes several brilliant, deeply thought-out pages to the

5. Izgoev is here referring to the German duelling fraternities, whose members wore uniforms and divided their time between drinking in the fraternity tavern (*Kneip*) and fighting saber duels (*Mensuren*). *Eds.*

6. "The Oaken Cudgel" [Dubinushka] and "Show Me One Abode" [Ukazhi mne takuiu obitel'] were familiar protest songs about the hardships of workers and peasants. The first was based on a poem by V. I. Bogdanov written in the 1860s, and the second came from a poem by Nekrasov. *Eds.*

subject of Russian students. This talented writer compares them to our old Zaporozhian Cossacks. In the contemporary Russian context he sees the students as a kind of Khortitsa Island, with its own special way of life and its own mores. "For these spiritual Cossacks," Rozanov writes, "and the needs of their level of maturity, we have an entire literature. No one notices that none of our so-called 'radical' journals contain anything essentially radical. . . . In their tone, viewpoint, and methods of attack and defense they are simply 'young people's magazines,' 'anthologies for young readers,' a species of 'kindergartens,' but in printed form and for children older than toddlers. These are not journals for merchants, officials and landowners, for our reading public; none of these people with adult interests, responsibilities and concerns ever open them, and the journals have no need of such readers. This is so well-known that it would be ludicrous to take the trouble to prove it. We have here not just a child's own history, told from a child's point of view, and a child's literary criticism, which totally excludes any aesthetic thought (a product solely of mature minds); we have a full-scale epos, with novels and stories drawn entirely from the life of young people, where adults play no part and are excluded. There are no heroes or even bystanders over thirty-five, and all who are approaching that age, and especially those who pass it, are painted in a form as ugly as children's notions of 'wicked strangers' and the image the Cossacks once had of the Turks. This literature is the most original product of our history and spiritual life, and everyone knows how pure and fresh it is; we would seek in vain for analogies to it in the aging life of Western Europe. In accord with the youthfulness of our nation, youth simply extends further here. It cuts a broader swath in the life of every Russian; it holds sway longer and on the whole is more vivid, active and significant than anywhere else. In point of fact, where else has it developed of and for itself almost all the creative genres, almost an entire little culture, with its righteous men and sinners, its martyrs and 'apostates,' its own songs, opinions, and even the rudiments of almost all branches of scholarship? 'Its own politics' are, in part, an aspect of this rudimentary scholarship, and in part its practical result."[7]

This artistic picture, drawn with delicate, good-natured irony, vividly and accurately characterizes our students and the special literature that has grown up to meet their intellectual needs. But Rozanov overlooked the fact that when the Russian *intelligent* emerges from this distinctive infantile culture he does not enter any other and remains, as it were, in a vacuum. The people still see him as a "master," while the great majority of educated men naturally find it impossible to continue leading a student's life after they have left the university. As a result, yesterday's radical, the ardent worshipper of the pub-

7. V. V. Rozanov, *Religion and Culture: A Collection of Articles* [Religiia i kul'tura: sbornik statei] (St. Petersburg: M. Merkushev, 1899), pp. 92-93. *Eds.*

lic good, today renounces all ideas and all civic activity. While he was at the university the special student culture appeared to give him a great deal, but no sooner has he left the classroom than he feels that he has received nothing.

He scorned "bourgeois" scholarship, learning only as much as he needed to get his degree, and drew up plans for a comprehensive program of self-education. But the result was that he did not even learn to express his thoughts intelligibly, and he does not know the ABC's of the physical sciences, the geography of his own country, or the basic facts of Russian history. And was university life itself, with its meetings, its mutual aid funds, and its societies, genuine civic activity or even a preparatory school for it? Or was it perhaps more truly just froth, that absorbed all the student's time and only appeared to have content? The constant bustle did not allow him to remain alone with himself for very long or to take stock of his life and of the baggage with which he was preparing to meet the future.

The meetings develop a taste for oratory in some of the students, and they do learn how to speak and master a crowd. But this training can in no way be compared with those mock parliamentary debates in great vogue in the English schools, which have produced the celebrated English debaters. Our student crowd is herd-like and intolerant; its judgments are simplistic and are supported by passion more than reason. The popular student orators always impress a listener with the wretchedness of their thought and the poverty and formlessness of their speech. They proceed according to a definite canon, speaking in aphorisms and dogmatic assertions. Graphic speech requires contact with many different kinds of people and the ability to observe life and understand the thoughts and feelings of others. These are certainly not the distinguishing characteristics of our student radicals. They live in their own narrow, exclusive circle and are perpetually caught up in its petty interests and intrigues. The arrogance which is already in evidence in the more mature upper-level gymnasium pupils reaches enormous proportions in the university students. They brand all colleagues who do not share the views of their own circle as not merely stupid but dishonorable. When they have the majority behind them they treat the minority like slaves and exclude its representatives from all student enterprises, even those concerned solely with financial aid.

"The one-sided freedom that dwells in the consciousness of the students is more bitter than any slavery," complains Vadim Levchenko, a student whose passionate and sincere article on youth was noted by almost the entire press.[8] "The whole system of student life is imbued with the denial of inner liberty. How dreadful not to think like the student crowd! They will banish

8. Vad. Levchenko, "The Crisis in University Life (Thoughts of a Student)" [Krizis universitetskoi zhizni (mysli studenta)], *Russian Thought* [Russkaia mysl'] (May 1908), p. 114. *Eds.*

you, accuse you of treason, and consider you an enemy. . . . Political doctrines are taken on faith, and the believers mercilessly punish the non-accep-
tance or renunciation of the new religious orthodoxy. Scholarly positions as
well as personal views are subjected to the same strict censorship. Among the
students the so-called boycott is the counterpart of administrative exile. . . .
An undercurrent of hostility surrounds and oppresses anyone who voices an
independent thought. Unverified rumors and slanderous accusations then suf-
fice to stigmatize the man who is guilty of displeasing the crowd.

"The Petersburg affair involving Professor Vvedenskii is common knowledge. This man, who is just about the best teacher of philosophy in Russia
since the death of Prince S. N. Trubetskoi, was subjected to the cruellest persecution both in the advanced courses for women and at the university, although no definite accusations of any kind were made against him. . . . The
women students' censure of Professor Sergeevich for his views is well known,
and we could also mention the 'rebellion' against Professor Ivaniukov by students who had just entered the Petersburg Polytechnicum. . . . The students'
criterion for evaluating a professor has nothing to do with his scholarly merits, they know and care very little about them. The primary, if not the sole,
standard is his political position . . . more or less accurately divined. . . ."[9]

The student chronicle has been further enriched since the appearance of
Levchenko's article. Young radicals hissed A. A. Manuilov, the rector of Moscow University; student delegates at the Women's Medical Institute of St. Petersburg spoke to the faculty council in a manner that forced the professors
to break off discussions, and so on, and so forth.

"An . . . indifference to questions of national honor, a narrowly self-indul-
gent notion of the principle of freedom, and a despotically fierce intolerance
for the opinions of others," Levchenko summarizes, "are the most typical
qualities that Russian student youth acquires from the intelligentsia milieu
that engendered it. These deadening principles have found their ultimate,
complete expression in the life of the university. The students absorb them
from the intelligentsia and then bring them back to it, dessicating the public
intellect and depriving social ideals of their luster."[10]

The intense, stimulating university life, which seems like grandiose civic
activity and takes up a great deal of time at the expense of studies, prevents
the students from examining their souls and giving themselves an exact and
honest reckoning of their actions and thoughts. And without this there is not
and cannot be any moral improvement. But in general, moral self-improve-
ment enjoys no credit among the radical youth, who for some reason are convinced that it is a "reactionary conceit." Ideally, they replace moral self-im-

9. *Ibid.*, pp. 114-15. *Eds.*
10. *Ibid.*, p. 119. *Eds.*

provement with a constant readiness to lay down their lives for their friends (more about this later); but in practice, the vast majority of—alas!—ordinary mortals replace it only with the shouting of thunderous words and the passing of radical resolutions at student meetings.

You can easily transport any cargo under a beautiful flag. The "great" Azev, the foremost hero of the day, began his career by stealing several hundred rubles. But since he explained that he needed the money to continue his education, and politically he was an extreme leftist, all was forgiven and people placed complete confidence in him. This episode was recalled only when the gentleman's long career as a *provocateur* was accidentally revealed. The same was true of another well-known *provocateur*, Gurovich, who conceived the idea of entrapping the Social Democrats by means of a legally published Marxist journal, *The Beginning*. Everyone knew that personally Mr. Gurovich was rather corrupt, but as long as he proclaimed himself a revolutionary and made revolutionary speeches at the top of his voice (he was trying to propagate the idea of terrorism among the Social Democrats), they forgave him everything and looked through their fingers at his "pecadilloes." They reminded him of all this, and of more besides, only after his provocation had been disclosed.

When a mature student, an *intelligent* with ideological principles, tries to "slip by" on an examination by cheating and deceiving his professor, you would think this should evoke a definite reaction from his comrades. But the students regard such feats with astonishing equanimity. Even cases of forged diplomas disturb no one. Levchenko, in the candid article we have already discussed, stresses how much lying there is in student circles. "They lie," he writes, "in polemical irritation, they lie to set a new record for leftism, they lie so as not to lose popularity. Yesterday's revolutionary, who thundered and cursed when he delivered an agitational speech from the platform of a student meeting, takes an examination today. In order to 'slip by' without knowing anything he resorts to pitiful, fraudulent tricks; while taking the examination he is pale and almost trembles; once he has 'slipped by' he is cocky and proud again."[11]

But the effects of this excitation are not always positive, even in the purely public sphere. At their meetings, "for fear of the Jews,"[12] the students very often adopt decisions which none of them individually believes in , and which each realizes he cannot put into effect. This explains their conduct during conflicts, conduct that throws their professors into despair and arouses honest indignation in those who love young people but do not wish to flatter them. When they gain any concessions, the students begin to think that peo-

11. *Ibid*., p. 120. *Eds.*
12. John 7:13, 19:38, 20:19. *Eds.*

ple are afraid of them; their demands grow, and their tone becomes insolent.
But when they encounter crude physical resistance they give way and withdraw, if possible covering their retreat with some ringing phrase, such as "the
students are preparing for battle." Are facts needed to confirm this? 1908
with its unfortunate student strike provided more than enough of them.[13]

These negative traits have become particularly conspicuous since 17 October 1905, which marked a fundamental turning point in Russian life. Prior to
that date Russian society and the Russian people could and should have forgiven their students everything, in view of the tremendous positive role they
played in national life. For all their grave faults—and they existed at that
period, too—the students were nonetheless almost the only group of educated
people who thought about the needs of the whole country and not just about
their personal interests. The students awakened social thought, harassed the
government, and continually reminded the autocratic bureaucracy that it was
not and never would be able to stifle the entire country. This was an enormous service, for which much will be forgiven.

Now the students have been relieved of this burden, which was too heavy
for their young shoulders, and society demands other things from them:
knowledge, industry and moral restraint.

IV

Whatever the convictions held by various groups of Russia's educated
youth, if you examine their mentality more deeply, you find that in the
final analysis they are all motivated by the same ideal. (By "ideal" I do
not mean speculative and more or less arbitrary constructs, but that real
force which irresistibly drives the will to specific actions.) Their ideal is
not some dream of mankind's future happiness, "when burdocks will
grow on my grave."[14] It is profoundly personal and intimate, and is
manifested in a striving toward death, in a desire to prove both to oneself
and to others that one does not fear death and is ready to meet it at any
time. In essence, this is what our revolutionary youth, in the person of its
purest representatives, regards as the sole logical and moral foundation
for its convictions. Your convictions will lead to your crucifixion: they are
holy, they are progressive, you are right. . . .

13. In the fall of 1908, the students at St. Petersburg University tried to start a nation-wide student strike in protest against the repressive policies of the Minister of Education, A. N. Schwarz. *Eds.*

14. In chapter 21 of Turgenev's *Fathers and Sons* [Ottsy i deti], Bazarov uses this
phrase in cynically rejecting visions of future progress. I. S. Turgenev, *Complete Collected Works* [Polnoe sobranie sochinenii], 3rd ed., 10 vols. (St. Petersburg: Glazunov, 1891),
II, 147. *Eds.*

Take a look at our generally accepted gradations of "leftism." What is their basis? Why are the Socialist-Revolutionaries considered "more left" than the Social Democrats (especially the Mensheviks), the Bolsheviks "more left" than the Mensheviks, and the anarchists and maximalists "more left" than the SR's? In fact, the Mensheviks are correct when they point out that the doctrines of the Bolsheviks, SR's and anarchists contain many petty-bourgeois elements. Clearly, the criterion for "leftism" lies in another sphere. He is "more left" who is closer to death, whose work is more dangerous—not to the social order against which he is struggling, but to his own person. In general, the Socialist-Revolutionary is closer to the gallows than the Social Democrat, and the maximalist and anarchist are still closer than the Socialist-Revolutionary. And it is this circumstance that exerts a magical influence on the most sensitive representatives of educated Russian youth. It bewitches their reason and paralyzes their conscience: everything that ends in death is sanctified, all is allowed the man who is going to his death and who daily risks his neck. Any objections are immediately cut off with a single phrase: that's an expression of your bourgeois fear for your own skin.

The maximalists, the most extreme and consistent "leftists," reproached even the Socialist-Revolutionaries for being liberal, bourgeois, even reactionary. The pamphlet, *A Reply to Viktor Chernov*, by the maximalist theoretician E. Tag—in, is an example. "In its final goal," Tag—in writes, "socialism threatens no one. Bourgeois democrats can easily become its (i.e., the Socialist-Revolutionary Party's) ideologues and seduce it from the true path. . . . We repeat: peasant and worker, when you go forth to struggle and *to die* in the struggle, go and struggle and *die*, but for your own rights and your own needs."[15] This "go and die" is the crux of the matter.

As long as the principle of "go and die" guided the actions of only a select few, it could maintain them at an extremely high moral level. But once the circle of the "doomed" widened, inner logic led inexorably to what occurred in Russia: all those instances of corruption, murder, looting and theft, and every sort of libertinism and provocation. People cannot live by the thought of death alone, nor make constant readiness to die the criterion of all their actions. Obviously, for the person who is ready to die momentarily neither the cares of daily life, nor moral problems nor questions of creativity and philosophy can have any value in themselves. But this is nothing but suicide—and undeniably, for many years the Russian intelligentsia has formed a peculiar monastic order of people who have condemned themselves to death, and, moreover, to the most rapid death possible. If one's object is to sacrifice oneself, why wait for maturity? Isn't it better to sacrifice young people, since they are more excitable?

15. E. Tag—in [A. G. Troitskii], *A Reply to Viktor Chernov* [Otvet Viktoru Chernovu] (St. Petersburg: n.p., 1906), p. 37n. *Eds.*

If this "doomed" quality did give youth a special moral tone, still it is clear that a life cannot possibly be built on the ideal of death. Naturally, I am speaking only of those *intelligenty* whose words did not diverge from their deeds. The moral position of the many others who were "sympathizers" and even instigators but did not themselves go to their death was doubtless tragic and horrifying. It is no wonder that "repentance," "self-indictment," and so forth, are always part of the Russian *intelligent*'s life, and particularly in times of special excitement. It goes without saying that a person who confessed that he "had no right to live" and who felt a continual divergence between his words, ideas and deeds could not create worthy forms of human life or be a true leader of his people. But even those whose sincerity was boundless and etched in their own blood were unable to play this role, for they could not teach others how to live but only how to die.

There are reasons for everything, of course, and there are profound historical reasons for the Russian intelligentsia's mental condition. But now there are only two alternatives: either all of Russia is condemned to death and there is no way to save her, or else there must be a radical change, an all-encompassing transformation in this fundamental and, to my mind, most deeply rooted feature of the Russian intelligentsia's psychological structure. Instead of love of death, the basic motive force behind its activity must become love of life, life in common with its millions of compatriots. Love of life is in no way equivalent to fear of death. Death is inevitable, and people must be taught to meet it with calm and dignity. But this is entirely different from teaching them to seek death and from evaluating every deed and thought according to whether or not it threatens to result in death. And doesn't this exalted view of death conceal a peculiar fear of it?

Russian educated society is now caught up in a profound ideological ferment. It will be fruitful and creative only if it generates a new ideal capable of arousing love of life in Russian youth.

This is the fundamental task of our time.

Despite everything, the great majority of our average *intelligenty* do live and desire to live, but in their hearts they confess that only the striving for self-sacrifice is holy. This is the tragedy of the Russian intelligentsia. The average *intelligent* is so impotent and so useless to the people because of this profound spiritual discord, in combination with the intelligentsia's lack of culture and education, the many negative qualities engendered by centuries of slavery, and its lack of serious training. *Intelligenty* who finish school and enter practical life do not make an intellectual and spiritual transition to another, higher plane. On the contrary, they frequently give up all spiritual interests. And for those who do not give them up, the ideal remains death, and the revolutionary work that leads to it. In the light of this ideal, any concern with putting one's personal life in order, fulfilling private and public obligations, or determining genuine standards for governing relations with one's neighbors is declared a bourgeois affair. A man lives, marries, fathers children—what can be done! This is an unavoidable but petty detail that ought not deflect him from his basic task. The same is true of work—the *intelligent* must work in order to eat, unless he can become a "professional revolutionary" living at his organization's expense.

There have been frequent attempts to identify the contemporary revolutionaries with the ancient Christian martyrs. But these are two completely different spiritual types. Their cultural fruits, too, are different. "For we know," wrote the Apostle Paul, "that if our earthly house of this tabernacle were dissolved, we have a building of God, an house not made with hands, eternal in the heavens." (II Cor. 5:1.) As we know, many of the Christian martyrs were mature or elderly, while among the contemporary revolutionary activists who end their lives on the scaffold, people over thirty-five or forty are very rare exceptions. The prevailing desire of Christianity was to teach man to *meet* death calmly and with dignity, and tendencies which spurred a person to *seek* death in Christ's name were comparatively infrequent. In the Church Fathers we even find those who seek death accused of arrogance.

I allowed myself this digression because it clarified my thought as to why the Russian intelligentsia could not create a serious culture. Christianity did create one because it made a just, righteous life on earth as well as an "honorable death" a requirement for heavenly bliss. It would be odd to console the contemporary revolutionary with a "house in the heavens."

Relations between the sexes, marriage, concern for one's children, a commitment to solid knowledge such as is acquired only through many years of persistent effort, a favorite project which one sees come to fruition, the beauty of life—how can there be any interest in these things if the educated man's ideal is the professional revolutionary who battles for a few anxious years and then dies on the scaffold?

Of course, absolutism's centuries-long sway over our life molded the Russian intelligentsia's spiritual physiognomy. Without these traits, could the intelligentsia have sustained for the last half century that heroic struggle which has attracted the attention of the entire world? But on 17 October 1905, we came to a turning point. And now, without in the least detracting from the service the Russian intelligentsia performed in the past, we must begin to take its dark sides into account as well. In the heat of struggle they could be overlooked. But now we are on the threshold of a new stage in Russian history, one marked by the overt appearance of public forces alongside the government (whatever these forces may be, and however distorted their legal representation), and we have to take stock of the harm inflicted on Russia by the historically molded character of her intelligentsia.

I would not for a moment deny that Russian *intelligenty*—revolutionary, socialist, and simply democratic—concerned themselves with creative organizational work in addition to seeking the great exploit that would earn them a martyr's death. There were *intelligenty* who labored in various ways to organize the working class, and others who united the peasants to struggle for their interests as consumers, tenants and hired workers. Still others worked to educate the people, while the *zemstvo* men labored over the rudiments of local self-government. Indubitably, all this is organic, creative work and constitutes an historic deed. But we all know that the results of this labor, which demanded tremendous energy and total selflessness, were, comparatively speaking, very meager; the country progressed but slowly. External causes alone cannot account for this. If we turn from the results of the work to the mentality of the workers, we shall see that they labored without complete faith in their cause or total devotion to it. They were oppressed and anguished by the thought that there was more important and serious work to be done, but unfortunately they could not accomplish it, either because of their own weakness or for some other reason.

We all know how the work of the first Social Democrats, the so-called "economists," was greeted. With a sure instinct, they understood that the most important task was to organize the working masses and train leaders from the ranks of the workers themselves. These first SD's went to prison and exile, but this did not prevent their views from being branded as pitiful, cowardly and servile. But even worse, the "economists" themselves neither understood nor believed in their cause sufficiently to defend their views openly and boldly. It took the horrors of our post-revolutionary reaction for P. B. Aksel'rod and some other **Mensheviks** to begin propounding once again the axiom that a Social-Democratic workers' party is inconceivable without workers. But even then they accompanied their argument with a mysterious lifting of the "veil of the future," tactical grimaces, and loud phrases. The Popular Socialists, who had so generously heaped reproaches on the Constitutional Democrats for cowardice, opportunism, and angling for ministerial portfolios, had to listen to their full share of these same accusations from their "friends on the left." The *zemstvo* workers were presented with this gift: "It was not the *zemstvo* liberals with their schools, which in fact were not very different from the church schools, who prepared the great revolution; if anything was done along these lines in the *zemstvo*, it was done by the 'third element.' The 'third element' provided Sipiagin and Plehve with whole carloads of material for resettlement in Siberia. The *zemstvo*'s secret work was valuable, not its open, audited activity."[16]

These reproaches are important not in themselves but because deep in their hearts their targets were crushed by them. They could never find a point of

---

16. *Conscious Russia: A Symposium on Contemporary Themes* [Soznatel'naia Rossia: sbornik na sovremennye temy], No. 3 (St. Petersburg: "Rabotnik," 1906), pp. 62-63. *Eds.*

principle that would give them the strength to defend their cause openly, acknowledge its self-sufficing value, and say they were consciously devoting *all* their energies to it and saw nothing wrong in so doing. No, they always tried to justify themselves and throw off the burden of these reproaches. The Social-Democratic "economists" sought to prove that they were not "economists" at all, but extreme revolutionaries. The Mensheviks tried to show that they were infected neither by revisionism nor by trade-unionism, but preserved the flame of the most fervent orthodox revolutionism. With the greatest scorn the Popular Socialists rejected any imputation of "Kadetism." The Kadets, too, sought for a time to dissociate themselves from analytic reason in order to fly on the wings of fantasy.

Two tremendously important consequences ensued. In the first place, in Russia the average, rank-and-file *intelligent* usually does not know his job and does not like it. He is a poor teacher, a poor engineer, a poor journalist, an impractical technician, etc. He regards his profession as something incidental, a sideline that does not deserve respect. If he is enthusiastic about his profession and devotes himself to it whole-heartedly, he can expect the cruellest sarcasm from his friends, the genuine revolutionaries and the phrase-mongering idlers alike. But a person can acquire serious influence in society and carry weight in contemporary life only if he commands solid, genuine, specialized knowledge. He cannot play a role in life for very long without it, by merely living off popular pamphlets. If you recall what a pitiful education our *intelligenty* receive in secondary school and university, you can understand how their indifference to their profession and the revolutionary superficiality they use to resolve all problems produced an anti-cultural impact. History has provided us with all too glaring proof of this. Finally, we must have the courage to admit that aside from some thirty or forty Kadets and Octobrists, the overwhelming majority of the deputies in our State Dumas have not exhibited the knowledge necessary to undertake the administration and reconstruction of Russia.

The second consequence is no less important. During crises, popular movements, or even mere public excitement, the extremist elements very quickly become dominant, since they meet almost no resistance from the moderates. With feverish rapidity, the intelligentsia rushes after those who constantly risk their own lives, not in word but in deed. A "sick conscience" makes itself felt: in a sudden transport a man will erase the work of many years, to which, apparently, he was never committed. Sometimes comedies occur, like the famous case of the Vice-Governor who, after some thirty years of service to the "autocratic government" in various capacities, converted to Social Democracy; but there are also serious tragedies in men's intellectual and personal lives. After 17 October, Russia proved to have too few strong, influential people to restrain the revolution with a strong hand and proceed at once to reforms. Then discerning individuals realized that the cause of freedom was played out for the present, and it would take many years of persistent struggle before the principles of the Manifesto were brought to life.

But perhaps the heaviest blow to the Russian intelligentsia was not the defeat of our liberation movement but the victory of the Young Turks, who were able to organize a national revolution and win an almost bloodless victory. Their success should force us to ponder deeply those aspects of the Russian intelligentsia's life and character that we have hitherto almost completely ignored.[17, 18]

17. *Note to the Second Edition.* Since the preceding lines were written, the Young Turks, after eight months of bloodless revolution, have passed to a second stage of their political life. Since they are a creative force, they were attacked from both the right and the left. This has always been the case, in all countries. The Turkish *Ahrar* played the role of our SR's and SD's. And if the Young Turks have been victorious once again, it is only because they embody the creative force of the Turkish nation-state. Of course, even the Young Turks may fall under the blows of the separatists and the masses deceived by black reaction. But their ruin will mean Turkey's ruin, and the history of the Young Turks is and always will be a shining example of the moral power that the nation-state idea gives to a revolution it inspires.

[The Young Turk movement originated at the end of the nineteenth century among young army officers and intellectuals who had been exposed to European influence. Resentful of the decay and weakness of the Ottoman Empire, the Young Turks demanded representative government, administrative and social reform, and the transformation of the Empire into a modern state. In 1908 the Committee of Union and Progress, the political organization of the Young Turks, forced the Sultan to restore constitutional rule and to convene a parliament. The *Ahrar*, or Liberal Union, formed the main opposition to the Committee of Union and Progress; it represented the subject nationalities of the Ottoman Empire and opposed the centralizing tendencies of the Committee. In 1909 opposition forces rebelled unsuccessfully against the domination of the Young Turks. *Eds.*]

18. I feel obliged to make a reservation in regard to the "platform" formulated in the Preface to this book: I fully accept the *basic thesis* propounded there, but disagree with the other authors on the *principles* used to support it.

IN DEFENSE OF LAW

The Intelligentsia and Legal Consciousness

Bogdan Kistiakovskii

Law cannot be ranked with such spiritual values as scientific truth, moral perfection and religious sanctity. It does not have the same absolute significance, and its content is in part determined by changeable economic and social conditions. This relative significance of law allows some theorists to assign it a very low value. Some see law as a mere ethical minimum, while others consider compulsion, that is, violence, one of its integral elements. If they are correct, there is no reason to reproach our intelligentsia for disregarding law. It aspired to higher, absolute ideals, and could overlook this secondary value on its way to them.

But spiritual culture does not consist of substantive values alone. The valuable formal properties of intellectual and emotional life make a significant contribution to it. And of all the formal values, law, since it is the most highly developed and is almost concretely tangible, is the most important. Law disciplines a person much more than does logic or scientific method or any systematic exercise of the will. Most importantly, in contrast to the individual character of these other systems, law is pre-eminently social and is, indeed, the only system that instills social discipline. Only law creates social discipline, and a disciplined society is identical to a society with a well-developed legal system.

From this point of view the substantive content of law also appears in a different light. Its primary and most essential element is freedom. True, this freedom is external and relative, and is determined by the social environment. But inner, more absolute spiritual freedom is possible only when external freedom is present, and the latter is the best school for the former.

If we keep in mind the law's general disciplinary function and consider the part it has played in the Russian intelligentsia's spiritual development, we will arrive at some highly disconcerting conclusions. The Russian intelligentsia consists of people who are undisciplined both personally and socially. This lack of discipline is related to the fact that the intelligentsia never respected law nor saw any value in it; of all cultural values, law was the one it relegated furthest to the background. Under these conditions our intelligentsia could not develop a sound legal consciousness. On the contrary, the level of its legal consciousness is extremely low.

I

The literary exposition of legal ideas might have fostered the intelligentsia's legal consciousness, and at the same time served as an index of our legal awareness. The strenuous activity of consciousness and the unremitting labor of thought in any field is always reflected in literature. It is the first place we must look for evidence about the nature of our legal consciousness. But here we encounter a striking fact: our "rich" literature of the past contains not a single treatise nor even a legal study of *public* interest. We had scholarly juridical research, of course, but this always remained the exclusive preserve of specialists. What interests us is literature of *public* relevance, and this contained nothing that might have stimulated our intelligentsia's legal consciousness. It may be said that not a single legal concept played a part in the intelligentsia's intellectual development, insofar as that development was reflected in literature. Even now, law is not a part of that set of ideas which goes into forming our intelligentsia's world-view. And literature is the witness to this gap in our public consciousness.

In this respect, how different our history has been from that of other civilized nations! In the corresponding period in England we find, on the one hand, Hobbes's treatises on the citizen (*De Cive*) and on the state (*Leviathan*) and Filmer's *Patriarcha*, and, on the other, Milton's works in defense of freedom of speech and the press, Lilburne's pamphlets and the legal ideas of the "Levellers." The most turbulent period in England's history also produced the most extreme contrasts in legal concepts. But these ideas did not destroy each other, and in due course a fairly tolerable compromise was effected and received literary expression in Locke's *Two Treatises of Government*.

In eighteenth-century France the discoveries of natural science and systems of natural philosophy by no means exhausted the intellectual range of educated people. On the contrary, a great portion of the complex of ideas that ruled the minds of Frenchmen in this century of enlightenment were undoubtedly derived from Montesquieu's *Spirit of the Laws* and Rousseau's *Social Contract*. These were purely legal ideas. Even the notion of the social contract, which in the mid-nineteenth century was incorrectly interpreted in a sociological sense as an explanation of the genesis of social organization, was pre-eminently a legal idea that established a superior standard for regulating social relations.

Legal concepts played no less important a role in Germany's spiritual development. Here a solid, centuries-old tradition had already been established by the end of the eighteenth century, thanks to Althusius, Pufendorf, Thomasius and Christian Wolff. Finally, in the pre-constitutional era,[1] when German culture attained its greatest flowering, law was recognized as an integral compo-

1. I.e., prior to 1850. *Eds.*

nent of that culture. Let us recall merely that three representatives of German classical philosophy, Kant, Fichte, and Hegel, assigned the philosophy of law a very prominent place in their systems. For Hegel it occupied quite an exceptional position, and he therefore hastened to expound it immediately after the *Logic*, or ontology, leaving unwritten the philosophy of history, the philosophy of art, and even the philosophy of religion; these were published only after his death, from students' notes.

Most other German philosophers, such as Herbart, Krause, and Fries, also cultivated the philosophy of law. In the first half of the nineteenth century a "philosophy of law" was undoubtedly the philosophical work most frequently encountered in Germany. Moreover, as early as the second decade of that century a celebrated dispute arose between two jurists, Thibaut and Savigny, "On the Vocation of our Era for Legislation and Jurisprudence." This purely juridical controversy had profound cultural significance; it attracted the interest of Germany's entire educated public and fostered a more intensive awakening of its legal consciousness. If it signaled the final collapse of the concept of natural law, it simultaneously led to the triumph of the new historical school of law. This school produced Puchta's remarkable book, *Customary Law*, and it was very closely associated with the development of the new Germanist school, whose members refined and defended German legal institutions, as opposed to Roman law. One of the Germanists, Beseler, in his remarkable *Popular Law and the Law of Jurists*, emphasized the significance of the people's legal consciousness even more than had Puchta in *Customary Law*.

We cannot point to anything comparable in our intelligentsia's development. We possess juridical faculties in all our universities, some of which are more than a century old, and five specialized juridical institutions of higher learning as well. This adds up to about 150 chairs of law in the whole of Russia. But not one of the men who have held these chairs has given us so much as a legal study, to say nothing of a book, that would have broad *public* significance and would influence our intelligentsia's legal consciousness. We cannot point to a single article in our juridical literature that first advanced a true and urgent legal concept, even one like Jhering's *Struggle for Law*, which is not really very profound. Neither Chicherin nor Solov'ev made any significant contribution to the field of law. And even the good work they did do proved almost sterile: their influence on our intelligentsia was infinitesimal, and their legal ideas had the weakest repercussions of all. Recently the idea of a revival of natural law and the notion of intuitive law have been broached here. It is still premature to speak of their importance for our public development, but so far there are no grounds for supposing it will be very great. Where is that external form, that definitive formula, which normally gives ideas elasticity and helps spread them? Where is the book capable of using these ideas to stimulate our intelligentsia's legal consciousness? Where is our *Spirit of the Laws*, our *Social Contract?*

It might be replied that the Russian people set out very late on their historical path, and that we have no need to develop the ideas of individual freedom and personal rights, the rule of law, and constitutional government on our own, because all these ideas have long since been proclaimed, elaborated in detail, and implemented; therefore, we need only borrow them. But even if this were the case, we would still have to live these ideas. Borrowing is not enough—it is necessary to be wholly seized by them at a certain moment in life. However old an idea may be, it is always new for the person experiencing it for the first time. It performs creative work in his consciousness as it is assimilated and transformed by the other elements present; it spurs his will to action, to deeds. But the Russian intelligentsia's consciousness has never been wholly seized by the ideas of individual rights and the legal state, and the intelligentsia has never fully lived them.

But in any case, ideas cannot simply be borrowed. The ideas of individual freedom, the rule of law and the constitutional state are not identical for every era, any more than capitalism or any other economic or social system is identical in all countries. All legal ideas take on their own special coloring and nuances in the consciousness of each individual nation.

II

The blunting of the Russian intelligentsia's sense of law and its lack of interest in legal concepts are the consequences of an age-old evil—the absence of any kind of legal order in the Russian people's daily life. As early as the beginning of the 1850s, Herzen had this to say: the legal insecurity which has weighed upon the people from time immemorial was a kind of school for them. "In submitting, they are submitting only to force; the flagrant injustice of one part of the laws has led them to scorn the other. Complete inequality before the law has killed the bud of respect for legality in them. The Russian, whatever his class, breaks the law wherever he can do so with impunity; the government acts in the same way." After providing this dismal characterization of our legal disarray, however, Herzen himself, as a true Russian *intelligent*, adds, "This is painful and sad for the moment, but there is an immense advantage for the future. In Russia, behind the visible state there is no invisible state, which is only the apotheosis, the transfiguration, of the existing order of things."[2]

2. Alexander Herzen [Aleksandr Gertsen], "Du développement des idées révolutionnaires en Russie," *Collected Works in Thirty Volumes* [Sobranie sochinenii v tridtsati tomakh] (Moscow: Akademiia nauk SSSR, 1954-65), VII, 121. Kistiakovskii indicates that the half sentence preceding the quotation is part of it; however, this does not appear in the above edition, nor is it given as a possible variant. In other respects, also, his citation of the passage is inaccurate. The translated version was taken from the original source, and not from Kistiakovskii's Russian rendering. *Eds.*

And so Herzen suggests that this fundamental defect of Russian civic life is in some way an advantage. He was not the only one to have this notion; it was an idea shared by the whole circle of men of the forties, and it was particularly strong in the Slavophile group. They saw something positive, not negative, in the weakness of our external legal forms, and even in the total absence of legality in Russian civic life. Thus, Konstantin Aksakov asserted that while "Western man" took "the way of formal justice, the way of the state," the Russian people took the way of "inner justice." Therefore in Russia, especially before Peter's reign, the relationship between people and Sovereign was based on mutual trust and a sincere reciprocal desire for the common good. "But," he suggested, they will tell us that "either the people or the authorities may betray the other. A guarantee is needed!" And to this he replied, "A guarantee is not needed. A guarantee is an evil. Where it is needed, there is no good; it is better for a life that contains no good to be destroyed than for it to endure with the help of evil."[3]

This denial of the need for legal guarantees, which went so far as to see them as an evil, inspired the humorist B. N. Almazov to put into K. S. Aksakov's mouth a poem which begins as follows:

> For reasons quite historical
> We have a lack intense
> Of that quality diabolical,
> Juridical common sense.
> Too lofty is our sense of right
> In this broad-natured nation
> To fit within the confines tight
> Of legal codification.[4]

This poem conveys the views of Aksakov and the Slavophiles fairly accurately, if in somewhat exaggerated form.

It would be a mistake to think the Slavophiles were alone in disregarding the significance of legal principles for social life. They merely expressed this view very sharply, and their epigones carried it to extremes. K. N. Leont'ev,

---

3. Konstantin Sergeevich Aksakov, *Complete Collected Works* [Polnoe sobranie sochinenii], 3 vols. (Vol. I: Moscow: P. Bakhmetev, 1861; Vols. II-III: Moscow: Universitetskaia tipografiia, 1875-80), I, 3, 9. *Eds.*

4. B. Adamontov [B. N. Almazov], *Dissonances: Poems* [Dissonansy: Stikhotvoreniia] (Moscow: F. B. Miller, 1863), pp. 114-15. Kistiakovskii misquotes the first line, substituting "organic" for "historical"; also, the original attributes the words to Ivan Aksakov, not Konstantin. Almazov (1827-76) was a minor poet with a flair for literary parody who achieved a measure of popularity in the early 1860s with his comic verse. The lines quoted are from "A Scholarly-Literary Masquerade," which features many of the leading intellectuals of the day in its cast of characters. *Eds.*

for example, practically glorified the Russian for being alien to the "counting-house morality" of the Western European bourgeois. But we know that Herzen too saw some advantage for us in our lack of a firm legal order. We must admit that our entire intelligentsia is united in its failure to understand the relevance of law for social life.

III

Freedom and inviolability of the person are the foundations of a sound legal order. One would think that the Russian intelligentsia has reason enough to be concerned with personal rights. From time immemorial we have recognized that all social development depends on the position of the individual. Consequently, changes in our social theories have always meant the replacement of one formula regarding the individual by another. Such formulas were advanced one after the other: the critically thinking, conscious, fully developed, self-perfecting, ethical, religious, and revolutionary individual. Then there were the opposing tendencies, which sought to submerge the individual in the claims of society, asserted that the individual is a *quantité négligeable*, and defended the collective personality. Finally and most recently, Nietzscheism, Stirnerism, and anarchism have advanced the new slogans of the self-sufficient individual, the egoistic individual and the superman. It would be difficult to find a richer and more comprehensive development of the ideal of the individual, and one might have thought that it was at least exhaustive. But this is just where we note the greatest lacuna, since our public consciousness never advanced the ideal of the *legal* person. Both aspects of this ideal, the person disciplined by law and by a stable legal order, and the person endowed with all rights and freely enjoying them, are alien to our intelligentsia's mentality.

A host of evidence establishes this conclusion beyond any doubt. The Russian intelligentsia's mentors have frequently either ignored the *legal* interests of the individual entirely or were overtly hostile to them. K. D. Kavelin, one of our most outstanding juridical thinkers, devoted a great deal of attention to the general problem of the individual. In his article, "A View of the Juridical Life of Ancient Russia," which appeared in *The Contemporary* back in 1847,[5] he was the first to point out that in the history of Russian legal institutions the individual had been overshadowed by the family, the commune and the state, and had not received a legal status of his own. Then at

5. "A View of the Juridical Life of Ancient Russia" [Vzgliad na iuridicheskii byt drevnei Rossii], reprinted in *Works* [Sochineniia], 4 vols. (Moscow: V. Grachev i Komp., 1859), I, 305-75. Konstantin Dmitr'evich Kavelin (1818-85), a historian and jurist, also wrote on ethics, philosophy, sociology, and current problems. He was a leading Westernizer, whose political outlook was moderately liberal. *Eds.*

the end of the sixties he began to study the problems of psychology and
ethics, hoping that a theoretical explanation of the relationship between the
individual and society would provide a key to the correct solution of all our
most urgent social problems. But this did not prevent him from displaying an
incredible indifference to guarantees of *individual rights* at the decisive moment in the early sixties when the question of completing the reforms of Alexander II first arose. In a pamphlet he published anonymously in Berlin in
1862, and especially in the correspondence he was then conducting with Herz-
en, he mercilessly criticized the constitutional projects being advanced by
the noble assemblies.[6] He felt that in Russia any representative institution
would consist of nobles and would lead, consequently, to noble dominance.
But in rejecting a constitutional state for the sake of his democratic aspirations
he ignored its legal significance. A truth that we consider indisputable—that
the freedom and inviolability of the person can be realized only in a constitutional state—seems not to have existed for Kavelin, insofar as he expressed
himself in this correspondence, for at the time the idea of struggling for the
rights of the individual was, generally speaking, totally foreign to him.

In the seventies the indifference, and sometimes outright hostility, to individual rights not only grew stronger but even acquired a certain theoretical
justification. N. K. Mikhailovskii was unquestionably the outstanding spokesman of this period; speaking for himself and his generation, his answer to
the question that concerns us was classic in its clarity and precision. He declared bluntly that "freedom is a great and tempting thing, but we do not
want freedom if, as in Europe, it only increases our age-old debt to the people." He added, "I am sure I have expressed one of the most intimate and
heartfelt ideas of our time, the one that gives an original stamp to the seventies, and for the sake of which the seventies made countless dreadful sacrifices."[7] With these words the rejection of a legal order was erected into a system, complete with foundation and superstructure. Mikhailovskii justified
this system in the following way:

> Sceptical about freedom, we were prepared to solicit no rights for our-
> selves; I don't meant privileges—that goes without saying—but even the
> most elementary paragraphs of what in the old days used to be called
> natural law. We were fully agreed that legally we would make do with

6. The anonymous pamphlet Kistiakovskii refers to was entitled *The Nobility and the
Emancipation of the Peasants* [Dvorianstvo i osvobozhdenie krest'ian] , published in Berlin in 1862. Kavelin's correspondence with Herzen was published in M. Dragomanov, ed.,
Letters of K. Dm. Kavelin and Iv. S. Turgenev to Al. Iv. Herzen [Pis'ma K. Dm. Kavelina
i Iv. S. Turgeneva k Al. Iv. Gertsenu] (Geneva: Ukrainskaia Tipografiia, 1892). *Eds.*
7. N. K. Mikhailovskii, *Works* [Sochineniia N. K. Mikhailovskogo] , 6 vols. (St. Petersburg: Russkoe Bogatstvo, 1896-97), IV, 949.

locusts and wild honey, and would personally endure all adversities. Of course our renunciation was platonic, so to speak, since no one ever offered us anything but locusts and wild honey. But I am referring to our state of mind, which went to improbable extremes that history will record some day. "They flog the *muzhik*, let them flog us," is an approximate expression of this state of mind in its extreme form. And all this was for the sake of the one possibility upon which we staked our entire life—the possibility of an immediate transition to a better, higher system, bypassing the intermediary stage of European development, the bourgeois state. We believed that Russia could break a new historical path distinct from that of Europe. But what mattered to us was not that this should be a national path, but only that it be a good one, and the path we considered good was one of conscious, practical adaptation of our national physiognomy to the needs of the people.[8]

The fundamental tenets of the Populist world-view, insofar as it was concerned with legal problems, are expressed in these lines. Mikhailovskii and his generation renounced political liberty and a constitution in view of the possibility of Russia's immediate transition to a socialist system. But this entire sociological construct was based on a complete misunderstanding of the nature of a constitutional state. Just as Kavelin opposed constitutional projects because in his day popular representation would have been confined to the nobility, so Mikhailovskii rejected a constitutional state as bourgeois. Because of the inherent weakness of our intelligentsia's legal consciousness, both men concentrated on the social aspect of the constitutional state and disregarded its legal character, even though its essence lies precisely in the fact that it is a legal state. And its legal character is most clearly expressed in the protection it accords the individual by guaranteeing his inviolability and freedom.

IV

The content of written statutes underlies three major definitions of law: law as the establishment and limitation of freedom (the natural law school and the German idealist philosophers); law as the demarcation of interests

---

8. *Ibid.*, p. 952. *Note to the Second Edition.* The article from which these excerpts were drawn was written in September of 1880. By that time the Populist world-view had lost its original integral character, since more than two years earlier the People's Will Party had arisen from the heart of the movement and begun the struggle for political liberty. Mikhailovskii sympathized with this struggle, and in his article he was polemicizing against the Slavophiles who, as usual, were trying to prove that guarantees are unnecessary. He spoke of the denial of the need for political liberty as a feature of the entire Populist intelligentsia in the past.

(Jhering); and, finally, law as a compromise between different claims (Adolf Merkel). The last of these merits special attention from the sociological standpoint. Every reasonably important new law in a contemporary constitutional state is a compromise worked out by different parties which voice the demands of the social groups or classes they represent. The contemporary state is itself based on compromise, and the constitution of each individual state is a compromise that reconciles the various aspirations of its most influential social groups. From the socio-economic point of view, therefore, the contemporary state simply happens to be predominantly bourgeois most of the time, but it might also be predominantly noble. Thus England prior to the Reform of 1832 was an example of a constitutional state in which the nobility ruled, and Prussia, despite a sixty-year-old constitution, is still a noble rather than a bourgeois state. But workers and peasants may also predominate in a constitutional state, as we see from the examples of New Zealand and Norway. Finally, the state may be devoid of any specific class coloration in those cases where there is an equilibrium between the classes and none has an unquestioned preponderance.

But if even the social character of the contemporary constitutional state is frequently based on compromise, this is still more true of its political and legal structure. This permits the socialists, despite their principled rejection of the constitutional state as bourgeois, to get along with it fairly easily and, by participating in parliamentary activity, to make use of it. Consequently, both Kavelin and Mikhailovskii were right when they assumed that a constitutional state in Russia would be either noble or bourgeois; but they were wrong in concluding that it must therefore be met with implacable hostility, and not permitted even as a compromise. Socialists the world over are compromising with the constitutional state.

But as we noted above, the most important thing is that Kavelin, Mikhailovskii, and after them the whole of the Russian intelligentsia, completely lost sight of the legal character of the constitutional state. We must have recourse to the concept of law in its pure form, that is, its true substance and not what it borrows from economic and social relations, if we are to analyze and elucidate the legal organization of the constitutional state. Starting from this pure concept, it is not enough to point out that law demarcates interests or effects a compromise between them; we must insist that law exists only where the individual is free. A legal order in this definition is a system of relationships whereby all members of a given society possess the greatest freedom of action and self-determination. But a legal order defined in this way cannot be contrasted to a socialist order. Quite the contrary, a more profound understanding of both leads to the conclusion that they are closely related, and that from the juridical point of view a socialist order is simply a more rigorously implemented legal order. Conversely, a socialist order can be brought into being only when all its institutions have received a most precise legal formulation.

So weak was the Russian intelligentsia's legal consciousness that even its leaders, like Kavelin and Mikhailovskii, could not attempt to provide legal expression for their aspirations, democratic in the first case and socialist in the second. They refused to press for even a minimum of legality, and Kavelin spoke out against a constitution while Mikhailovskii was sceptical about political liberty. True, at the end of the seventies events did force the leading Populists, and Mikhailovskii among them, to begin to fight for political liberty. But since the Populists were drawn into this struggle by force of external circumstances and historical necessity, and not as a result of their ideological development, it could not, of course, be crowned with success. The personal heroism of the members of the People's Will Party could not compensate for this basic ideological defect of the Populist movement and of the entire Russian intelligentsia. The reaction which set in in the second half of the eighties was all the starker and gloomier because, in the absence of the legal foundations and guarantees needed for normal civic life, our intelligentsia could not even fully comprehend the extent to which the Russian people were deprived of rights. They had no theoretical formulas to define this rightlessness.

Only the new wave of Westernism that flooded the country in company with Marxism in the early nineties began to sharpen the intelligentsia's legal consciousness somewhat. Gradually it began to assimilate truths which were elementary for Europeans but were the greatest discoveries for us. Our intelligentsia finally understood that every social struggle is a political struggle; that political liberty is a prerequisite for a socialist system; that a constitutional state, despite bourgeois predominance, gives the working class greater scope to struggle for its interests; that the primary needs of the working class are inviolability of person and freedom of speech, strike, assembly and organization; that the struggle for political liberty is the first and most essential task of any socialist party; and so forth, and so on.

One might have expected that our intelligentsia would finally recognize the absolute value of the individual and demand implementation of his rights and inviolability. But the flaws in the intelligentisa's legal consciousness were not eliminated so easily. Even though it had passed through the school of Marxism, its attitude to the law remained unchanged. The ideas that prevail in our Social-Democratic Party, which not long ago enjoyed the sympathy of the majority of our intelligentsia, provide evidence of this. The protocols of the so-called second regular congress of the Russian Social-Democratic Workers' Party, which met in Brussels in August, 1903, and drew up the party program and statutes, are particularly interesting in this regard. No protocols were preserved from the party's first congress, which took place in Minsk in 1898; and the manifesto issued in its name was not drawn up and ratified by the congress, but was composed by P. B. Struve at the request of a member of the Central Committee.[9] Thus, the *Complete Text of the Protocols of the Second Regular Congress of the RSDWP*, published in Geneva in 1903, is of special interest as the earliest record of how the Social-Democratic section of the intelligentsia thinks about law and politics. (In his article, "Sectarian Marxism and Intelligentsia Social Democracy,"[10] Mr. Starover [A. N. Potresov], a participant at the congress and at the time one of the intellectual leaders of Russian Social Democracy, certifies that these protocols contain the opinions of intellectuals, and not of the members of a "workers' " party in the strict sense of the word.)

We cannot, of course, indicate every instance in the debates when individual participants displayed a striking absence of legal sensitivity and a complete misunderstanding of the significance of legal justice. But we need only show that even the party's intellectual and political leaders frequently defended positions that contradicted the fundamental principles of law. One of these leaders was G. V. Plekhanov, who did more than anyone else to expose the Russian intelligentsia's Populist illusions, and whose twenty-five years of expounding Social-Democratic principles deservedly make him the party's most eminent theorist. At the congress he gave a sermon on the relativity of all democratic principles which amounted to the rejection of a firm and solid legal order and of the constitutional state itself. In his view,

every democratic principle must be looked at not in the abstract, but in relation to what may be called the fundamental principle of democracy, namely, *salus populi suprema lex*. Translated into the language of the revolutionary, this means that the success of the revolution is the highest law. And if the need arose to restrict the operation of one or another democratic principle temporarily for the sake of the revolution, it would be criminal to hesitate at such a restriction. My own personal opinion is that we cannot exempt even universal suffrage from that fundamental principle of democracy I have just stated. Let us consider a hypothetical case when we Social Democrats might come out against universal suffrage. The bourgeoisie of the Italian republics once deprived nobles of political rights. The revolutionary proletariat might limit the political rights of the upper classes, just as the upper classes

9. Struve (who did not attend the congress) was invited to draft the Manifesto by Stepan Radchenko, one of the founders of the St. Petersburg League of Struggle for the Emancipation of the Working Class and a member of the new party's central committee. *Eds.*

10. A. N. Potresov [Starover], "Sectarian Marxism and Intelligentsia Social Democracy" [O kruzhkovom marksizme i ob intelligentskoi sotsial-demokratii], *Studies of the Russian Intelligentsia: A Collection of Articles* [Etiudy o russkoi intelligentsii: sbornik statei], 2nd ed. (St. Petersburg: O. N. Popova, 1908), pp. 253ff.

once limited the political rights of the proletariat. The suitability of such a measure could be decided only from the standpoint of the rule, *salus revolutiae suprema lex*. And we would have to take the same position on the question of the duration of parliaments. If the people, in a burst of revolutionary enthusiasm, elected a very good parliament—a species of *chambre introuvable*—then logically we should try to turn it into a long parliament; but if the elections were unsuccessful, we would have to try to dissolve it, not in two years but, if possible, in two weeks.[11]

The idea proclaimed in this speech—that force and usurped power are supreme, and not the principles of law—is simply monstrous. This way of posing the problem aroused opposition even among the delegates to the Social-Democratic congress, who were accustomed to worshipping social forces alone. Eyewitnesses report that after the speech the Bundists, who represented social elements more like those of the West, shouted: "And wouldn't Comrade Plekhanov deprive the bourgeoisie of freedom of speech and inviolability of person as well?" But since these shouts were out of order they were not recorded in the protocols. To the honor of the Russian intelligentsia, however, it must be noted that there were also recognized speakers who protested Plekhanov's words, although it is true they belonged to the minority opposition at the congress. One delegate, Egorov, remarked that "the laws of war are one thing, and constitutional laws another," and that Plekhanov had failed to take into account the fact that the Social Democrats were drawing up their program "on the assumption of a constitution." Another, Goldblatt, found Plekhanov's words "an imitation of bourgeois tactics. If we were to be consistent, then on the basis of Plekhanov's words the demand for universal suffrage would have to be stricken from the Social-Democratic program."[12]

Be that as it may, Plekhanov's speech unquestionably shows that our intelligentsia's legal consciousness is not only extremely weak, but distorted as well. Even the most outstanding leaders of the intelligentsia are ready to renounce the immutable principles of legal procedure for the sake of temporary advantage. It is not surprising, therefore, that during the liberation period the Russian intelligentsia could not put into practice even the most elementary rights of the individual—freedom of speech and assembly. Only speakers acceptable to the majority enjoyed free speech at our rallies; anyone who disagreed was drowned out by shouts, whistles, cries of "that's enough," and sometimes even physical coercion. Holding rallies became the privilege of small groups,

11. Russian Social-Democratic Workers' Party, *Second Regular Congress. Complete Text of the Protocols* [Rossiiskaia Sotsial-Demokraticheskaia Rabochaia Partiia, Vtoroi ocherednoi s"ezd. Polnyi tekst protokolov] (Geneva: Tipografiia Partii, 1903), p. 169.
12. *Ibid.*, p. 170. [Kistiakovskii has slightly altered the original wording. *Eds.*]

with the result that they lost much of their meaning and value, and ultimately nobody set much store by them. Clearly, genuine freedom for the public discussion of political issues could not develop when a few groups monopolized the privilege of organizing rallies and enjoying free speech at them. All that happened was that this privilege was extended to other social groups with opposing views, which occasionally received permission to hold meetings of their own.

Our wretched legal consciousness also explains why our revolutionary years were so sterile in regard to law. At the time the Russian intelligentsia displayed total misunderstanding of the legislative process; it was ignorant even of the elementary truth that an old law cannot simply be repealed, since repeal cannot take effect until the old law is replaced by a new one. Quite the contrary, the only result of simple repeal is that the law appears inoperative temporarily, but later is restored in full force.

The spontaneous introduction of freedom of assembly showed this especially clearly. Our intelligentsia proved incapable of giving this freedom immediate legal formulation and even wished to elevate the absence of legal forms into law, as can be seen from the extremely characteristic debates on the freedom of assembly "bill" in the First State Duma. An outstanding jurist who was a member of the First Duma remarked with perfect justice that "the bare proclamation of freedom of assembly would mean in practice that in certain cases the citizens themselves would begin to take action against abuses of this freedom. And however imperfect the organs of the executive power may be, in any case it is safer and more reliable to entrust them with defending citizens from such abuses than to leave it to the discretion of private reprisals." He observed that "the same people who in theory were in favor of non-interference by the authorities, in practice complained bitterly and interpellated the ministers in regard to official inaction every time the government refused to take steps to defend individuals' life and liberty." "This was thoroughly inconsistent," he adds, and he attributes it to a "lack of legal knowledge."[13]

We have now gotten to the point where complete and equal freedom of speech does not exist even within the chamber of the Third Duma, since the dominant party and the opposition are not equally free to discuss the same questions.[14] This is all the sadder since the popular representative body,

13. P. Novgorodtsev, "The Legislative Activity of the State Duma" [Zakonodatel'-naia deiatel'nost' Gosudarstvennoi Dumy], *The First State Duma* [Pervaia gosudarstvennaia duma], 3 vols. (St. Petersburg: privately printed by A. A. Mukhanov and V. D. Nabokov, 1907), II, 22.

[Kistiakovskii is referring here to the opposition the Kadets met when they introduced a bill in the First Duma regulating freedom of assembly. The leftist parties, which had not opposed other Kadet proposals in principle, now argued that no regulation of assembly was needed. *Eds.*]

14. The Third Duma excluded the Kadets and the socialist parties from participation in the parliamentary committee concerned with national defense. *Eds.*

whatever its composition, ought at the least to reflect the entire nation's legal consciousness, as the minimum expression of its ethical conscience.

V

A nation's legal consciousness is always reflected in its ability to create organizations and give them a formal structure. Since organizations cannot exist without formal rules to govern them, the establishment of organizations must be accompanied by the development of such rules. The Russian people as a whole do not lack talents in this sphere; doubtless, they even have an innate inclination for particularly intensive forms of organization. Their striving for a communal way of life, as manifest in their agrarian communes, *artel*'s and so on, provide sufficient evidence on this point. The life and structure of these organizations are determined by the inner consciousness of right and non-right dwelling in the national soul. The people's attitude to the law was interpreted erroneously because of the predominantly inner quality of their legal consciousness. First the Slavophiles and then the Populists assumed that "juridical principles" are alien to the Russian people and that, guided only by their inner consciousness, they act solely from ethical motives. Indeed, the Russian people do not make a clear enough distinction between legal and moral standards, and the two are fused in their minds. This probably explains the deficiencies of Russian customary law; it lacks unity, and uniform application, the hallmark of any customary law, is even more foreign to it.

But this is precisely the area where the intelligentsia should have come to the people's aid; it should have assisted them in making the final distinction between the standards of customary law and ethics, in applying this law more consistently, and in developing it further. Only then could the Populists have carried out the task they set themselves of helping to consolidate and develop communal principles; at the same time, it would have become possible to transform the communes into higher forms of social life that would approximate socialism. The Populists' false point of departure, the assumption that our people's thinking is molded solely by ethics, prevented them from completing their task and shattered their hopes. Concrete social forms cannot be built on ethics alone. To attempt to do so is unnatural, for it destroys and discredits ethics and leads to the ultimate deadening of all legal consciousness.

Every social organization needs *legal* norms, that is, rules that regulate people's external conduct, and not their internal conduct, which is governed by ethics. Although they determine external behavior, legal rules themselves are not something external, since they first exist in our consciousness and are as much inner elements of our spirit as are ethical rules. They assume an external existence as well only when they are expressed in legal statutes or applied in practice. But our intelligentsia ignored all inner, or, in the current expression, intuitive law; it thought of law only in terms of those external, lifeless rules that fit so neatly into the articles and paragraphs of a written statute.

It is most characteristic of our intelligentsia that along with its desire to build complex social structures on ethical principles alone it displays a striking predilection for formal rules and detailed regulations in its own organizations; there it puts unusual faith in the articles and paragraphs of organizational statutes. This phenomenon, which might seem an incomprehensible contradiction, can be explained by the fact that our intelligentsia regards a law not as a legal conviction but simply as a rule which has received external, formal expression.

We have here one of the most typical symptoms of an undeveloped sense of law. It is common knowledge that a police state has a tendency to engage in detailed regulation of all social relations by means of written laws, and that this is the hallmark that distinguishes it from a legal state. It can be said that our intelligentsia's legal consciousness is at the police-state level. All of the police state's typical features are reflected in the intelligentsia's susceptibility to formalism and bureaucratism. The Russian bureaucracy is usually contrasted to the Russian intelligentsia, and in a certain sense this is justified. But a number of questions might be raised in regard to this contrast: is the intelligentsia's world really so foreign to that of the bureaucracy? isn't our bureaucracy an outgrowth of our intelligentsia, nourished by its sap? and finally, isn't the intelligentsia responsible for the fact that we have such a powerful bureaucracy? One thing, at least, is beyond question—the intelligentsia is completely permeated with its own bureaucratic spirit, which finds expression in all its organizations and especially in its political parties.

Our party organizations date back to the pre-revolutionary period. Their members were people who were sincerely idealistic, were free of all prejudices, and had made great sacrifices. Such people might have been expected to incorporate at least some of the ideals for which they were striving in their own free organizations. But instead we see only a slavish aping of the monstrous practices that characterize the Russian state.

Let us again take the Social-Democratic Party as an example. The second congress, as we said, formulated the party statutes. The statutes of a private organization correspond to the constitution of a state. The statutes chosen determine, as it were, whether the party will have a republican or monarchical structure; they give its central institutions an aristocratic or democratic character; and they establish the rights of individual members *vis-à-vis* the party as a whole. One would think that the statutes of a party composed of convinced republicans would assure its members of at least minimal guarantees of freedom of person and due process. But apparently the representatives of our intelligentsia find free self-determination of the individual and a republican system details unworthy of attention—at least they deserve none when it is a question of putting them into everyday practice, rather than proclaiming them in programs. No free institutions of any kind were established by the statutes of the Social-Democratic Party adopted at this congress. Martov, leader of the congress minority, characterized the statutes as follows: "Along with the majority of the old editorial board [of the newspaper *The Spark*], I thought the congress would put an end to the 'state of siege' within the party and introduce normal conditions. In actuality the state of siege, with exceptional laws against particular groups, has been continued and even intensified."[15]

But Lenin, the majority leader, who insisted on adopting the statutes containing the state of siege, was in no way embarrassed by this description. "I am not at all frightened," he said, "by the terrible words 'state of siege,' 'exceptional laws' against particular individuals and groups, etc. When it comes to unstable and wavering elements we not only can, but we must create a 'state of siege,' and our party statutes as a whole, the centralism of which this congress has henceforth confirmed, are nothing but a 'state of siege' against the many sources of political vagueness. It is against vagueness that we need special, even exceptional laws, and the step taken by this congress has correctly charted our political course by creating a solid basis for such laws and measures."[16] But if a party of educated republicans cannot do without a state of siege and exceptional laws, it is understandable why Russia is still administered with the aid of "extraordinary protection" and martial law.[17]

The party's state-of-siege statutes were passed by a majority of only two votes, showing the kind of legal concepts that prevail among our radical intellectuals. This violated the cardinal legal principle that a society's statutes, like a constitution, be ratified on a special basis by a qualified majority. The leader of the congress majority did not compromise even when everyone realized that

15. *Second Congress Protocols*, p. 331.

[Martov (Iulii Osipovich Tsederbaum, 1873-1923) became the leader of the Mensheviks when the Social-Democratic Party split at this congress, and he remained their foremost spokesman and theorist until his death in Germany. *The Spark* (Iskra), published 1900-05, was recognized at this congress as the official newspaper of the party. Both Lenin and Martov were members of the original editorial board, but after the party split Lenin resigned. "Exceptional laws" and "state of siege" are references to the anti-socialist law of 1878 in Germany, which outlawed the Social-Democratic Party. It remained in effect until 1890, and one of its provisions permitted the authorities to proclaim a "minor state of siege" in areas where Social-Democratic influence was particularly strong and expel persons deemed dangerous to public security. *Eds.*]

16. *Ibid.*, pp. 333-34.

17. "Extraordinary protection" [chrezvychainaia okhrana] and "martial law" [voennoe polozhenie] refer to the Extraordinary Temporary Law of 14 August 1881, which was renewed every three years until 1917. This law allowed disturbed areas, declared to be in a state of "reinforced" or "extraordinary" protection or under martial law, to be exempted from normal legal procedure: trials could be transferred to courts-martial, with closed sessions; arrests could be made on mere suspicion; the right of search of private domiciles was uncontrolled; and the local authorities could arbitrarily impose administrative sentences of exile for up to five years. After 1905, most of the empire was governed under these measures. *Eds.*

the statutes with the state of siege would lead to a party split, a situation that absolutely demanded compromise. As a result a split actually did occur between the majority ("Bolsheviks") and the minority ("Mensheviks"). But most interesting of all is the fact that the statutes which caused the split turned out to be perfectly worthless in practice. Consequently, less than two years later, in 1905, the so-called third congress, consisting solely of Bolsheviks (the Mensheviks declined to participate, in protest against the method of selecting the delegates), rescinded the 1903 statutes and replaced them with new ones acceptable to the Mensheviks as well.

But this still did not lead to re-unification. After originally splitting on organizational issues, the Mensheviks and Bolsheviks later carried their animosity to extremes and extended it to all tactical questions. In accord with certain socio-psychological laws, once the discords and antagonisms had arisen, they continued to deepen and broaden as a result of people's innate personal qualities. True, individuals with a highly developed awareness of legal propriety can suppress these socio-psychological emotions and keep them in check. But only those who are clearly aware that every organization, and social life in general, is based on compromise can do this. Our intelligentsia cannot do it, of course, since it has not yet developed its legal consciousness to the point where it frankly acknowledges the necessity of compromise. Among these people of principle compromises are always covert and based solely on personal relations.

The Russian Social Democrats are not at all unique in their faith in the omnipotence of statutes and the force of binding rules. It afflicts our entire intelligentsia. None of our parties has a truly vital and active legal consciousness. We could take analogous examples from the history of our other socialist party, the Socialist-Revolutionaries, or our liberal organizations, such as the Union of Liberation. But unfortunately we must dispense with such a cumbersome apparatus of facts. Let us note just one highly characteristic feature of our party organizations. In no other country is there so much talk about party discipline; at every congress of every party there are interminable discussions of the obligations to be imposed on the members. Of course, many would explain this on the grounds that open organizations are new to us, and there is some truth in this. But it is neither the whole nor the main truth. The more essential reason is that legal convictions, which would have provided internal discipline, are foreign to the intelligentsia. We need external discipline precisely because we have no internal discipline. In this area too we perceive law not as a legal conviction but as a binding rule. And this is additional testimony to the low level of our legal consciousness.

VI

In our discussion of the Russian intelligentsia's legal consciousness we examined its attitude toward the two basic aspects of law—individual rights and the objective legal system. In particular, we tried to determine how this legal consciousness is reflected in the solution of organizational problems, in the broad sense of the word, since these are the fundamental problems of constitutional law. Using its own organizations as an example, we tried to ascertain the extent to which our intelligentsia is capable of taking part in the legal reorganization of the state, the transformation of *a regime of force* into *a regime of law*. But our discussion would be incomplete if we ignored the intelligentsia's attitude to the courts.

The court is the most important institution in stating and establishing the law. In all nations, before the legislative method had developed, the laws were clarified and sometimes even created by judicial decisions. The parties bringing their disputes to court defended their own personal interests, but each of them tried to prove his "right" by pleading that he had an objective law on his side. In his decision the judge gave an authoritative definition of the law in force, basing himself on the society's legal consciousness. A judge could hold aloft the banner of law and create new law only if he were aided by the vital and active legal consciousness of the nation.

Later on, this law-creating activity of court and judge was partially overshadowed by the legislative activity of the state. The introduction of constitutional forms led to the creation of the state's legislative organ, the popular representative body, that was called on to give direct expression to the nation's legal consciousness. But not even the legislative activity of the representative body can do away with the court's significance in implementing the rule of law. In the contemporary constitutional state the court is primarily the custodian of existing laws; but in applying the law it continues to create new law as well. In recent decades legal theorists have turned their attention to the fact that the court has preserved this function, even though the present legislative system gives predominance to written law. Within the context of the idea of the constitutional state this is a novel view of the court, but it is even beginning to find its way into the most recent legislative codes. The Swiss civil code, unanimously passed by both chambers of the national legislature on 10 December 1907, puts it in contemporary terms: the first article of the code prescribes that in those cases where a law is lacking the judge shall make his decision on the basis of the rule he would lay down "if he were the legislator." Thus, the most democratic and progressive European nation recognizes that the judge is as much a spokesman for the nation's legal consciousness as the elected deputy in the legislature. Sometimes an individual judge has still greater importance, for in certain cases he decides issues by himself; he does not, however, make a final decision, for thanks to the appellate system a case can be taken to a higher instance. All of this demonstrates that a nation with a well-developed legal consciousness must concern itself with its courts and value them as custodians and executives of its legal system.

But what is our intelligentsia's attitude to the courts? Let us note that our court system, as established by Alexander II's Judicial Statutes of 20 November 1864,[18] is based on judicial principles fully consonant with those required by a legal state. A court system of this kind is very well adapted to the establishment of a true legal order. The architects of the judicial reform were inspired by the desire to use the new courts to prepare Russia for the rule of law. The initial appointments to the reorganized courts aroused the most glowing expectations for them. And at first the public regarded them with lively interest and affection.

But now, more than forty years later, we must sadly admit that it was all an illusion and we do not have a good court system. True, people point to the fact that from the time the Judicial Statutes went into effect right up to the present the courts have frequently been subject to so-called "corruption." This is absolutely true. There have been two major types of "corruption." First, a great number of cases, primarily political, were removed from the jurisdiction of the courts and submitted to special forms of investigation and trial. Secondly, the independence of the judges was progressively curtailed, and the courts were placed in an ever more dependent position. The government was pursuing strictly political ends in taking these measures. And it is remarkable how it was able to hypnotize the public, too, into focusing solely on the courts' political role. We even viewed trial by jury from just two perspectives, the political and the humanitarian; at best we saw trial by jury as a court of conscience, an expression of passive humanitarianism rather than of an active legal consciousness.

Of course, with our social conditions it was perhaps inevitable that we should have a political attitude toward the criminal courts. In this area the struggle for law necessarily turned into a struggle for one or another political ideal. But the public's indifference to the *civil* courts is striking. Broad segments of society have absolutely no interest in their organization or activity. Our non-specialized press never concerns itself with their relevance to the development of Russian law, nor does it report those decisions that are of the greatest legal importance. If the papers refer to the civil courts at all, it is only in connection with sensational cases. And yet our civil courts are relatively independent, and if they were controlled and regulated by the intelligentsia they might have an enormous impact on the consolidation and development of our legal system.

When the instability of our system of civil law is discussed, people are usu-

18. The Judicial Statutes of 1864 were one of a series of far-reaching administrative and social reforms that followed the emancipation of the serfs. Though subsequently marred by the developments Kistiakovskii mentions below, the judicial reform reorganized and streamlined the courts, instituted jury trials in major criminal cases, established the independence of judges, and created the Russian bar. *Eds.*

ally referring to the defects of our property law. And in fact our civil code is archaic, we have no commercial code at all, and several other areas of civil life are almost without regulation by the precise norms of written law. But this should make our civil courts all the more important. Under the same circumstances peoples with a highly developed legal consciousness, the Romans and the English, for example, produced well-balanced systems of unwritten law, but our civil law is still as unstable as ever. Of course, we do have law created by judicial decisions; we could not survive without it, and it arises from the fact that there is a certain consistency in the activity of the courts. But in no other country is the practice of the supreme appellate court so unstable and contradictory; no appellate court reverses its own decisions as often as our Senate.[19] Recently, too, the decisions of the Civil Cassation Department of the Senate have been strongly influenced by motives that have nothing whatever to do with law. We need recall only the sharp *volte-face* after 1907 in regard to Article 683 of our civil code, which regulates the compensation for injuries suffered on the railroads. But there is no doubt that much of the blame for the inconsistency of our supreme appellate court lies with the public, which is indifferent to the soundness and rationality of the system of civil law that governs it. Even our legal theorists take little interest in it, and the Senate's appellate practice has therefore received hardly any scrutiny. We lack even the specialized periodicals to carry out these functions. *Law*, our one weekly devoted to the defense and improvement of *formal* law, is only ten years old.

The public's indifference is all the more striking since civil law affects its most essential and vital interests. It deals with the everyday, prosaic problems which must be solved if we are to put our social, family, and material life in good order.

Our courts can be no better than society's legal consciousness. A few individuals did have a beneficial influence on our public's legal consciousness, but they were all members of the first reformed courts. In the past two decades our courts have not produced a single judge capable of obtaining universal recognition and sympathy from the Russian public. And as for the judicial colleges,[20] of course, there is nothing to be said.

"Judge" is not the honorable title here that it is in other countries, where it signifies impartiality, disinterestedness, and noble service to the law alone. Our criminal courts are not impartial, and they have even turned into something of an instrument of vengeance. This is, of course, the area where political factors play the most decisive role. But even our civil courts are far from

19. The Senate, through its Civil and Criminal Cassation Departments, functioned as the supreme court of Imperial Russia. *Eds.*

20. Important cases were heard by a college, or panel, of judges, consisting of a president of the court and two other members. *Eds.*

equal to their tasks. The ignorance and negligence of some judges is notorious, but the majority regard their work, which demands unceasing intellectual labor, with no interest, thoughtfulness, or awareness of the importance and responsibility of their position. People who know our courts well assert that even the most complex and intricate cases are decided not on the basis of law, but by the force of circumstances. At best, a talented and diligent lawyer will advance a few details advantageous to his client in the course of the trial. But often the decisive element is not even the semblance of law, but wholly extraneous considerations.

Broad segments of Russian society have neither a genuine understanding of the significance of the court nor respect for it, and this has an especially marked effect on two elements of the public who participate in every trial—witnesses and experts. Most often our trials leave one convinced that the witnesses and experts are totally unaware that their true function is to aid in uncovering the truth. Just how frivolously certain circles regard this function is shown by such improbable but current terms as "trustworthy" or "honest" perjuror.

It has been a long time since we provided a "speedy trial" in civil cases; our courts are so overloaded that it takes about five years for a case to go through all the appellate instances. An objection can be raised that the courts' excessive case-load is the major reason for the judges' negligent, mechanical attitude to their work. But if the judges were better trained and informed, and if both judicial officers and the public took an interest in the courts, the work would go smoothly and cases would be decided more easily, fairly, and quickly. Ultimately, these conditions would lend so much weight to the claims of the legal system that something would also have to be done about the understaffing of the courts.

The judicial reform of 1864 also created a class of free servants of the law—the lawyers. But in this respect, too, we must sadly acknowledge that although the bar has existed for over forty years it has done little to develop our legal consciousness. We did and do have eminent criminal and political defenders, among them some ardent proponents of a humane attitude to the criminal. But most of them fought only for a particular political ideal, for a "new law," if you like, but not for "law" in the strict sense of the word. Too involved in the struggle for a new law, they often forgot about the claims of formal law or of law in general. Ultimately they sometimes rendered poor service to the "new law" itself, since they were guided more by political than by legal considerations. Our legal establishment has done even less to improve our system of civil law. In this sphere the struggle for law is all too easily supplanted by other motives, and our eminent attorneys frequently turn into plain businessmen. This is irrefutable proof that the atmosphere in our courts, as well as our public's legal consciousness, not only fail to support the struggle for law but often have precisely the opposite effect.

The courts cannot occupy the high position intended for them unless the public is fully cognizant of their real functions, and there is boundless evidence that our intelligentsia lacks this awareness. As examples, let us take some of the views expressed in passing by members of the State Duma, as spokesmen of the nation's legal consciousness. Aleksinskii, a representative of the extreme left in the Second Duma, threatened the enemies of the people with a "people's court," asserting that "this court is the most terrible of all." Several sessions later in the same Duma a representative of the extreme right, Shul'gin, justified the field courts-martial on the grounds that they were preferable to the "people's mob law," and maintained that their abolition would result in "mob law in its most terrible form," from which even the innocent would suffer.[21] This abuse of the word "court" shows that our deputies' thinking still reflects the period when the courts sentenced the condemned to "banishment and confiscation."

Political conditions alone cannot be blamed for our bad courts; we too bear the responsibility. Under wholly analogous political conditions other nations have had courts that nonetheless upheld the law. The saying "there is a judge in Berlin" dates from the late eighteenth and first half of the nineteenth centuries, when Prussia was still an absolute monarchy.

Nothing that I have said about our intelligentsia's weak legal consciousness was said either in judgment or in condemnation. The defeat of the Russian revolution and the events of the last few years are in themselves a harsh enough sentence against the intelligentsia. Now the intelligentsia must withdraw into itself and plunge deeply into its own inner world in order to bring fresh air and health to it. In the course of this inward labor, a genuine legal consciousness must finally awaken in the Russian intelligentsia. These lines were written with the faith and fervent hope that the time is near when our intelligentsia's legal consciousness will create and shape our new social life. Through a series of bitter experiences, the Russian intelligentsia must come to the realization that along with the absolute values of personal self-perfection and a moral world order there are also relative values, such as a very prosaic but solid and inviolable legal order.[22]

21. Second State Duma, *Stenographic Account* [Gosudarstvennaia Duma: vtoroi sozyv, stenograficheskie otchety] (St. Petersburg: Gosudarstvennaia Tipografiia, 1907), I, 248, 377-78. The field courts-martial were introduced by emergency decree in August, 1906. In areas under "extraordinary protection" and martial law, the cases of civilians who committed crimes deemed by the authorities to be so obvious as to need no investigation could be transferred to field courts-martial. The membership of these courts was kept secret; the accused had no counsel or right of appeal; and sentence was carried out within twenty-four hours. About 1,000 persons were executed by this means in the eight months the law functioned. *Eds.*
22. *Note to the Second Edition.* Many people feel that it is unjust to blame our intelligentsia for its weak legal consciousness, since the blame lies instead in external circum-

stances—the absence of rights that prevails in our lives. The effect of these circumstances cannot be denied and was noted in my article. But they cannot be blamed for everything and we cannot reassure ourselves with the thought that "the actions of the state, for too long, for generations, have corrupted instead of educating us," and that "entire generations of Russians were brought up to disregard the principle of legality and acknowledge its impotence and uselessness." (V. Maklakov, "Legality in Russian Life" [Zakonnost' v russkoi zhizni], *Messenger of Europe* [Vestnik Evropy] [May 1909], pp. 273-74.) If we have become aware of this evil we can no longer reconcile ourselves to it; we cannot salve our conscience, but must carry on an inner struggle against the principle that is corrupting us. It is unworthy of thinking people to say: we are corrupted and will continue to be corrupted until the cause of our corruption is removed. Every person is obliged to say: I must not be corrupted any longer, now that I have recognized what it is that is corrupting me and where the source of my corruption lies. We must now strain all the forces of our intellect, feeling, and will to free our minds from the baneful effect of unfavorable circumstances. That is why the task of the time is to arouse the Russian intelligentsia's legal consciousness and summon it to life and action.

THE INTELLIGENTSIA AND REVOLUTION

Petr Struve

The Russian masses had been shaken by two revolutionary crises prior to our recent revolution, which was related to the outcome of the Russo-Japanese War. They were the Time of Troubles, with the Razin rebellion as its aftermath, and the Pugachev uprising. These were great upheavals in our national life, but we would search them in vain for any religious or political idea that would make them comparable to the great turning points in the West. Cannot the participation of the Schismatics in the Pugachev revolt be ascribed to a religious idea? No, rather, these revolutions demonstrated the destructive force of the struggle of class interests, and since they could not counterpose any alternative to the historical principle of the state they dashed themselves to pieces against it.

The revolution of the turn of the seventeenth century is highly instructive when compared to the events of our own time. Usually reaction in one form or another triumphs after the victory of a revolution. The Time of Troubles is unique in this respect: in the revolution as such, as a mass movement, the sound, state-oriented elements prevailed immediately, without a period of reaction. This is related to another, no less important characteristic: the Troubles were not just a social movement or a struggle for political power, but a gigantic movement of national and religious self-defense. Without the Polish intervention the great Troubles of 1598-1613 would have been nothing but a series of palace intrigues and *coups d'état* alternating with impotent and sporadic revolts of the anarchical elements of society. Polish intervention transformed the Troubles into a national liberation struggle in which the nation was led by conservative social forces capable of organizing the state. If this was a great epoch, it was not because the lower depths rose up. Their uprising achieved nothing.

Thus, the Time of Troubles demonstrates the incalculable importance of state and national principles with striking force and clarity. From this point of view, the moment when the state-oriented militia elements diverged from and began to struggle against the anti-state Cossacks is especially important.

---

1. The following reflections were written two years ago as the draft of a chapter of a book I was then contemplating in which I wished to review our cultural and political development and evaluate the revolution we had experienced.
Note to the Second Edition. Reprinted without changes.

Prokopii Liapunov, the first militia leader, paid for his illusion that common cause could be made with the "thieves" with his own life and with the total failure of the national effort he had conceived. Then, under the leadership of Minin and Pozharskii, the "last-ranking people of the Muscovite state" rose to save it at the call of Patriarch Hermogen, and they succeeded in liberating the nation and restoring the state. But they did so in opposition to the anti-state "thievery" of the anarchical elements.[2] We can sense something contemporary, too contemporary, in the general psychology of this crucial moment in our pre-Petrine Troubles.

For the lower classes the social consequences of the Troubles were not simply insignificant, they were negative. By their anarchical revolt against the state the peasants merely intensified their own enserfment and augmented the social power of the "masters." And the second wave of social unrest of the seventeenth century, the Sten'ka Razin movement, although it exacted a multitude of sacrifices and was senselessly cruel and utterly "thievish" in its methods, broke just as impotently against the power of the state.

In this regard there is nothing new in the Pugachev rebellion that would distinguish it in principle from the Troubles of 1598-1613 and the Razin revolt. Nonetheless, all these movements, and especially the Pugachev rebellion, do have tremendous social significance and social content. It can be expressed in two words—peasant emancipation. In his Manifesto of 31 July 1774, Pugachev, in an attack on the state, anticipated the Manifesto of 19 February 1861.[3] The failure of his "thievish" movement was inevitable. If, for economic and other reasons, it was fearfully difficult for states and sovereigns to carry

2. In 1611, when the central government was paralyzed and Moscow was in the hands of a Polish garrison, a militia arose in the provinces to liberate the country from foreign domination. Its leader was Prokopii Liapunov, a member of the provincial service gentry. His forces were joined by Cossack elements who also rallied to the defense of Orthodoxy against the Catholic Poles. Although temporarily united, the two groups represented mutually antagonistic strata of Muscovite society. While they were camped near Moscow discords erupted, in the course of which Liapunov was murdered and the militia disintegrated. In response to a fervent appeal from Patriarch Hermogen, then a prisoner in Moscow, a second militia was organized, the initiative being taken by the town of Nizhnii-Novgorod. The leaders were Prince Dmitrii Pozharskii, another provincial serviceman, and Kuz'ma Minin, a butcher and municipal leader. This militia succeeded in freeing Moscow and establishing the conditions for the election of a new tsar. Like the first militia, though more successfully, the forces of Pozharskii and Minin acted in uneasy cooperation with the Cossacks—who were often referred to as "thieves," in view of their predilection for plunder and banditry. (One of the pretenders to the throne during this period, whose entourage consisted mainly of Cossacks and adventurers, was commonly called The Thief.) *Eds.*

3. The Manifesto of 19 February 1861 was the act freeing the serfs. Pugachev's manifesto declared the serfs free from further obligations to the landlords or the state, turned the land over to them, and urged them to seize and punish their masters. *Eds.*

out peasant emancipation in the eighteenth and early nineteenth centuries, it certainly could not be achieved *against* the state and sovereign. The cause of peasant emancipation was not only crushed, it was perverted into its opposite by the "thievish," anti-state methods used in the struggle for it.

In the seventeenth and eighteenth centuries the Cossacks were the agents of this anti-state "thievery." At that time "cossackdom" was not a military caste, as it is today; it was a social stratum, the one farthest removed from the state and most hostile to it. It did have military habits and tastes, but these remained on the level of organized, collective banditry.

The Pugachev rebellion was the Cossacks' last attempt to rouse the lower classes and lead them against the state. With its failure the Cossacks abandoned their role as the agents spreading anarchical, anti-state ferment among the masses. The Cossacks themselves were integrated into the state, and until they were replaced by another force the masses were left *alone* in their struggle.[4] Once the Cossacks' revolutionary role was nullified, a new element emerged in Russian life which—however dissimilar to the Cossacks in its social status and way of life—replaced them in the political sense and served as their historical successor. This element is the intelligentsia.

The word "intelligentsia" can, of course, be used in various senses. The history of this word in colloquial and literary Russian might be the subject of an interesting specialized study. We recall the sense in which the landowner-tax farmer used it in Turgenev's "A Strange Story." " 'We live quietly here: the governor is a melancholic, the marshal of the nobility a bachelor. But there's to be a big ball at the Nobles' Assembly the day after tomorrow. I advise you to attend: we are not without pretty girls here. And, you will see all of our *intelligentsia*.' My acquaintance, as a man who had once studied at the university, loved to use erudite expressions. He pronounced them with irony, but also with respect. Besides, everyone knows that in addition to reliability the occupation of tax-farming bred a certain profundity of thought in people."[5]

Obviously, by "intelligentsia" we do not mean the guests attending balls at the Nobles' Assembly. Nor do we even mean the "educated class." An intelligentsia in that sense has long existed in Russia, there is nothing remarkable about it, and it fulfills no Cossack mission. To a certain extent part of the

4. In the eighteenth century the Russian government gradually extended its authority over the Cossacks of the Don and the Ukraine; the officer class was assimilated into the nobility, the autonomy of the Cossack communities was curtailed, and they were absorbed into the administrative structure of the Empire. In 1775 the Zaporozhian *sech'* was broken up entirely and its members resettled. The Cossacks remained a hereditary military caste, however. *Eds.*

5. I. S. Turgenev, "A Strange Story" [Strannaia istoriia], *Complete Collected Works* [Polnoe sobranie sochinenii], 3rd ed., 10 vols. (St. Petersburg: Glazunov, 1891), VII, 173. *Eds.*

clergy always constituted the "educated class"; later the nobility attained primacy in this respect. In every state the role of the educated class has been and remains very great; in a backward state which only recently lay on the extreme periphery of European culture, its role is quite naturally immense. The role played by this class in connection with its cultural function of spreading enlightenment is obvious and historically comprehensible, but this is not our present concern. The intelligentsia is a totally unique factor in Russian political development, its historical significance stemming from its attitude to both the idea and the actuality of the state.

The intelligentsia, in this political definition, made its appearance in Russian life only during the era of reforms, and it became fully manifest in the revolution of 1905-07. But its intellectual foundations date back to the "remarkable era"[6] of the forties.

In viewing the intelligentsia as an ideological and political force in Russian history we can distinguish both a constant element, the stable *form*, as it were, and a more changeable element, its transitory *content*. The Russian intelligentsia's ideological form is its *dissociation*, i.e., its alienation from the state and hostility to it.

The intelligentsia's spiritual history reveals two types of dissociation, absolute and relative. The absolute type appears as anarchism, the denial of the state and of any social order *per se* (Bakunin and Prince Kropotkin). The various forms of Russian revolutionary radicalism, and I have in mind here mainly the varieties of Russian socialism, are manifestations of relative dissociation. *Historically*, there is no essential difference between absolute and relative dissociation (although the anarchists insist there is). For anarchism's rejection of the state in principle is extremely abstract, while the recognition of the need for public authority (in essence, the state) in principle by revolutionary radicalism is equally abstract, and fades away in the face of its hostility to the state in all its concrete attributes. Consequently, in a certain sense Marxism, with its doctrines of class struggle and of the state as the organization of class domination, was the most intense and complete embodiment of the intelligentsia's anti-state dissociation.

But our definition of the intelligentsia's essence would be incomplete if we confined ourselves to just this one aspect of its dissociation. The intelligentsia's dissociation is not merely anti-state but atheistic as well. The intelligentsia denies the state and struggles against it, but it rejects the mystique of the state not in the name of some other mystical or religious principle, but for the sake of a rational, empirical one.

---

6. A reference to the intellectual ferment of the 1840s. Pavel Vasil'evich Annenkov (1812-87) coined the term in his memoirs, *The Remarkable Decade* [Zamechatel'noe desiatiletie]. *Eds.*

This is the most profound philosophical and psychological contradiction burdening the intelligentsia. It denies the world in the name of the world, and thereby serves neither the world nor God. To be sure, our literature follows Vladimir Solov'ev in fostering a legend of sorts about the Russian intelligentsia's religiosity. Essentially, this is an application to the Russian intelligentsia of the same view—which to my mind is superficial and will not withstand criticism—that led Solov'ev to his famous rehabilitation of anti-religious thinkers from a religious, Christian point of view. The only difference is that eighteenth-century Western European positivism and rationalism are not so completely alien to the religious idea as are the nineteenth-century Russian positivism and rationalism which nourished our entire intelligentsia. Recently the intelligentsia has exhibited a maximalism that gives it a formal similarity to Ibsen's Brand ("all or nothing!")[7] and that bears the stamp of this contradiction, which is in no way abstract. On the contrary, its vital meaning permeates everything the intelligentsia does and explains all its political reverses.

People argue that the Russian intelligentsia's anarchism and socialism are a form of religion, and that it is just this maximalism that reveals the presence of a religious principle. Moreover, anarchism and socialism are only special forms of individualism, and like it aspire to the utmost fullness and beauty of individual life, and this, the argument goes on, is their religious content. The concept of religion behind all these and similar assertions is entirely formal and has no intellectual content.

Christianity teaches not only submission to but also love for God, and since its appearance in the world the fundamental, irremovable element of every religion must be, cannot but be, faith in the redemptive power and decisive importance of personal creation, or, more truly, of personal achievement accomplished in conformity with the will of God. It is interesting that those dogmatic forms of modern Christianity like Calvinism and Jansenism, which in theory pushed the idea of determinism to its limit with the doctrine of predestination, both psychologically and in practice established and promoted the idea of personal achievement alongside it. Religion cannot exist without the idea of God and the idea of personal achievement.

Religious dissociation from the state is entirely possible—Tolstoi is an example. But precisely because Tolstoi is religious, he is ideologically hostile both to socialism and to atheistic anarchism, and he stands outside the Russian intelligentsia.

The basic philosopheme of socialism, its ideological axis as a world-view, is the principle that human good and evil ultimately depend on external condi-

---

7. Brand, the hero of Henrik Ibsen's verse-play of the same name, destroys his own and his family's life by his demand for total moral commitment to his idea of religion, as expressed in his slogan, "all or nothing." He was frequently used as a symbol of intelligentsia intransigence by the *Vekhi* authors. *Eds.*

tions. It is no coincidence that the founder of socialism was Robert Owen, a follower of the French Enlightenment thinkers and of Bentham, and that he advanced a doctrine on the formation of human character which rejected the idea of personal responsibility. Religion in any form acceptable to contemporary man teaches that human goodness depends entirely on a person's free submission to a higher principle. The fundamental philosopheme of any religion predicated not on fear but on love and reverence is, "The Kingdom of God is within you."[8] For the religious mind, therefore, nothing can be more valuable and important than a person's individual self-perfection, which socialism disregards on principle.[9]

As a purely economic doctrine socialism does not contradict any religion, but neither is it in any way a religion itself. A religious person cannot believe in socialism ("I believe, Lord, and I confess")[10] any more than he can believe in railroads, radio, or proportional representation.

The spiritual birth of the Russian intelligentsia, in our use of the word, took place when progressive Russian intellects accepted Western European atheistic socialism. The first Russian *intelligent* of this type was Bakunin, a man whose crucial role in the development of Russian social thought is still far from adequately appreciated. Without Bakunin, Belinskii would not have "swung left,"[11] nor would Chernyshevskii have continued a certain *tradition* of social thought. We need only compare Novikov, Radishchev, and Chaadaev with Bakunin and Chernyshevskii to understand the ideological gulf that separates the luminaries of the Russian educated class from the luminaries of the Russian intelligentsia. Novikov, Radishchev, and Chaadaev were men truly enraptured by God, while atheism in the most profound philosophical sense of the word was the real spiritual element that sustained Bakunin in his final phase and Chernyshevskii from the beginning to the end of his career. The difference between Novikov, Radishchev, and Chaadaev, on the one hand, and Bakunin and Chernyshevskii on the other is not simply "historical." They are not links in the same chain but represent two essentially irreconcilable spiritual currents which must struggle against each other at every stage of development.

---

8. Luke 17:21. Also the title of one of Tolstoi's moral tracts. *Eds.*

9. See my article, "Lev Tolstoi," *Russian Thought* [Russkaia mysl'] (August 1908), pp. 218-30.

10. See Acts 19:18. *Eds.*

11. In the late 1830s Belinskii, at this time strongly influenced by Bakunin, went through a period of what he called "reconciliation with reality." A static interpretation of Hegel's philosophy led him to accept existing political and social conditions as a necessary manifestation of the Absolute. By 1840 or 1841 he had freed himself from this conservative position and was beginning to view Russia's shortcomings with a critical eye, even to the point of embracing socialism. By this time Bakunin had gone abroad, however, and Belinskii's "move to the left" owed more to Herzen's influence than to Bakunin's. *Eds.*

The intelligentsia's spiritual uniqueness, which clearly distinguishes it from the educated class, became evident in the sixties with the growth of radical journalism. It is remarkable how our national literature remains a preserve the intelligentsia cannot capture. The great writers, Pushkin, Lermontov, Gogol', Turgenev, Dostoevskii, and Chekhov, do not have the lineaments of *intelligenty*. Belinskii's greatness is not as an *intelligent*, as Bakunin's pupil, but chiefly as the interpreter of Pushkin and his national significance. Even Herzen, despite his socialism and atheism, waged a constant inner struggle with his *intelligent*'s image. Or, rather, he sometimes wore the uniform, as it were, of the Russian *intelligent*. But again, Herzen's break with the men of the sixties was not simply an historical or historically determined case of conflict between people of different periods of cultural development and social thought, but something much more serious and substantive. In his whole essence Chernyshevskii is a different man from Herzen. He is not just a different individual, but another spiritual type altogether.

In the subsequent history of Russian social thought, Mikhailovskii is an example of a typical *intelligent*—of a much finer individual stamp than Chernyshevskii, of course, but nonetheless an *intelligent* from head to toe. In complete contrast, Vladimir Solov'ev is not an *intelligent* at all. Saltykov, who as an individual has little in common with Herzen, is very similar to him in one regard: although he was in no way an *intelligent*, he too wore the intelligentsia uniform, and quite submissively. Dostoevskii and Tolstoi, each in his own way, tore this uniform off and threw it far away. Meanwhile, Russian liberalism as a whole—this is its essential difference from Slavophilism—feels dutybound to wear it, although the acute dissociation that is the essence of the *intelligent* is completely foreign to it. Gleb Uspenskii's enigmatic image is enigmatic because his true face is entirely hidden behind the intelligentsia mask.

* * *

The Russian intelligentsia's atheistic dissociation from the state is the key to an understanding of the revolution we have experienced and are experiencing yet.

All Russian political movements between the Pugachev uprising and this revolution were movements of the educated, privileged part of Russia. The officers' revolution of the Decembrists is a perfect example. By 1862 Bakunin thought that a social and political movement had already begun in the masses themselves. One could probably argue endlessly about when the movement that erupted as the 1905 revolution really did begin. But in 1862 Bakunin said: "Many people are discussing whether or not there will be a revolution in Russia, without realizing that there already is a revolution in Russia," and went on: "There will be terrible trouble in Russia in 1863 unless the Tsar decides to convene a national assembly."[12] Surely he did not think then that the revolution would drag on for more than forty years.

Intelligentsia thought and popular thought came together only in our revolution; for the first time in Russian history it happened in this sense and took this form. The revolution rushed to the attack on the political and social structure of autocratic, aristocratic Russia. 17 October 1905 marks the radical transformation in principle of the political order that had developed in Russia over the centuries. This transformation was extremely rapid in comparison with the long preceding period, when the regime's entire policy was aimed at cutting the nation off from all avenues leading to such change. The turning point came during the short-lived "period of confidence"[13] and was brought on, of course, by the bankruptcy of the old regime's foreign policy.

The last phase of this transformation, the act of 17 October, took place under the pressure of the spontaneous outburst that inspired the general strike, and the speed with which these events were played out intoxicated the intelligentsia. It imagined itself the master of the historical stage, and this wholly determined the "tactics" it used as it set out to realize its ideas. We have already characterized these ideas in general terms. The key to understanding what happened lies in the combination of the tactics and the ideas, and not in the tactics alone.

The revolution should formally and actually have come to an end with the act of 17 October. What made the situation before 17 October intolerable for both nation and state was the fact that the autocracy absolutely restricted the life of the nation and the development of the state within predetermined limits. Anything that, *de jure* or *de facto*, extended or even threatened to extend these limits was treated with intolerance and oppression. I characterized and condemned this policy in my preface to the foreign edition of Witte's famous memorandum on autocracy and the *zemstvo*.[14] The collapse of this policy was inevitable, and as a result of the war and of society's increasing complexity it occurred, we repeat, very quickly.

12. M. Bakunin, *The People's Cause: Romanov, Pugachev or Pestel'?* [Narodnoe delo: Romanov, Pugachev ili Pestel'?] (London: Trübner, 1862), pp. 6, 21. *Eds.*

13. The "period of confidence" refers to the ministry of Prince P. D. Sviatopolk-Mirskii, between the assassination of the arch-reactionary Viacheslav von Plehve in July, 1904, and the events following the Bloody Sunday massacre of 9 January 1905. Sviatopolk-Mirskii promised reforms and declared his confidence in the public. *Eds.*

14. Sergei Iul'evich Witte, *Autocracy and the Zemstvo* [Samoderzhavie i zemstvo] (Stuttgart: "Zaria," 1901). Witte was one of the outstanding officials of the last decades of tsarist Russia, serving as Minister of Finance under Alexander III and Nicholas II, and as Prime Minister in 1905-06. His confidential memorandum argued against the extension of *zemstvo* institutions on the grounds of the fundamental incompatibility between autocracy and the self-government organs. It was smuggled abroad and published by Struve with a long introduction. *Eds.*

At the moment when the state was being transformed in 1905, broad sections of Russia's educated public were wholly dominated by the ideology and mentality of dissociation. A regime which had taken shape historically, over the centuries, was supposed to fall to pieces as soon as it had made the concession which settled in principle the question of a Russian constitution. In the actual words of Social-Democratic propaganda of the period, there was talk of "giving the cur a final kick." Statements like this were made before the representative body had been convened and before anyone knew the real mood of the nation as a whole; most importantly, they were made before anyone knew the country's readiness for political life and capacity for political self-control. No one has ever called for massive political and social changes with such unbounded frivolity as our revolutionary parties and their organizations during the "days of freedom."[15] We need only point out that the idea of overthrowing the monarchy did not appear as a preliminary slogan in any of the great revolutions. Both in seventeenth-century England and in eighteenth-century France the monarchy was overthrown as the result of a fatal conjunction of events which no one foresaw, no one provoked, no one "made."

Parliament had already existed for centuries when the short-lived English republic was born, in the midst of a great religious and political struggle and through the efforts of men whose leader, perhaps the most forceful and brilliant embodiment of the English state idea, raised the power of England to an unprecedented height. The French monarchy fell in consequence of its purely political unreadiness for a revolution which it had itself set in motion. And the republic established in its place and forged in the struggle for national existence seems to have lived only to give way to a new monarchy that ultimately fell in combat with foreign enemies. Napoleon I built an entire legend around himself, in which his person was closely intertwined with the idea of the power and greatness of the state. The dynasty that was restored when he fell had been recalled and placed on the throne by foreigners, and as a result it was politically weak from the outset. But the Bourbons, represented by the Orleanist branch, would have returned to the French throne after 1848 had they not been forestalled by the little Napoleon, whose strength came from the national and political fascination of the First Empire. The fall of Napoleon III took place in this atmosphere ripe for revolutions, and was occasioned by the state's total, historically unprecedented military defeat. Thus, modern French history consists of nearly a century of continuous political alternations, filled with great state events, from republic to monarchy and back again.

The revolutionary experience of other countries provides the best com-

---

15. "Days of freedom" refers to a period of several weeks after the issuing of the October Manifesto when, as a result of administrative confusion and the faltering of the government, the customary restrictions on civil liberties virtually disappeared. *Eds.*

mentary on our own. The intelligentsia found in the masses only inchoate instincts that spoke in remote voices, merging into a vague hum. Instead of taking up systematic educational work to transform this hum into the conscious articulate sounds of national identity, the intelligentsia just tacked its short, bookish slogans onto it. When the hum subsided, the slogans were left hanging in midair.

After 17 October, the struggle against the historic Russian state and the "bourgeois" social structure was conducted with still greater passion and revolutionary intensity than before; the intelligentsia brought to this struggle the tremendous fanaticism of its hatred, the murderous logic of its conclusions and constructs—and not a glimmer of a religious idea. On the face of it, the intelligentsia's religiosity or non-religiosity has no bearing on politics. But only on the face of it. It is no coincidence that while the Russian intelligentsia was irreligious, in our substantive sense of the word, at the same time it was dreamy, impractical, and frivolous in politics. Credulity without faith, struggle without creation, fanaticism without enthusiasm, intolerance without reverence—in a word, here were all the external features of religiosity without its content. This contradiction is of course inherent in any radicalism colored by materialism and positivism. But never has it weighed down any living historical force so heavily as it does the Russian intelligentsia.

Radicalism or maximalism can be justified only by a religious idea, by devotion and service to some higher principle. In the first place, a religious idea can blunt the sharp edges of this kind of radicalism, with its harshness and cruelty. But in addition, and most importantly, religious radicalism appeals to a person's inner essence, for the religious outlook regards the external organization of life as a secondary matter. Therefore, no matter how decisively religious radicalism may pose political and social problems it cannot fail to see them as problems of a person's education. Even if this education is accomplished through direct communion with God, by superhuman means, so to speak, it remains human education and improvement; it is addressed to the individual person, his inner powers and his sense of responsibility. Conversely, all forms of atheistic maximalism brush aside the problem of education in politics and social reform, replacing it with the external organization of life.

When we assert that the Russian intelligentsia's former or present ideology rejects personal achievement and responsibility, we appear to contradict its actual history of service to the people, and the examples of heroism, asceticism and self-denial that marked this service. But it must be understood that the actual practice of self-denial does not necessarily imply recognition of the idea of personal responsibility as a principle governing private and public life. His reflections on his duty to the people never brought the *intelligent* to the realization that the idea of personal responsibility implicit in the principle of duty should apply not only to himself, the *intelligent*, but to the people as well, that is, to every individual regardless of his origins and social status. Thus, for all their attractiveness, the heroism and asceticism of the intelligentsia, which devoted its powers to serving the people, were deprived of any principled moral significance and educational force.

During the revolution this became quite clear. The intelligentsia's doctrine of service to the people presupposed no obligations on their part and assigned them no educational tasks of their own. And since the people are individuals, motivated by interest and instinct, the intelligentsia ideology could scarcely produce an idealistic result once it had filtered down to them. Translated into real life, the teaching of the Populists, not to mention that of the Marxists, turned into license and demoralization.

There are only two alternatives to the idea of education in politics: despotism or ochlocracy. By making the most extreme demands and calling the people to action in their name, our radical intelligentsia totally rejected education in politics and replaced it with agitation. But agitation was soon played out and could do no more. By the time it had waned the moment had passed, and reaction was triumphant. But this was not just a case of lost opportunity.

The detestable triumph of reaction has moved many of us to forget or keep silent about the mistakes of our revolution. Nothing could be more dangerous than forgetfulness, nothing more thoughtless than silence. "Political impressionism" is the only name for this attitude; it must be opposed by an analysis that transcends the impressions of the moment in order to study the moral essence of the political crisis into which the intelligentsia has led our country.

What propelled the masses into this crisis? The very same things that propelled them into the revolutionary movements of the seventeenth and eighteenth centuries: their sufferings and the social demands that grew spontaneously from them, their instincts, appetites and hatreds. There were no religious ideas at all. This was extremely favorable terrain for the intelligentsia's atheistic radicalism, which set to work with an assurance worthy of better application.

The political radicalism of the intelligentsia's ideas was grafted onto the social radicalism of the people's instincts with stunning rapidity. How lightly and boldly the intelligentsia pushed the exhausted, suffering masses onto the path of political and social revolution! This was not simply a political error or tactical lapse; it was a moral error. It was based on the notion that society's "progress" need not be the fruit of human improvement, but could be instead a jackpot to be won at the gambling table of history by appealing to popular unrest.

Political foolishness and ineptitude compounded this fundamental moral error. If the intelligentsia possessed the form of religiosity without the content, its "positivism," on the contrary, was totally formless. Here were "positive" ideas that were in no way authentically positive, "scientific" ideas that lacked any knowledge of life and people, "empiricism" without experience, and "rationalism" without wisdom or even common sense.

They made the revolution badly. It is now becoming quite clear that cleverly staged provocation played a role in the making of it. But this is only a vivid illustration of the revolutionaries' striking ineptitude and helplessness in practical affairs; it is not the crux of the matter. The point is not how they made the revolution, but *that* they made it at all. They made a revolution when their job was to concentrate all their energies on political education and self-education. The war had opened the people's eyes and aroused the national conscience, creating possibilities for political education that promised the most fruitful results. But instead, what did we see? Two general strikes accompanied by revolutionary agitation of the workers (a Soviet of Workers' Deputies!);[16] a series of senseless, pitiful mutinies in the armed forces; the Moscow uprising,[17] which was much worse than it appeared at first; the boycott of the elections to the First Duma;[18] and the preparation (with the help of provocateurs!) of further armed uprisings, which broke out when the Duma had already been dissolved.[19] All this was supposed to terrorize the regime and ultimately bring it down. The regime was in fact terrorized. The field courts-martial and endless executions followed. And then fear became the state's normal political condition, which it remains to this day, and in this atmosphere the government put through the change in the electoral law.[20] Now it will take years to get the country moving again.

And so the atheistic dissociation from the state that characterizes the Russian intelligentsia's political outlook also caused both its moral frivolity and its political impracticality.

16. The St. Petersburg Soviet (Council) of Workers' Deputies, composed primarily of worker delegates from the various factories of the capital, arose spontaneously during the general strike of October, 1905, as a strike committee and coordinating center; for a brief period it was the most authoritative public body in Russia. The Soviet was dispersed and its members arrested on 3 December 1905. *Eds.*

17. The Moscow uprising of December, 1905, was touched off by the news of the arrest of the St. Petersburg Soviet and marked the culmination of the revolution of 1905. It was suppressed only after the artillery siege of one of the working-class quarters of the city and the loss of at least 500 and perhaps as many as 1,000 lives. *Eds.*

18. Elections to the First State Duma were boycotted by the Socialist-Revolutionaries and the bulk of the Social Democrats, in the belief that an armed uprising to force the calling of a constituent assembly was still possible. *Eds.*

19. The dissolution of the First Duma after a session of only two months was followed by several naval mutinies, some agrarian unrest, and a new wave of terrorist acts, the most spectacular of them an attempt on the life of Prime Minister Stolypin which killed a number of bystanders. *Eds.*

20. The government followed the dissolution of the unruly Second Duma in June, 1907, with a new electoral law that increased the representation of landowners and decreased that of peasants, workers, and national minorities. The change was technically illegal, since it was made without the consent of the Duma, and it is often referred to as a *coup d'état. Eds.*

What follows from this diagnosis of our illness? First of all, and I stressed this before, it means that the ailment is deep-seated, and it is ridiculous to discuss it in terms of political tactics. The intelligentsia must re-examine its entire attitude, and especially the primary buttress of this attitude—socialism's denial of personal responsibility which we discussed earlier. With the removal of this stone—and it must be removed—the entire intellectual structure will collapse.

When this happens the very role of "politics" in the intelligentsia's ideological perspective will have to change. On the one hand, politics will cease to be an isolated sphere, independent of all other aspects of spiritual life, as it has been hitherto. For it too will be based on the idea of a person's inner improvement rather than the external arrangement of society. And, on the other hand, the domination of politics over all the non-political aspects of spiritual life must come to an end.

The Russian intelligentsia developed an attitude toward politics which, in the last analysis, is distorted and fundamentally contradictory. While reducing politics to the external organization of life—which it is from the technical point of view—the intelligentsia simultaneously viewed it as the alpha and omega of its own and the people's entire existence. (I am using the word politics here precisely in the broad sense of the external social organization of life.) Thus, a limited means was turned into an all-embracing end—an obvious, though in human affairs extremely common, distortion of the relationship between means and ends. If politics is subordinated to the idea of education, however, it can break out of the isolation to which the "external" conception necessarily condemns it. Then politics cannot simply be reduced to a contest of social forces, to a class struggle, for example, which will ultimately be decided by physical superiority. On the other hand, it becomes impossible to subordinate all spiritual life to politics in the external sense.

Of course, there can be an external concept of education as well. Such a concept underlies the kind of social optimism that assumes that a person is always ready, always sufficiently mature, for a better life, and that only an irrational social structure prevents him from manifesting his innate virtues and potentialities. From this point of view, "society" is the educator, good or bad, of the individual. Our concept of education has nothing to do with the "organization" of the social environment and its pedagogical effect on the personality. This is the "socialist" idea of education, and it has nothing in common with the idea of education in the religious sense. The latter is completely alien to socialist optimism. It believes not in organization but only in creation, in a person's positive labor on himself, in his inner struggle for the sake of creative tasks.

* * *

Once the Russian intelligentsia renounces its atheistic dissociation from the state, it will cease to exist as a special cultural category. Can it accomplish the enormous feat of transcending its unsound essence? To a considerable extent the fate of Russia and her culture depends on the answer to this question. Can any definite answer be given right now? It is very difficult, but we do have some indications.

There is reason to believe that the change will come from two sources and will accordingly have a dual character. First, as economic development proceeds the intelligentsia will be "bourgeoisified"; that is, through a process of social adjustment it will become reconciled with the state, and it will organically and spontaneously be drawn into the existing social structure and distributed among the different classes of society. Strictly speaking, this will not be a spiritual revolution; the intelligentsia will simply adapt its spiritual physiognomy to the given social structure. The rapidity of this process will depend on the pace of Russia's economic development and the pace at which her entire state structure is reorganized in a constitutional spirit.

But the intelligentsia may also undergo a real spiritual upheaval, the product of a struggle of ideas. In the present instance we are interested only in this upheaval. What horoscope can be cast for it?

A profound ferment has already begun in the intelligentsia; new ideas have come to life, and its old ideological foundations have been shaken and compromised. This process has only just begun, and it is still impossible to say what success it will have or where it will stop. But we can already state that insofar as Russian intellectual life is linked with the spiritual development of other, more advanced countries, processes taking place abroad cannot fail to be reflected in Russian minds. The Russian intelligentsia, as a special cultural category, is the offspring of the interaction of Western socialism and the unique conditions of our cultural, economic and political development. Before the introduction of socialism into Russia, the Russian intelligentsia did not exist; there was only an "educated class," which followed various trends of thought.

At present, no process is more portentous and fraught with consequences for the spiritual development of the West than the crisis and disintegration of socialism. Socialism in decay is being absorbed by social policy. Bentham has conquered Saint-Simon and Marx. Syndicalism is the last effort to save socialism. On the one hand it is an attempt to bring about a romantic regeneration of socialism by overtly grounding it on elemental, irrational principles. But on the other hand, it marks just as overt an appeal to barbarism. It is perfectly obvious that this effort is impotent and sterile. Under these circumstances, socialism can scarcely remain the life-blood of the spiritual and social existence of those elements of Russian society that make up the intelligentsia.[21]

The crisis of socialism is not so evident in the West because of the absence of an intelligentsia there. The West has no sensitive nerve comparable to our intelligentsia. The crisis of socialism must, therefore, have a greater ideological impact in Russia than elsewhere. This crisis raises the very same problems that underlie the Russian revolution and its reverses. But even though our intelligentsia may be more sensitive to the crisis of socialism than Westerners, it is also concealed from us by our ill-starred "politics," by the revival of an undefeated absolutism, and by the frenzy of reaction. The principles at issue and the organic nature of the crisis are therefore much clearer in the West.

Neither a camomile tea of tactical directives nor a bland diet of non-ideological cultural work can cure an ideological crisis of this magnitude. Of course, we do need persistent cultural work. But just so that we can keep our balance and not get lost in this work, we need ideas and the creative struggle of ideas.

21. See my article, "Facies hippocratica," *Russian Thought* [Russkaia mysl'] (October 1907), pp. 220-32.

THE ETHIC OF NIHILISM

A Characterization of the Russian Intelligentsia's Moral Outlook

Semen Frank

> The earth turns—*inaudibly*—not around the inventors of new noises but around the inventors of new values.

> And suppose one goes through fire for his teaching—what does that prove! It would be better in truth, if his own teaching were to rise from his own fire.
>
> Friedrich Nietzsche, *Thus Spoke Zarathustra*[1]

Anyone who is both willing and able to carry on a free, truthful discussion of the present state of our society and the means of regenerating it must focus his attention on two extremely important developments: the collapse of the promising social movement that was guided by the intelligentsia's consciousness, and the subsequent rapid disintegration within the intelligentsia of its firmest moral traditions and concepts. Essentially, both testify to the same thing: they expose the hitherto concealed impotence, ineffectiveness, and unsoundness of the Russian intelligentsia's traditional cultural philosophy and moral outlook.

In regard to the first development, the failure of the Russian revolution, the banal "explanation" that the perfidy of "reaction" and "the bureaucracy" are responsible cannot satisfy anyone attempting a serious, conscientious, and, above all, productive discussion of the problem. It is not so much factually incorrect as methodologically erroneous. It is not a theoretical *explanation* at all, but merely a totally one-sided moral *accusation*, which has harmful effects. Of course, the party defending the "old order" against the liberation movement indisputably did everything in its power to curb the movement and rob it of its gains. It can be charged with egotism, short-sighted statesmanship, and disregard for the nation's interests. But to hold it responsible for the failure of a struggle that was waged in outright opposition to it and was at all times aimed at its destruction is to argue either with bad faith or with childish thoughtlessness. It is equivalent to blaming the Japanese for the unfortunate outcome of the Russo-Japanese war. The common tendency to console oneself in every instance with the cheap notion that "the authorities are to blame"

1. Friedrich Nietzsche, *Thus Spoke Zarathustra*, translated by Marianne Cowan (Los Angeles: Henry Regnery, 1957), pp. 163, 106. *Eds.*

bespeaks a degrading slave mentality, one devoid of a sense of personal responsibility and accustomed to attributing its good or ill to the mercy or wrath of an alien, external force. The contrary proposition, that "every nation has the government it deserves," is wholly and unconditionally applicable to the present situation.

The old regime's actual strength in the pre-revolutionary period perhaps made it impossible to recognize its historical inevitability. But now that the struggle that temporarily gripped the whole of society and made its voice politically decisive has ended in the failure of those who defended new ideas, society no longer has the right to disclaim responsibility for the quality of life that emerged from the ferment. Society's impotence, as revealed in this political clash, is neither an accident nor a simple misfortune; from the historical and moral point of view it is a *sin*. In the final analysis, the intelligentsia's spiritual forces—its beliefs, its life experiences, its values and tastes, its intellectual and moral tone—guided and defined the entire movement, its objectives as well as its tactics. The political problem thereby becomes one of morals and cultural philosophy; the failure of the intelligentsia's *actions* raises the more general and important question of the value of the intelligentsia's *faith*.

The other development we mentioned brings us back to the same question. How could the intelligentsia's moral foundations, apparently so solid and firm, be undermined so quickly and radically? How could the pure and honest Russian intelligentsia, raised on the precepts of the best people, have sunk even for a moment to robbery and brute licentiousness? Why did political offenses merge so imperceptibly with ordinary crimes, and how did "Saninism" and the vulgarized "sex problem" become ideologically interwoven with revolutionism? Mere moral condemnation of these phenomena would not simply be unproductive, it would obscure their most characteristic trait. For the striking thing about them is that these were not simple violations of morality, possible anywhere and at any time, but outrages with pretensions to ideological significance that were advocated as new ideals. The problem is how such advocacy could succeed, and why the intelligentsia lacked moral traditions strong and stable enough to offer it vigorous resistance. Awareness of this problem implies an intuitive understanding that, to say the least, all is not well with the intelligentsia's world-view. Both the political and the moral crisis demand with equal urgency that we subject the Russian intelligentsia's spiritual life to a thoughtful and dispassionate examination.

The following lines are devoted to just one part of this broad and complex task, a critical analysis and evaluation of the intelligentsia's *moral* outlook. Of course, the various aspects of spiritual life do not exist in isolation from one another; a living soul cannot be disassembled and then put back together like a machine. We can only separate out the parts intellectually, by the artificial process of abstraction. The moral world-view is especially closely interwoven into the whole spiritual fabric. It is inseparably linked with religious and philosophical beliefs and values on the one hand, and, on the other, with a person's spontaneous psychic impulses and his general awareness of the world and feeling for life. Therefore, a self-contained theoretical representation of it must inevitably remain schematic, a mere diagrammatic sketch rather than an artistic portrait. And a pure, isolated analysis that consciously and consistently ignores the vital bonds linking the moral outlook with other spiritual motifs that in part underlie it and in part result from it is neither possible nor desirable.

It is extremely difficult to unravel the vital skein of spiritual life and trace the interlacings of its separate threads—that is, moral and philosophical motifs and ideas, and we can expect to achieve only approximate precision. But even an imperfect analysis is terribly important and urgently needed. The Russian intelligentsia's moral world—its essential features have remained unchanged for many decades, despite the variety of social doctrines the intelligentsia has professed—developed into a vast, living system, a kind of organism that maintains its existence and possesses the instinct of self-preservation. To understand this organism's diseases—we have just pointed out their obvious and threatening symptoms—we must attempt to anatomize it mentally and penetrate to its deepest roots.

I

Morality, moral judgments and moral themes occupy quite an exceptional place in the Russian *intelligent*'s soul. If it were possible to characterize our intelligentsia's cast of mind in one word, it would have to be *moralism*. The Russian *intelligent* knows no absolute values, standards or orientation in life other than the moral differentiation of people, actions and circumstances into good and bad, benevolent and malicious. If we are to realize that there are, or can be, other values and standards in addition to moral ones, and that along with the good, the ideals of truth, beauty and Divinity too can affect the soul and stir hearts to great deeds, we must have special, insistent signals and unusually loud appeals—and these always strike most of us as rather unnatural and affected. Theoretical, aesthetic and religious values have no power over the heart of the Russian *intelligent*; his perception of them is weak and confused, and in any case he always sacrifices them to moral values.

Theoretical, scientific truth, rigorous and pure knowledge for its own sake, and the disinterested search for a satisfactory intellectual image of the world and mastery over it were never able to take root in the intelligentsia's consciousness. Our entire intellectual development is painted in the vivid color of moral utilitarianism. From the ecstatic worship of natural science in the sixties to the latest scholarly fads such as empirio-criticism, our intelligentsia has sought in thinkers and their systems not scientific truth but practical usefulness, the justification or sanction of some moralistic social tendency. This was precisely the psychological trait that Mikhailovskii tried to substantiate and legitimize with his notorious doctrine of "subjective method." This characteristic feature of the Russian intelligentsia's thinking— its failure to develop what Nietzsche called "intellectual conscience"—is so well-known and obvious that there can be no disagreement over the fact itself, only over its evaluation.

Muffled and uncertain, the voice of aesthetic conscience sounds even more faintly and more timidly in the Russian *intelligent*'s soul. In this respect Pisarev and his puerile dethronement of our greatest national artist,[2] and the entire Pisarev episode, that turbulent revolt against aesthetics, was not merely an isolated incident in our spiritual development. It was, rather, a lens that focused the rays of the barbaric iconoclasm that still burns unquenched in the intelligentsia's consciousness onto a single bright point. Aesthetics is an unnecessary and dangerous luxury, and art is permissible only as an outer form for moral instruction; in other words, it is pure art that we reject, while permitting its tendentious distortion. For long decades this belief dominated our progressive public opinion, and even now, when people are ashamed to profess it openly, it continues to cast a shadow over the whole of our spiritual life.

As for religious values, it has recently become fashionable to claim that the Russian intelligentsia is profoundly religious and fails to realize it only through a misunderstanding; but this view rests entirely on an inaccurate use of words. Semantic arguments are futile and boring. If by religiosity we mean *fanaticism*, then, of course, the Russian intelligentsia is religious to the highest degree: that is, it is possessed of a passionate devotion to a favorite idea that verges on an *idée fixe*; it leads a person to self-sacrifice and great achievements on the one hand, and, on the other, to an abnormal distortion of his whole perspective on life and the intolerant annihilation of everything that does not agree with his idea. But in fact the concept of religion must have a more precise definition than this free and metaphorical, though inevitable and often helpful usage. For all the diversity of religious views, religion always involves faith in the real existence of the absolutely valuable and the recognition of a principle whereby the real force of material existence and the ideal truth of the spirit are merged into one. Essentially, the religious attitude consists of an awareness of the cosmic, superhuman significance of higher values, and any world-view based on an ideal that has only relative, human meaning will be irreligious and anti-religious, whatever the psychological force of the passions accompanying it and generated by it.

---

2. This is a reference to Pisarev's attack on Pushkin in an 1865 article which dismissed the poet as a trivial versifier without social consciousness and took Belinskii to task for considering him an important artist. D. I. Pisarev, "Pushkin and Belinskii" [Pushkin i Belinskii], *Works: A Complete Collection in Six Volumes* [Sochineniia D. I. Pisareva: Polnoe sobranie v shesti tomakh], 4th ed. (St. Petersburg: F. Pavlenkov, 1903-05), V, 9-129. *Eds.*

If the intelligentsia's view of life is foreign and hostile to theoretical and aesthetic themes, it rejects and banishes religious themes and values still more forcefully. Anyone who loves truth or beauty is suspected of indifference to the people's welfare and is condemned for ignoring vital needs for the sake of illusory interests and luxurious diversions; but anyone who loves God is considered an outright enemy of the people. This is not a simple misunderstanding, nor[3] is it just foolishness and myopia reinforcing the dogma, unsubstantiated by theory or historical experience, of the eternally and immanently "reactionary" character of every religion. On the contrary, we see here the inherent and inevitable metaphysical repulsion of two modes of contemplating and perceiving the world; it is the primordial and irreconcilable struggle between the religious attitude that strives to draw human life closer to a superhuman, absolute principle and to discover an eternal and universal support for it, and the *nihilistic* attitude that strives to immortalize and absolutize what is only "human, too human." Let us grant that the dogma of an intrinsic bond between religion and reaction is only a naive illusion based on intellectual prejudice and historical ignorance. There is, nonetheless, an incontrovertible and profoundly important truth in the view that love for "heaven" forces a person to have an entirely different attitude toward "earth" and earthly affairs. Religiosity is incompatible with the practice of according absolute significance to earthly, human interests, or with a nihilistic, utilitarian worship of the external blessings of life. And here we have arrived at the deepest and most crucial motif of the intelligentsia's conception of life.

The Russian intelligentsia's *moralism* is only the expression and reflection of its *nihilism*. To be sure, if one reasons according to strict logic, then in the sphere of morals, too, one can derive from nihilism only nihilism, that is, amorality, and Stirner had little trouble explaining this logical conclusion to Feuerbach and his students. If existence has no intrinsic meaning, and subjective human desires are the only rational criterion for the way a person lives his life, then why must I recognize any obligations? Wouldn't a simple, egotistic enjoyment of life, an ingenuous and natural *"carpe diem,"* be my legitimate right? Our Bazarov, too, was irrefutably logical when he refused to serve the interests of the *muzhik* and professed the most thorough indifference to the human prosperity that would ensue when "burdocks would be growing" from him, Bazarov.[4] We shall see later on that this contradiction finds quite palpable expression in the practical consequences of the intelligentsia's world-view.

3. The Russian text reads *no* ["but"], evidently a misprint for *ne* ["nor" in this context]. *Eds.*

4. I. S. Turgenev, *Fathers and Sons* [Ottsy i deti], *Complete Collected Works* [Polnoe sobranie sochinenii], 3rd ed., 10 vols. (St. Petersburg: Glazunov, 1891), II, 147. Izgoev quotes the same phrase in his article above, p. 84. Bazarov, the hero of *Fathers and Sons*, was regarded as the archetypal Russian nihilist. *Eds.*

But at this point let us assume that one can make a logical leap and psychologically get from egotism to altruism, and from concern with one's own ego to concern for the daily bread of everyone, or of the majority—or, to put it another way, let us assume that the irrational instinct of tribal or social solidarity replaces rational proof. Then we can derive all the rest of the Russian intelligentsia's world-view perfectly clearly from its *nihilism*.

To the extent that any *universally obligatory and binding faith* is associated with nihilism, this faith can only be moralism.

By nihilism I mean the denial or non-recognition of absolute (objective) values. Generally speaking, human activity is guided either by a striving for certain *objective* values (for example, theoretical scientific truth, artistic beauty, the object of religious faith, state power, national pride) or by subjective motives, the inclination to satisfy the personal needs of oneself and others. Any faith, whatever its content, creates a corresponding morality; that is, it imposes certain obligations on the believer and determines what he must consider good and evil in his life, activity, interests and impulses. A morality derived from a faith in objective values, from the recognition of the intrinsic sanctity of some goal, serves as an auxiliary to the faith, a kind of technical norm and hygiene for a fruitful life. Therefore, although the life of every believer is subject to a strict morality, it has only an instrumental, and not a self-sufficient, importance in his life; every moral demand can be based upon and deduced from the ultimate goal, and consequently does not claim to have a mystical, incontrovertible meaning in itself. But whenever the object of aspiration is a relative good without absolute value—specifically, the satisfaction of subjective human needs and demands—a logically invalid but psychologically unavoidable process of thought absolutizes morality and places it at the *basis* of the entire practical world-view.

When a person must subordinate the spontaneous impulses of his "I" to the subjective interests of "thou"—even a collective "thou"—instead of to an absolute value or goal, he subordinates himself to interests which are essentially equal in value (or of equal insignificance) to his own. Then the obligations of self-denial, disinterestedness, ascetic self-restraint and self-sacrifice necessarily assume the character of absolute, self-sufficient commandments, for otherwise no one would be bound by them or fulfill them. In this case, it is not the goal or ideal that is recognized as an absolute value, but *service* to it in itself. And if Stirner's question, "Why am 'I' less valuable than 'thou' that I must be sacrificed to him?" remains unanswered, the authority that surrounds moral *practice* is made all the more mystical and indisputable, in order to forestall this kind of acute perplexity. This attitude, in which morality not only predominates but possesses unlimited, autocratic power over a consciousness lacking faith in absolute values, may be termed *moralism*. It is precisely this nihilistic moralism that constitutes the essence of the Russian *intelligent*'s world-view.

The Russian *intelligent*'s symbol of faith is *the people's welfare*, the satisfaction of the needs of the "majority." He feels that serving this goal is a person's highest and, indeed, sole obligation, and anything beyond it is demonic. For this reason he does not simply reject or refuse to accept other values—he actually fears and hates them. It is impossible to serve two gods at once, and if God, as Maksim Gor'kii has openly declared, is "the people's essence,"[5] then all others are false gods, idols or devils. Activity guided by love for science or art, a life illumined by religious light in the proper sense of the word, that is, by communion with God, distracts attention from service to the people, weakens or destroys moralistic enthusiasm, and signifies, from the perspective of the intelligentsia's faith, a dangerous pursuit of phantoms. Therefore the intelligentsia rejects such activity, partly as stupidity or "superstition," and partly as an immoral proclivity.

Of course, this does not mean that scientific, aesthetic and religious interests and experiences are *in fact* alien to the Russian intelligentsia. The spirit and its primordial needs cannot be suppressed, and it is only natural that the living people who have garbed their soul in the *intelligent*'s moral uniform should retain all the innate human feelings. But these feelings persist in the Russian *intelligent*'s soul in much the same way as the feeling of pity for the enemy in the soldier's soul, or the desire for the free play of fantasy in the consciousness of a rigorously scientific thinker; they are an illegitimate, though ineradicable, weakness, something that is at best merely tolerated. Scientific, aesthetic and religious experiences are always relegated, as it were, to a person's private, intimate life. More tolerant people regard them as a luxury, a leisure-time diversion, or a mild eccentricity, while the less tolerant condemn them in others and bashfully conceal them in themselves. But the *intelligent qua intelligent*, that is, in his conscious faith and public activity, must be alien to them; his world-view and ideal are hostile to these aspects of human life.

From science the *intelligent* takes a few propositions—popularized, distorted, or fabricated *ad hoc*—and although he is frequently even proud of how "scientific" his faith is, he indignantly rejects both scientific criticism and all pure, disinterested scientific thought. Aesthetics and religion he does not need at all. Pure science, art and religion are all incompatible with *moralism* and service to the people; they all rest on love for objective values and conse-

5. M. Gor'kii, *Collected Works in Eighteen Volumes* [Sobranie sochinenii v vosemnadtsati tomakh] (Moscow: Gosudarstvennoe izdatel'stvo khudozhestvennoi literatury, 1960-63), V, 266. In fact, the spokesman for Gor'kii's views in his "god-building" novel *The Confession* [Ispoved'] (1908) says that it is the building of God that is the people's essence. Gor'kii [A. M. Peshkov, 1868-1936] was regarded as the spokesman of Russia's lower classes with his stories, novels and plays depicting the life of vagabonds and the wretchedly poor. He was the most important writer associated with the Social-Democratic Party—however, the book which Frank quotes was decidedly unacceptable to the party orthodoxy of Lenin. *Eds.*

quently are alien and thereby hostile to the utilitarian faith which the Russian *intelligent* professes. *The religion of service to earthly needs* and *the religion of service to ideal values* clash at this point. However complex and multifarious their irrational psychological interaction within the soul of the *intelligent* as a human being, in the realm of *intelligentsia consciousness* their conflict leads to the utter annihilation and proscription of ideal demands in the name of the integrity and purity of the moralistic faith.

Nihilistic moralism is the most profound and basic feature of the Russian *intelligent*'s spiritual physiognomy. Denial of objective values leads to deification of the subjective interests of his fellow man ("the people"), whence follows recognition of service to the people as a person's highest and sole mission; this in turn leads to ascetic hatred of everything that hinders, or merely does not aid, the accomplishment of this mission. Life has no objective, intrinsic meaning; its sole boon is material security and the satisfaction of subjective needs. A person must therefore devote all his energy to improving the lot of the majority, and anything that distracts him from this pursuit is evil and must be mercilessly extirpated. That is the strange chain of reasoning, weak logically but firmly welded psychologically, that guides all the behavior and value judgments of the Russian *intelligent*. Nihilism and moralism; nonbelief and fanatically stringent moral demands; lack of principle in the metaphysical sense—for nihilism is the denial of judgments made on principle and of the objective distinction between good and evil—and the fiercest conscientiousness in observing empirical principles, which are in essence conditional, non-principled demands: this distinctive, rationally incomprehensible and yet vitally powerful fusion of antagonistic elements into a mighty psychological force is the mentality that we term nihilistic moralism.

II

This cast of mind either produced or is related to other features of the intelligentsia's world-view, and most importantly the essential fact that the concept of *culture* in the precise, strict sense of the word is alien to the Russian *intelligent* and even somewhat inimical to him. This judgment may appear erroneous, for is it not this same Russian *intelligent* who speaks so often of the desirability of culture, the backwardness of our way of life, and the need to raise it to a higher level? But once again our concern is not with words, but with concepts and actual value judgments.

The pure concept of culture is organically rooted in the consciousness of the educated European; but it is neither native nor dear to the Russian, and it scarcely touches the inner man. The objective, intrinsically valuable development of the external and internal conditions of life; increased material and spiritual productivity; perfection of political, social and domestic forms of intercourse; progress in morality, religion, science and art; in a word, the multifarious labor of raising collective existence to an objectively higher level—this is the vital concept of culture, with its powerful intellectual influence, that inspires the European. But this concept is, once again, based entirely on faith in *objective values* and on service to them, and we can give a straightforward definition of culture in this sense as the *aggregate of objective values which have been actualized by the historical development of social life.* From this point of view, culture exists not for some good or purpose, but only for itself; cultural creation signifies the improvement of human nature and the embodiment of ideal values in life, and as such it is in itself a superior and self-sufficient object of human activity.

In contrast to this concept, culture as we usually understand it here is stamped with utilitarianism throughout. When our people speak of culture they mean either railroads, sewage systems and highways, or the development of popular education, or the improvement of the political mechanism. They always offer us something useful, a *means* for achieving some other end—namely the satisfaction of life's subjective needs. But a wholly utilitarian concept is incompatible with the pure idea of culture, just as a wholly utilitarian concept of science or art destroys the very essence of what we call science and art.

It is precisely the pure concept of culture that has no place in the Russian *intelligent*'s intellectual framework; it is psychologically alien and metaphysically hostile to him. The squalor, the spiritual poverty of our entire life, prevents a forthright love for culture from arising and taking root; it appears to kill the instinct for culture and to immunize us against the very idea of it. Furthermore, nihilistic moralism sows animosity toward culture as its metaphysical antithesis. To the extent that the Russian *intelligent* can grasp the pure concept of culture at all, he finds it profoundly antipathetic. He instinctively senses in it an enemy of his world-view, and he feels that culture is an unnecessary and morally impermissible aristocratic luxury; he cannot cherish it since he recognizes none of the objective values of which it is the aggregate. The struggle against culture is one of the characteristic traits of the intelligentsia generally, and is logically derived from nihilistic moralism. The traditional absence of culture in our everyday life and the metaphysical aversion to the idea of culture in the intelligentsia's world-view merge psychologically and work together to perpetuate the low cultural level of our entire existence.[6]

If we add this anti-cultural tendency to the features of nihilistic moralism outlined above, we get a more or less comprehensive diagram of the traditional intelligentsia world-view, the most appropriate designation for which is *populism*. The concept of "populism" draws together all the basic symptoms of the spiritual temper we have been describing: *nihilistic utilitarianism*, which denies all absolute values and regards service to the subjective, material interests

6. See below for a discussion of our so-called "cultural workers."

of the "majority" (or the people) as the only moral goal; *moralism*, which demands from an individual strict self-sacrifice and the unconditional subordination of his own interests (even the highest and purest) to the cause of public service; and, finally, an *anti-cultural tendency*, a desire to turn everyone into a "worker," to curtail and minimize higher claims for the sake of universal equality and solidarity in the fulfillment of moral demands. Populism in this sense is not a specific socio-political orientation, but a broad spiritual current that combines with quite diverse socio-political theories and programs.

Marxism would seem to combat populism, and in fact the themes of respect for culture and for raising productivity (material, but spiritual along with it), which are alien to the intelligentsia's consciousness, did sound for the first time with the appearance of Marxism. For the first time it was observed that the moral problem is not universal and in a certain sense is even subordinate to the problem of culture, and that ascetic renunciation of the higher forms of life is always an evil, not a good. But these themes did not dominate the intelligentsia's thinking for long. The victorious and all-devouring populist spirit swallowed up and assimilated Marxist theory, so that by now the difference between conscious populists and populists professing Marxism at most comes down to a difference in political program and sociological theory. In no way does it signify disagreement over cultural and philosophical principles.

In his ethical core the Russian *intelligent* has remained a stubborn, inveterate *populist* from the 1870s, approximately, to the present day. His God is the people, his one aim is the happiness of the majority, and his morality consists of service to this goal combined with ascetic self-restraint and with hatred or disdain for spiritual interests of intrinsic value. The Russian *intelligent* preserved his populist soul inviolate over the decades, despite the great variety of political and social theories he professed. Until quite recently populism formed the *intelligent*'s all-embracing and unshakable life program. He piously defended it from temptation and violation, saw its fulfillment as the sole rational purpose of his life, and judged others by its purity.

But in the course of the Russian intelligentsia's history, this general populist spirit has taken two sharply distinct forms: *direct, altruistic service to the needs of the people*, and *the religion of absolute achievement of the people's happiness*. Within the confines of the general populist ethic, this is, so to speak, the distinction between "loving one's neighbor" and "loving those farthest from you."[7] Let us be frank: the so-called "cultural worker," who is

7. See Nietzsche, *Thus Spoke Zarathustra*, pp. 67-68: "My brothers, I do not advise you to love your neighbor: I advise you to love those farthest from you." This was part of the epigraph Frank chose for his contribution to the 1902 symposium *Problems of Idealism*, "Fr. Nietzsche and the Ethic of 'Love for the One Farthest Away' " [Fr. Nitsshe i etika 'liubvi k dal'nemu,' in P. Novgorodtsev, ed., *Problemy idealizma*], where his evaluation of this position was very different. *Eds.*

now almost forgotten, quite rare, and in any case has been displaced from the center of public attention, the *intelligent* who was inspired by idealistic impulses to go "to the people" with his knowledge and his love in order to help the peasant satisfy his ordinary, essential needs, was the highest, purest, and morally most valuable fruit of our populism. "Cultural workers" was, strictly speaking, a misnomer; although spreading popular education was an essential part of their program, their concept of culture, as always in populism, was purely utilitarian. They were inspired not by love for pure knowledge but by a vital love for people, and they valued education only as one of the means (though the most important) of improving the people's welfare. The life mission of these unselfish, loving individuals was to alleviate the people's need in all its forms and daily manifestations.

There was much in this movement that was ridiculous, naive, one-sided, and even theoretically and morally wrong. The "cultural worker" shared all the illusions and narrowness of the populist in general. Often he went to the people to repent and used his activity to minimize, as it were, the "sin" of his former participation in more cultivated forms of life. In his relations with the people there was a conscious effort to merge with peasant spontaneity, since he was governed by the belief that on the whole this spontaneity was the ideal form of human existence. Absorbed in his own mission, like a monk he censured the vanity of all aspirations toward broader and more distant goals. But one thing atoned for all this—his spontaneous sense of vital love for people. This type of *intelligent* revealed and embodied all that was positive and fruitful in populist morality; it was as though he had absorbed and actively cultivated the most nourishing root of populism, its *altruism*.

A few of these individuals are probably still scattered across Russia, but the current of social morality that created them ran dry long ago, partly driven out and partly distorted and absorbed by the other variant of populism, *the religion of the absolute achievement of the people's happiness*. We are referring to that militant populism that has played such an incalculably important role in the public life of recent decades in the form of *revolutionary socialism*. To understand and assess this most powerful form of populism, one which may be considered fatal for contemporary Russian culture, we must trace the spiritual channels by which the moral well-spring of the intelligentsia's mentality flows into the stream of socialism and revolutionism.

III

The Russian intelligentsia's nihilistic moralism or utilitarianism is not just an ethical doctrine or moral sentiment, and it does not merely *establish a moral obligation* to work for the people's welfare. It merges psychologically with the dream, or faith, that the object of one's moral efforts—the happiness of the people—can be achieved, and, moreover, in an absolute and eternal form. This faith really is psychologically analogous to religious faith, and it takes the place of authentic religion in the consciousness of the atheistic intelligentsia. Here is the clear demonstration that while the intelligentsia rejects any religion or metaphysics, it is in fact wholly dominated by a certain social metaphysics, and, moreover, one which contradicts its philosophical nihilism even more glaringly than does its moralistic world-view.

If the universe is chaos and is determined only by blind material forces, then how is it possible to hope that historical development will inevitably lead to the reign of reason and the building of an earthly paradise? How can one conceive of this "state within a state," this controlling force of reason among the blind and mindless elements, this serene paradise of human well-being in the midst of the omnipotent, chaotic clash of cosmic forces which have nothing to do with man, his aspirations, his misfortunes or his joys? But the thirst for universal human happiness and the need for a metaphysical substantiation of one's moral ideal are so great that this difficulty simply goes unnoticed, and atheistic materialism is calmly combined with the staunchest faith in future world harmony. The "scientific socialism" professed by the vast majority of the Russian intelligentsia even assumes that this metaphysical optimism is "scientifically proven."

In fact, the roots of this "theory of progress" go back to Rousseau and the rationalistic optimism of the eighteenth century. Contemporary social optimism, like Rousseau's, is convinced that all the misfortunes and imperfections of human life stem from the errors or malice of specific individuals or classes. Essentially, the natural conditions for human happiness are always at hand; all that is needed to inaugurate the reign of the earthly paradise is to do away with the injustice of the oppressors or the incomprehensible stupidity of the oppressed majority. Social optimism thus rests on a *mechanistic, rationalistic theory* of happiness. The problem of human happinesss, from this point of view, is a problem of the external organization of society; and since happiness is guaranteed by material goods, it is a problem of *distribution*. The minority that unjustly owns these goods needs only to be dispossessed, and deprived of the possibility of owning them once and for all, and human prosperity will be assured. Such is the simple but powerful train of thought that links nihilistic moralism with the *religion of socialism*.

Once a person has been seduced by this optimistic faith, he can no longer be satisfied with direct, altruistic, day-to-day service to the people's immediate needs. He is intoxicated with the ideal of the radical, universal achievement of the people's happiness. In comparison with this ideal, simple, individual, person-to-person aid, mere relief of current sorrows and anxieties, not only pales and loses its moral attractiveness but even seems a harmful waste of time and energy on petty, useless concerns, a betrayal of all mankind and its eternal salvation for the sake of a few individuals close at hand. And in fact, militant socialist populism not only displaced altruistic populism but morally slandered it as well, branding it as cheap and trivial "philanthropy." Holding as it does the simple and true key to the universal salvation of mankind, socialist populism cannot help but scorn and condemn prosaic, unending activity of the kind that is guided by direct altruistic sentiment. So widespread and intense is this attitude that by now even the "cultural workers" themselves generally are ashamed to acknowledge openly the simple, genuine meaning of their activity, and they justify themselves by referring to its usefulness for the common cause of the universal organization of mankind.

In theory, the same utilitarian altruism—the striving for the well-being of one's neighbor—lies at the basis of the socialist faith. But the abstract ideal of absolute happiness in the remote future destroys the concrete moral relationship of one individual to another and the vital sensation of love for one's neighbor, one's contemporaries and their current needs. The socialist is not an altruist. True, he too is striving for human happiness, but he does not love living people, only his *idea*, the idea of universal human happiness. Since he is sacrificing himself to this idea, he does not hesitate to sacrifice others as well. He can see his contemporaries only as victims of the world's evil that he dreams of eradicating, or as perpetrators of that evil. He pities the former but can provide them with no direct aid, since his activity will benefit only their remote descendants; consequently, there is no *genuine* feeling in his attitude toward them. The others he hates, and he regards the struggle against them as his immediate task and the fundamental means of achieving his ideal. It is this feeling of hatred for the enemies of the people that forms the concrete, active psychological foundation of his life. Thus, great love for future humanity engenders great hatred for people, the passion for building the earthly paradise becomes a passion for destruction, and the faithful populist-socialist becomes a *revolutionary*.

We must make a reservation at this point. When we speak of *revolutionism* as a typical feature of the Russian intelligentsia's mentality, we are not referring to its participation in political revolution, nor are we thinking of its political party complexion at all; our sole concern is the intelligentsia's *moral and social world-view*. One can participate in a revolution without having the world-view of a revolutionary, and, conversely, one can be a revolutionary in principle yet reject the necessity or timeliness of revolutionary action from considerations of tactics or expediency. Revolution, and specific activity in pursuit of goals that are revolutionary in regard to the existing order, are political phenomena, and as such they lie wholly outside the confines of our theme. Here we are speaking of revolutionary activity only in the sense of *revolutionism on principle*, the conviction that social struggle and the violent destruction of existing societal forms constitute the basic and intrinsically necessary means for achieving one's moral and social ideal. This conviction is an essential aspect of the world-view of socialist populism, where it has all the force of religious dogma. We cannot understand the Russian intelligentsia's moral life unless we take this dogma into account and understand its connection with the other elements of the intelligentsia's *profession de foi.*

The same motif that constitutes the driving force of the socialist faith underlies revolutionism: social *optimism*, and the *mechanistic, rationalistic theory of happiness* derived from it. According to this theory, as we have just noted, the intrinsic conditions for human happiness are always at hand, and the factors preventing the establishment of the earthly paradise lie not within man but outside him—in his social conditions or the imperfections of the social mechanism. And since these factors are external they can be removed by external, mechanical means. From this viewpoint, therefore, the promotion of human happiness is essentially not a creative or, strictly speaking, a constructive task, but merely a matter of clearing away and removing obstacles, in other words, of destruction. This theory—which, by the way, is usually not formulated explicitly but lives in people's minds as an unconscious, self-evident and tacitly implied truth—presumes that the harmonious organization of life is a natural condition, as it were, that will inevitably set in of its own accord once the obstacles barring the way have been swept aside; progress does not demand any creation in the strict sense of the word, or positive construction, only demolition, the destruction of the external barriers that obstruct it. "Die Lust der Zerstörung ist auch eine schaffende Lust," said Bakunin,[8] but the qualifier "auch" has long since disappeared from this aphorism; destruction is no longer seen as *one* of the means of creation, but has been identified with it altogether, or, more accurately, has completely replaced it. Here before us is an echo of the Rousseauism that inspired Robespierre with the conviction that the reign of reason could be ushered in only by the merciless elimination of the enemies of the fatherland.

Revolutionary socialism is permeated with the same faith. In order to establish the ideal order it is necessary to "expropriate the expropriators," which requires the "dictatorship of the proletariat," which in turn demands the elimination of all political obstacles and of external obstacles in general. Thus revolutionism merely reflects the metaphysical absolutization of the value of destruction. The intelligentsia believes that struggle, annihilation of the enemy, and the forcible, mechanical destruction of the old social forms are sufficient to guarantee the achievement of its social ideal; this belief accounts for all its political and social radicalism and its tendency to regard political struggle, and especially the most extreme techniques—conspiracy, insurrection, terrorism, etc.—as the shortest and most important path to the people's welfare. This is an entirely natural and logical belief, given the mech-

8. "The passion for destruction is also a creative passion," the concluding sentence of Bakunin's "The Reaction in Germany." *Eds.*

anistic, rationalistic theory of happiness. Mechanics does not provide for the creation of the new in the proper sense of the word. All man can do in regard to natural substances and forces is distribute them in a way he finds advantageous and destroy combinations of matter and energy that are harmful to him. If we view the problem of human culture as a mechanical problem, we are left with only two tasks: destruction of the old, harmful forms and redistribution of their elements into new, useful combinations. One must have an entirely different conception of human life in order to realize that in the cultural sphere these mechanical methods alone are unavailing and a new principle is needed—that of creative construction.

Hatred is always the psychological incentive and accompaniment of destruction, and to the degree that destruction overshadows other forms of activity, hatred displaces other impulses in the psychic life of the Russian *intelligent*. We have already remarked in another context that hatred for the enemies of the people is the basic passion motivating the populist revolutionary. In saying this we have absolutely no intention of "defaming" the *intelligent* or condemning him morally. By nature the Russian *intelligent* is most often a gentle, affectionate person, and if hatred has entrenched itself in his soul, the fault does not lie with his personal defects, nor is it in any way a personal or selfish hatred. His faith *obliges* him to hate; hatred serves as the most profound and passionate *ethical* impulse in his life, and, therefore, subjectively he cannot be blamed for it. Furthermore, we must admit that even from an objective point of view such a feeling of hatred, inspired by ethical motives, is often morally valuable and socially useful.

But if we proceed not from narrowly moralistic considerations but from broader philosophical ones, we must recognize that when hatred becomes entrenched at the center of spiritual life and consumes the love that engendered it, a harmful, abnormal degeneration of the moral personality takes place. We repeat: hatred corresponds to destruction and is the motive force in destruction, just as love is the motive force of creation and consolidation. Destructive energies are sometimes necessary in the economy of human life, and they can serve creative purposes. But to replace all creation by destruction, to supplant all the socially harmonizing passions with the discordant principle of hatred, distorts the proper and normal balance of forces in moral life. It is impossible to spend without accumulating; it is impossible to develop centrifugal forces without paralyzing them with a corresponding development of centripetal ones; it is impossible to concentrate on destruction without justifying it by creation and confining it to the narrow limits within which it really is necessary for creation; and it is impossible to hate without subordinating hatred, as an auxiliary accompaniment, to an active feeling of love.

Human life, like cosmic life, is permeated by the element of struggle. In a sense, struggle is an immanent form of human activity, and whatever a person may strive for, whatever he may create, he forever encounters obstacles and confronts enemies, and he must continually beat the plowshare and the pruning hook into the sword and the spear.[9] Nevertheless, there remains a radical difference between constructive labor and the labor of struggle, between productive work and warfare; only the former is intrinsically valuable and bears real fruit, while its needs provide the sole justification for the latter. This relationship applies to all areas of human life. Foreign war is sometimes necessary to secure the freedom and success of national life, but a society perishes when war keeps it from productive labor; internal war—revolution—can never be more than a temporarily necessary evil, and it cannot block social cooperation for long without harming the society; literature, art, science and religion degenerate when polemical struggle displaces the autonomous creation of new ideas; morality perishes when the negative forces of censure, condemnation and indignation begin to predominate over the positive impulses of love, approval and recognition. Struggle is always a necessary, but not a directly productive form of activity. It is not a good, but only an unavoidable evil, and wherever it supplants genuinely productive work it results in the impoverishment and decline of that area of life.

We can take production and war as symbols of the two primordial principles of human life. The normal relationship between them is the subordination of war to production, and this is always the condition for progress, for the accumulation of both material and spiritual wealth, and for genuinely successful human life. To sum up, we can now say that the fundamental moral and philosophical error of revolutionism is that it absolutizes the principle of struggle and consequently disregards the higher, universal principle of productivity.

When choosing between these two forms of human activity—destruction and creation, or struggle and productive labor—the intelligentsia wholly commits itself to the first; similarly, when confronted with the two basic methods for the social acquisition of goods (both material and spiritual), *distribution* and *production*, it again recognizes only the first. Distribution, like struggle or destruction, is a mechanical rearrangement of ready-made elements, in contrast to production, the creative formation of the new. And socialism is a world-view in which the idea of distribution has replaced the idea of production. True, as a socio-political program socialism proposes the reorganization of all aspects of economic life, and it protests against the notion that its goals can be reduced to taking wealth away from those who have it and giving it to those who do not. This is indeed a distorted simplification of socialism as a sociological or economic theory. Nonetheless, it does convey the spirit of socialism's social morality with total accuracy. The theory of economic organization is merely socialism's technique; its *soul* is the ideal of distribution, and its ultimate desire does in fact amount to taking goods from some in order to give them to others.

9. See Isaiah 2:4, Micah 4:3. *Eds.*

The moral pathos of socialism focuses exclusively on the idea of distributive justice. This morality too has its roots in the mechanistic, rationalistic theory of happiness, in the conviction that on the whole there is no need to *create* the conditions for happiness, since they can simply be seized or taken back from those who illicitly usurped them for their own benefit. The socialist faith is not the *source* of this idolatry of the principle of distribution. On the contrary, it is supported by it, like a sociological fruit borne by the metaphysical tree of mechanistic ethics.

The intelligentsia's exaltation of distribution over production is by no means restricted to material goods. It appears most vividly and is most essential in this sphere because on the whole the utilitarian ethic regards material security as the basic problem of human organization. But it is important to note that the same tendency governs the Russian intelligentsia's entire conception of the world. In all areas of life it values the production of goods less than their distribution. The intelligentsia is almost as unconcerned about spiritual production, the accumulation of ideal values, as it is about material production; the development of science, literature, art, and culture in general are much less dear to it than the distribution of ready-made spiritual goods to the masses. What it calls "cultural activity" is in fact merely the distribution of cultural goods, not their creation; it is not the person who creates culture, the scholar, artist, inventor or philosopher, who earns the honorable title of "cultural worker," but the person who distributes piecemeal to the masses the fruits of other people's creation, the teacher, popularizer, or propagandist.

A restatement of our earlier remarks on the relationship between struggle and productive labor will serve to evaluate this tendency. Distribution is unquestionably a necessary function of social life, and a just distribution of life's blessings and burdens is a legitimate and obligatory moral principle. But it is a philosophical error and a moral sin to absolutize distribution and forget production or creation for its sake. In order to distribute anything one must first possess, and in order to possess one must create or produce. An organism cannot survive without the proper exchange of substances, but in the last analysis it does not survive by exchange alone, but by consuming the requisite nutriments which come to it from outside. The same applies to the material and spiritual needs of the social organism. The spirit of socialist populism, which scorns production for the sake of distribution and regards it not just with indifference but with outright hostility, ultimately undermines the people's strength and perpetuates their material and spiritual poverty. Instead of participating in the *creation* of national wealth, the socialist intelligentsia dissipates its enormous energy on unproductive political struggle motivated by the idea of distribution. Thus it remains sterile, metaphysically speaking, and despite its cherished and most valuable aspirations it leads a parasitic existence on the body of the nation.

It is time we finally understood that our life is not simply unjust, but is primarily poor and squalid, and that the poverty-stricken cannot become rich if they devote all their attention solely to the equal distribution of their few pennies. We must realize that the notorious distinction between "national wealth" and "popular welfare"—the distinction between accumulating goods and supplying the people with them—is only relative, and is of vital importance only for the truly rich nations. Thus, if occasionally it is appropriate to recall that national wealth does not in itself ensure popular welfare, for us it is infinitely more important to keep in mind the simpler and more obvious truth that without national wealth popular welfare is quite inconceivable. It is time we reduced the number of middlemen, conveyors, watchmen, administrators, and distributors of all kinds in the total economy of our national culture and increased the number of genuine producers. In a word, it is time we advanced from distribution and the struggle for it to cultural creation and the production of wealth.

IV

But in order to produce wealth, one must love it. We are here using the concept of wealth not in the sense of mere material riches, but in a broader philosophical sense which includes the possession of both material and spiritual goods, or, more precisely, which regards material well-being as only an accessory and a symbolic index of spiritual power and productivity. This metaphysical concept of wealth coincides with the idea of culture as the aggregate of ideal values embodied in historical life. Hence, in connection with what we said earlier, it is clear that the intelligentsia's disregard of the principle of productivity or creation for the sake of the principle of struggle and distribution is neither a theoretical error nor simply a miscalculation of the way to achieve the people's welfare. On the contrary, it rests on a delusion in the sphere of morality or religious philosophy. It results, in the final analysis, from nihilistic moralism, the non-recognition of absolute values and aversion to the idea of culture that is based on them. But this reveals a novel and curious intellectual nuance of nihilistic moralism.

The Russian intelligentsia does not love wealth. In the first place, it does not value spiritual wealth, or culture—the ideal force and creative activity of the human spirit that impels it to master and humanize the world and to enrich its life with the values of science, art, religion and ethics. What is more remarkable, it even extends this dislike to material wealth, instinctively recognizing its symbolic connection with the general idea of culture. The intelligentsia loves only the just distribution of wealth, not wealth itself, which it actually hates and fears. In its soul, love of the *poor* turns into love of *poverty*. It dreams of feeding all the poor, but its deepest metaphysical instinct unconsciously opposes the propagation of genuine wealth in the world. In his remarkable essay, *The Soul of Man under Socialism*, Oscar Wilde says, "There is only one class of people more selfish than the rich, and that is the *poor*."[10] In the Russian *intelligent*'s soul, however, from an obscure cranny the opposite evaluation issues, indistinctly, but powerfully and persistently: "there is only one condition worse than poverty, and that is wealth." Anyone who can read between the lines will easily discern this sentiment in the acts and thoughts of the Russian intelligentsia.

This internally contradictory attitude reflects what we may term the fundamental antinomy of the intelligentsia's world-view: the interweaving of the irreconcilable principles of nihilism and moralism into a single whole. The intelligentsia's nihilism leads to utilitarianism and forces it to regard gratification of material interests as the only authentic and truly necessary concern, while its moralism impels it to a renunciation of material gratification, a simplification of life, and an ascetic rejection of wealth. This contradiction is frequently avoided by applying the two principles to different spheres of life. Asceticism becomes the ideal of *personal* life, and is justified on the moralistic grounds that personal enjoyment of life's blessings is impermissible until they have become the property of everyone. Meanwhile, the ultimate ideal, what might be called the principled ideal, remains wealth and the broadest satisfaction of needs. Most *intelligenty* consciously believe and profess just this kind of rational combination of personal asceticism and universal utilitarianism, and apparently it also forms the rational first premise in the intelligentsia's philosophy.

But of course this only evades the logical contradiction between nihilism and moralism that we discussed at the beginning of this article, it does not eliminate it. In the final analysis, each of these elements contains a self-sufficient, primary quality which naturally tries to gain complete possession of the consciousness and displace its opposite. If there are no universally binding values in the world and everything is relative and conditional, determined by human needs and the human thirst for happiness and enjoyment, then on what grounds must I renounce the satisfaction of my own needs? This is the argument nihilism uses to destroy moralism. In literature this tendency is personified in the nihilist (in the narrow sense of the word) figure of Bazarov; in real life it has become very widespread today in the phenomena of "Saninism," vulgarized "Nietzscheism" (which clearly has nothing in common with Nietzsche and which also terms itself, more legitimately, "Stirnerism"), "expropriationism," etc.

But the classic Russian *intelligent* undoubtedly leans in the other direction, toward the displacement of nihilism by moralism. That is, he transforms asceticism from a personal practice justified on utilitarian grounds into a universal

10. The original reads: "There is only one class in the community that thinks more about money than the rich, and that is the poor." *The Complete Works of Oscar Wilde*, 12 vols. (Garden City, N.Y.: Doubleday, Page, 1923), X, 18. *Eds.*

moral outlook. This tendency was expressed consciously only in the brief episode of Tolstoyism, and this was quite natural since asceticism as a conscious dogma must have a religious foundation. But it can be said that unconsciously the entire Russian intelligentsia has it in its blood. Asceticism gradually passes from the realm of personal practice to the realm of theory, or, to be more precise, it becomes an all-embracing and self-sufficient, if unsubstantiated, faith, a general spiritual outlook, an organic moral instinct that determines all practical value judgments.

The Russian *intelligent* feels a positive love for the simplification, impoverishment and constriction of life. A social reformer, he is also, and even more so, a monk who hates worldly vanity and diversions, all luxury, whether material or spiritual, all wealth and substance, all power and productivity. He loves the weak, the poor, the wretched in body and spirit, but not just as unfortunates whom he can help make strong and rich, thereby eliminating them as social or spiritual types; he loves them precisely as ideal types of humanity. He wants to make the people wealthy but fears wealth itself as a burden and temptation, and he believes that all the rich are evil while all the poor are good and kind. He strives for the "dictatorship of the proletariat" and dreams of giving power to the people, yet fears any contact with power; he considers it evil and all who wield it oppressors. He wants to give the people enlightenment, spiritual benefits and spiritual strength, but in the depths of his soul he feels that spiritual wealth, too, is a luxury and believes that purity of intention can compensate for and outweigh any knowledge or skill. The ideal of a simple, guileless, squalid but innocent life attracts him. The Russian national hero Ivanushka the Fool, "the blessed," whose simplicity of heart and holy naiveté conquer all the strong, rich, and clever ones, is the Russian intelligentsia's hero as well.

Thus, in both the material and the spiritual realms the intelligentsia values only distribution and not production or accumulation, only equality in the enjoyment of goods and not their actual abundance. Its ideal is a life that is innocent and pure, though poor, rather than a life that is truly rich, abundant and powerful. But while asceticism clashes with and opposes utilitarianism in the appreciation of material wealth, creating a kind of unstable equilibrium, when it comes to appreciating spiritual wealth or the general idea of culture, on the other hand, ascetic self-restraint is reinforced by nihilistic unbelief and materialism; these two elements then join forces in endorsing a negative attitude toward culture, consolidating barbarism and giving it a principled justification.

In summary, we can define the classic Russian *intelligent* as a *militant monk of the nihilistic religion of earthly well-being*. If there are contradictions in this combination of traits, they are the living contradictions of the *intelligent*'s soul. First of all, the *intelligent* is a monk both in his outlook and in his way of life. He shuns reality, flees the world, and lives apart from actual, historical, everyday life in a world of phantoms, dreams and pious faith. The intelligentsia is like an autonomous state, a separate little world with its own very strong and rigorous traditions, its own etiquette, mores and customs, almost its own culture. It can be said that nowhere in Russia are there such firmly established traditions, such a clear and strict regulation of life, such categorical judgments of people and situations, and such loyalty to the corporate spirit as in this all-Russian spiritual monastery, the Russian intelligentsia. And in conformity with this monastic isolation it adheres to a monastically strict asceticism, exalts poverty and simplicity, and avoids all the temptations of vain, sinful worldly life.

But although he is secluded in his monastery, the *intelligent* is not indifferent to the world. On the contrary, he wishes to rule the world from his monastery and to propagate his faith in it. He is a militant monk, a monk-revolutionary. For the intelligentsia the political goal is not so much the introduction of some objectively useful reform, in the worldly sense, as the destruction of the enemies of its faith and the forcible conversion of the world. This monastically religious spirit is responsible for the intelligentsia's entire approach to politics— its fanaticism and intolerance, its impracticality and ineffectiveness in political affairs, its unbearable tendency to factionalism, and its lack of political common sense.

Finally, the *content* of this faith is the idolatry of earthly material wellbeing, an idolatry based on religious unbelief. All the enthusiasm of this monastic army is devoted to earthly, material interests and needs, to the creation of an earthly paradise of satiety and security. It regards anything transcendental, otherworldly or authentically religious, any faith in absolute values, as its outright, hated enemy. With ascetic rigor toward itself and others, fanatical hatred for enemies and heretics, sectarian bigotry, and unlimited despotism feeding on the awareness of its own infallibility, this monastic order labors to satisfy earthly, too "human" concerns about "bread alone." It uses all its asceticism and religious ardor, all the strength of its self-sacrifice and its resolve to sacrifice others, to serve subjective, relative, transitory interests—the only ones that nihilism and materialist unbelief can acknowledge. The most worldly matters and needs become the object of religious devotion, to be fulfilled in accordance with a universal plan drawn up by means of metaphysical dogmas and strict monastic regulations. A handful of monks, alien to the world and scorning it, declare war on the world so as forcibly to bring it great benefits and gratify its earthly, material needs.

V

It was only natural that sooner or later this mass of contradictions, this merging of divergent and, in principle, antagonistic elements that we find in the intelligentsia's traditional intellectual framework, would become manifest, and that their mutually repellent force, so to speak, would explode, shattering that framework. And this happened, as soon as the intelligentsia had the opportunity to test its faith in actual practice. The fate of our recent social movement has profound cultural and philosophical significance primarily because of the way it revealed the unsoundness of the Russian intelligentsia's world-view and its entire spiritual constitution. All the blindness and inherent contradiction of the intelligentsia's faith became apparent when the small underground sect emerged into the light of day, attracted a multitude of followers, and for a time acquired intellectual influence and even real power. Above all, this showed that monastic asceticism, fanaticism, solitude and hatred for the world are incompatible with genuine social creativity.

To a certain extent, public opinion has already recognized this aspect of the situation and taken it into account. Another, which is essentially more important, has not yet been assessed at its proper worth. That is the contradiction between moralism and nihilism, between the universally binding, religiously absolute *character* of the intelligentsia's faith and its nihilistically unprincipled *content*. The significance of this contradiction is by no means merely theoretical or abstract; it produces real, poisonous fruits. The non-recognition of absolute, truly binding values, and the cult of the material benefit of the majority, provide justification for the primacy of might over right and for the dogmas of the supremacy of the class struggle and the "class interest of the proletariat"; in practice, this means the idolatrous worship of party interests, and results in that unprincipled "hottentot" morality that judges deeds and thoughts from the point of view of their partisan usefulness or harm, rather than objectively or substantively. These dogmas are also responsible for the monstrous, morally inadmissible inconsistency in regard to terrorism from the right or the left, black or red pogroms, and for the fact that a just, unbiased attitude toward one's opponents is not simply absent but is rejected in principle.[11]

11. With remarkable insight, the late A. I. Ertel' long ago noticed the Russian intelligentsia's lack of principle, and he described it in a recently published letter of 1892: ". . . any protest that claims to be productive must originate . . . in the philosophical and religious convictions of the protestor himself. . . . Most of our 'protestants' fail to realize why the arbitrariness, coerciveness and high-handedness of the authorities outrage them, for while they are angered at these qualities in one instance, in another they are delighted *by the very same ones*—as long as they are exhibited not by Pobedonostsev, but by Gambetta, or someone of that sort. . . . The keystone of public conduct must be established not by statistics or the peasants' conditions, nor by some defect or other in the national economy or politics in general, but by a philosophical and religious understanding of one's own personal task." *The Letters of A. I. Ertel'* [Pis'ma A. I. Ertelia], edited and with an introduction by M. O. Gershenzon (Moscow: I. D. Sytin, 1909), pp. 294-95.

[Aleksandr Ivanovich Ertel' (1855-1908) was a Populist author, primarily of sketches and short stories, and a critic of the intelligentsia. Konstantin Petrovich Pobedonostsev

But this is not all. As soon as party ranks were disrupted, partly by failure and partly by a large influx of less disciplined, intellectually more primitive members, the same lack of principle led to the replacement of class and party nihilism by personal nihilism, or, in plain words, by hoodlum violence. The subjectively pure, disinterested, self-sacrificing devotees of the social faith turned out to be not only the political allies but the spiritual kin of robbers, murderers, hoodlums, and debauchees—this is the most tragic and, on a superficial level, surprising development of our recent cultural history. But it followed logically from the very content of the intelligentsia's faith, and specifically from its nihilism, and this must be acknowledged frankly, without gloating but with the deepest sorrow. The worst part of it is that the nihilism of the intelligentsia's faith seems involuntarily to sanction criminality and hooliganism and allows them to wear the mantle of ideological commitment and progressive thought.

The total sterility and impotence of the intelligentsia's consciousness when it came into contact with the real forces of life, and, on the other hand, the moral rottenness which practical activity revealed in some of its roots, are symptoms that cannot disappear without a trace. Indeed, we are witnessing the collapse and disintegration of the traditional intelligentsia spirit. The Russian *intelligent* as we have tried to portray him, a complete and integral moral character-type despite all his contradictions, is beginning to disappear before our eyes and soon will exist only as an ideal, a glorious memory of the past. In fact, this model has already lost its former unlimited sovereignty over people's minds, and only rarely is it embodied in pure form in the younger generation. Right now everything is confused: the Social Democrats are discussing God, studying aesthetics, fraternizing with "mystical anarchists," losing faith in materialism, and reconciling Marx with Mach and Nietzsche; a peculiar mystical socialism is becoming popular in the guise of syndicalism; "class interests" are somehow being combined with the "sex problem" and decadent poetry. Only a few old representatives of the classical Populism of the seventies wander about despondently and futilely in this dissonant babel of tongues and beliefs, like the last members of a once-powerful but now unproductive and soon-to-be-extinct cultural species.

There is no reason to be surprised at this crisis of the old intelligentsia consciousness, and still less to be grieved. On the contrary, we should be surprised at how slowly and unconsciously it is proceeding, more like an involuntary organic disease than a conscious cultural and philosophical reorganization. And there is cause for regret that despite the steady disintegration of the old

(1827-1907), professor of law and Procurator of the Holy Synod from 1880 to 1905, was the outstanding reactionary political figure of the reigns of Alexander III and Nicholas II. Léon Gambetta (1838-82), a radical lawyer and statesman, was one of the founders of the Third French Republic. *Eds.*]

faith, new ideas and ideals are emerging too weakly and vaguely, so that we cannot yet foresee the end of the crisis.

We need one thing to speed up this agonizing transitional period: conscious elucidation of the foundations of the prevailing ideas in morality and religious philosophy. In order to understand why an idea is erroneous or one-sided and find a corrective to it, it is usually enough to be fully aware of its ultimate premises, to touch its deepest roots, as it were. Our ideological chaos and turmoil has thus been prolonged by an inadequate concern with moral and metaphysical problems and an exclusive concentration on the technical problem of means rather than on ultimate goals and first causes.

Perhaps the most remarkable trait of the recent Russian social movement, and one that has had a telling impact on its fate, is its *lack of philosophical reflection and understanding*. Such historical movements as, for example, the great English or French revolutions tried to bring to life new, independently reasoned and developed philosophical ideas and values, and to lead national life onto the still untrodden paths revealed by the profound, bold investigations of creative political thought. Our social movement, by contrast, was guided by old themes which had been taken on faith, and not even from their original sources but at second- or third-hand. The absence of independent intellectual activity in our social movement, its profound philosophical conservatism, is so generally acknowledged and undisputed that it attracts scarcely any attention and is considered natural and normal.

The socialist idea that dominates our intelligentsia's mind was adopted whole, without criticism or verification, in the form in which it had crystallized in the West after a century of intellectual ferment. Its roots go back to the individualistic rationalism of the eighteenth century, on the one hand, and, on the other, to the philosophy of reactionary romanticism that arose out of intellectual dismay at the outcome of the great French Revolution. In believing in Lassalle and Marx, essentially we are believing in the values and ideas developed by Rousseau and de Maistre, Holbach and Hegel, Burke and Bentham; we are feeding on scraps from the philosophical table of the eighteenth and early nineteenth centuries. And when we assimilate these venerable ideas, the majority of which are already more than a century old, we pay absolutely no attention to these roots; we use the fruits without even asking from what tree they were picked, and we blindly assert their value without questioning their foundations. It is very typical of this philosophical mindlessness that of all the formulations of socialism the one that acquired overwhelming sovereignty over our minds was Marx's doctrine—a system which, despite the breadth of its scientific structure, not only lacks any philosophical and ethical basis whatsoever, but rejects it on principle. (Of course, this does not prevent it from actually resting on the crude, unverified premises of the materialist, sensationalist faith.)

Insofar as a striving for new values, intellectual initiative, and a thirst to organize one's life in accordance with one's own independently derived concepts and convictions still survive, this vital agitation of the spirit instinctively avoids the high road of life and confines itself to the isolated individual. Still worse, if it does occasionally succeed in penetrating the accretion of prevailing ideas and attracting attention, it is perceived superficially, in a purely literary manner; it turns into a fashionable novelty that makes no demands and is denatured by being interwoven with the old intellectual traditions and mental habits.

But here, as always, it is well to recall Nietzsche's penetrating words: "the earth turns not around the inventors of new noises, but around the inventors of new values!" The Russian intelligentsia, for all the defects and contradictions of its traditional mentality, has hitherto possessed one precious formal quality: it always sought a faith and tried to subordinate its life to its faith. And so it stands now before the very great and important task of reviewing its old values and creatively mastering new ones. To be sure, this revolution may prove so decisive that once the intelligentsia has accomplished it, it will cease to be an "intelligentsia" in the old, customary Russian sense of the word. But that would be all to the good! Perhaps a new intelligentsia is waiting to replace the old, one that will purify the intelligentsia's name of the historical sins heaped upon it while preserving inviolate the word's noble connotation. Once it has broken with the tradition of the immediate past it will be able to support and consolidate a longer and deeper tradition, extending its hand across the seventies to the thirties and forties to revive in new form what was eternal and of absolute value in the quest of the spiritual pioneers of that era. If we may note aphoristically what this revolution must involve, let us conclude our critical reflections with one positive suggestion. We must pass from unproductive, anti-cultural *nihilistic moralism* to creative, culturally constructive *religious humanism*.

A GUIDE TO NAMES AND TERMS

AKSAKOVS, THE, were a noble family whose origins went back to pre-Petrine times. Sergei Timofeevich (1791-1859), author of the autobiographical novel *The Family Chronicle*, has been called the first Slavophile. His sons, Konstantin (1817-60) and Ivan (1823-86), were two of the leading spokesmen of the Slavophile group.

AKSEL'ROD, PAVEL BORISOVICH (1850-1928), was one of the founders of Russian Social Democracy and later a leader of the Mensheviks. After the party split of 1903, and particularly in the wake of the 1905 revolution, Aksel'rod became one of the leading advocates of an open, mass workers' party in place of the narrow elite of professional revolutionaries defended by Lenin.

ALEKSINSKII, GRIGORII ALEKSEEVICH, was the leader of the Bolshevik group in the Second Duma, but he soon broke with Lenin and became the principal spokesman for the extreme left-wing faction of the Bolsheviks before World War I.

ALTHUSIUS, JOHANNES (1557-1638), was a legal philosopher with Calvinist and republican convictions. His major work was a general study of politics, *Politica Methodice Digesta et Exemplis Sacris et Profanis Illustrata* (1603).

ARTEL': a traditional form of peasant labor cooperative, used especially by itinerant groups of artisans or industrial laborers.

AVENARIUS, RICHARD (1843-96), was the founder of empirio-criticism, an epistemological theory which regarded "pure experience," i.e., experience cleansed of all metaphysical ingredients, as the sole source of knowledge. His principal work was *Kritik der reinen Erfahrung*, published in two volumes (1888-90).

AZEV, EVNO (1869-1918), was a leader of the Socialist-Revolutionary Party and the chief of its Fighting Organization, the party's terrorist arm, which carried out a number of political assassinations in the early years of the twentieth century. In 1909 it was disclosed that throughout his career as a revolutionary Azev had doubled as an agent of the tsarist secret police.

BAKUNIN, MIKHAIL ALEKSANDROVICH (1814-76), was one of the key figures in the development of socialist anarchism. His conflict with Marx split and ultimately destroyed the First International. The keynote of Bakunin's anarchism was revolt, a passionate, destructive, elemental rejection of social and political authority in general, and of its focal point, the state, in particular. He was especially interested in arousing the most down-trodden and potentially explosive elements of the population, those who he believed could be counted on to carry out the most thorough destruction of the old order. He was an uncompromising atheist, contending that the idea of God was the origin and justification of all hierarchical authority, and thence of human oppression. "The passion for destruction is also a creative passion" ("Die Lust der Zerstörung ist auch eine schaffende Lust") is from "The Reaction in Germany" [Die Reaktion in Deutschland], which Bakunin published under the pseudonym Jules Elysard in *Deutsche Jahrbücher für Wissenschaft und Kunst*, V, No. 247-52, 17-21 Oct. 1842, pp. 985-1002.

BELINSKII, VISSARION GRIGOR'EVICH (1811-48), was the most influential literary critic of the 1840s. His passionately written articles and reviews stressed the social responsibility of the writer, whose duty it was to reflect the progressive aspirations of society. Emphasizing the ideological rather than aesthetic content of literature, Belinskii helped to determine the radical intelligentsia's standard of literary judgment.

BEL'TOV: See Plekhanov

BERGSON, HENRI (1859-1941), was the most influential French philosopher of the turn of the century. In his doctrine of vitalism he emphasized the primacy of intuition and instinct over intellect and urged that life be experienced directly rather than dissected by rational analysis.

BERNSTEIN, EDUARD (1850-1932), a leading figure in the German Social-Democratic Party, aroused a major controversy with his attempt to "revise" Marxism by changing it from a revolutionary to a gradualist doctrine. Bernstein's criticisms of Marxism had, in fact, been anticipated slightly by the Russian "Legal Marxists," who included Struve, Berdiaev, Frank, and Bulgakov himself. In his article Bulgakov implicitly accepted Bernstein's "revisionist" view that the goal of the socialist movement is immaterial, it is the movement itself, with its successive partial victories, that constitutes the essence of socialism.

BESELER, KARL GEORG CHRISTOPH (1809-88), in *Volksrecht und Juristenrecht* (1843), argued in favor of studying the indigenous element in German law. His major theoretical contribution to jurisprudence was the development of "association law," based on the old Germanic ideas of association. As a member of the Prussian parliament he contributed to the Prussian code of 1851.

BLACK HUNDREDS were right-wing bands of ruffians which appeared during the 1905 revolution. They specialized in attacks on Jews and liberal intellectuals, and were responsible for many of the anti-Semitic *pogroms* that marked the period.

BOGDANOV [MALINOVSKII], ALEKSANDR ALEKSANDROVICH (1873-1928), was a leading Bolshevik until 1909, when he and Lenin parted ways. Strongly influenced by Mach and Avenarius, he considerably modified the philosophical bases of Marxism, most notably by denying the relevance of the concept of matter and, consequently, of materialism.

BOLSHEVIKS: See Russian Social-Democratic Workers' Party

BUKHAREV, ALEKSANDR MATVEEVICH, Archimandrite Fedor (1822-71), was a student and teacher in the theological seminaries. Central to his thinking was the acceptance of secular culture and the denial that it was opposed to Christianity. His views evoked opposition within the Church hierarchy, and Bukharev, unable to publish as a monk, gave up monastic life in the name of religious freedom.

BUNDISTS were members of the General Union of Jewish Workers in Russia and Poland, or, as it was more commonly known, the Jewish Social-Democratic *Bund*. The Bund represented most of the organized Jewish workers of the Pale of Settlement. It consistently adopted a moderate line, and it left the Russian Social-Democratic Party (temporarily) at the Second Congress when it lost its fight to be acknowledged as the sole representative of the Jewish workers.

CAUSE, THE [DELO] : See Shelgunov

CHAADAEV, PETR IAKOVLEVICH (1794-1856), occupies a central position in nineteenth-century Russian thought. His first "Philosophical Letter," written in 1829 and published in 1836, electrified its readers with its severely negative view of Russia as a cultural backwater, while expressing deep admiration for the unity and cultural achievements of the Christian West. It raised two fundamental questions that would continue to preoccupy Russian thinkers: the relationship between Russia and the West, and that between religion and culture.

CHERNYSHEVSKII, NIKOLAI GAVRILOVICH (1828-89), was a journalist who specialized in economic and social problems and became one of the leading radical writers of the sixties. Philosophically a materialist, he viewed man as a biological organism and the natural sciences as the proper tool for the study of man. In his utopian novel *What Is to Be Done?* (1863), however, he also concerned himself with the moral features of the new socialist order he hoped would arise in Russia.

CHICHERIN, BORIS NIKOLAEVICH (1828-1904), a university professor and mayor of Moscow, was a Russian "liberal conservative" who believed in the possibility of achieving liberty along with order and resolutely opposed socialism. His philosophy was a variant of Hegelianism, modified in particular by the stress he placed on the absolute significance of the human personality.

COHEN, HERMAN (1842-1918), was the leader of the Marburg school of neo-Kantianism, which concentrated on inquiry into the logical foundation of the natural sciences.

CONSTITUTIONAL-DEMOCRATIC PARTY (commonly called the Kadets, from the Russian initials of the party's name) was Russia's leading liberal party and the dominant group in the first two State Dumas (1906–07). Most of the *Vekhi* contributors were associated with the Kadets at one time.

CORNELIUS, HANS (1863-1947), was a neo-Kantian positivist.

DECEMBRISTS: army officers, mostly of noble birth, who staged the Decembrist revolt of 14 December 1825, an unsuccessful attempt at a *coup d'état* which was to be followed by liberal political and social reforms. Their attempt is often considered the first modern revolutionary movement in Russia.

DMITRII DONSKOI: in 1380 Dmitrii, Grand Prince of Moscow and Vladimir (1359-89), defeated the forces of the Golden Horde at Kulikovo Field on the Don River (and was thenceforth known as Dmitrii "of the Don," or Donskoi). Dmitrii's victory was the first serious challenge to the Tatars since their conquest of Russia a century and a half earlier; although they soon reasserted their supremacy, it marked the beginning of the end of their domination.

DOBROLIUBOV, NIKOLAI ALEKSANDROVICH (1836-61), until consumption cut short his brief career, was one of the most influential radical journalists of the reform period. Along with Chernyshevskii and Pisarev, he was a leading exponent of "nihilism." He was particularly noted for his literary reviews, which he used as springboards for social criticism.

"ECONOMISTS" were exponents of a school of thought within the Social-Democratic Party at the turn of the century. "Economism" regarded labor organization and the struggle for economic betterment of the workers as the immediate tasks of Social Democracy. The "economists" were vehemently and successfully opposed by the more politically-minded wing of the party, and especially by Lenin, whose *What Is to Be Done?* (1902) is an extended diatribe against them.

"EXPROPRIATIONS": a euphemism employed by the revolutionary parties to describe bank robberies perpetrated to gain funds for political activities.

FARABEUF, LOUIS-HUBERT, was a leading French surgeon and professor of medicine at the turn of the century.

FET, AFANASII AFANAS'EVICH (1820-92), was a major lyric poet with reactionary political views.

FEUERBACH, LUDWIG (1804-72), was one of the leaders of the Young Hegelian group of German philosophers of the early 1840s. His political radicalism and philosophical materialism constituted the major link between Hegel and Marx, although Marx later repudiated his views.

FICHTE, JOHANN GOTTLIEB (1762-1814), was a German romantic idealist philosopher who tried to resolve some of the basic problems left by Kant. He is now remembered chiefly for being one of the founders of virulent German nationalism.

FRIES, JAKOB FRIEDRICH (1773-1843), was primarily a critical philosopher. However, his progressive political views were expressed in his *Ethik* (1818), which stressed the ideals of individual liberty and political equality.

GARSHIN, VSEVOLOD MIKHAILOVICH (1855-88), is best known for his short stories. He attempted to share the life of the people and told of this life in highly symbolic prose. Oppressed by a sense of guilt, he became insane and committed suicide.

GEPNER, KARL FEDOROVICH, served as professor of surgery at the St.

Petersburg Medical-Surgical Academy and was the author of *A Concise Guide to Operative Surgery* (1876-80).

GUROVICH, M., was a police agent who financed and published *The Beginning* [Nachalo], the organ of the "Legal Marxists" at the end of the nineties.

GYMNASIUM, THE, was a secondary school that prepared students for university.

HERBART, JOHANN FRIEDRICH (1776-1841), was a philosopher, psychologist and educational theorist.

HERZEN, ALEKSANDR IVANOVICH (1812-70), was perhaps the single most important member of the early intelligentsia. A Westernizing opponent of the Slavophiles in the Moscow circles of the 1840s, Herzen emigrated to Western Europe in time to observe the revolutions of 1848 and became disillusioned with Western life. He laid the foundations for Populism with his belief that Russia would lead the West in the revolution to destroy middle-class civilization. Herzen not only disseminated his own views for many years, but also published newspapers and magazines which provided a forum for the views of other revolutionaries. His great personal wealth also enabled him to provide support to a considerable segment of the revolutionary intelligentsia.

IURKEVICH, PAMFIL DANILOVICH (1827-74), studied and taught at the Kiev Theological Academy before becoming professor of philosophy at Moscow University in the early 1860s. Iurkevich alienated the radical intelligentsia of the time with a criticism of Chernyshevskii's materialism. His philosophical work was grounded in the belief that the focal point of man's existence is not his intellectual life but the spiritual life of the heart.

IVANOV, VIACHESLAV IVANOVICH (1866-1949), was a symbolist poet and one of the leaders of the St. Petersburg intellectual elite of the Silver Age.

JAMES, WILLIAM (1842-1910), brother of novelist Henry James, was the first American philosopher to receive international attention. His theory of pragmatism was an attempt to avoid the problems of epistemology by arguing that a proposition is true if believing it is useful to the believer.

JHERING, RUDOLF von (1818-92), was noted particularly for his work on Roman law. In opposition to the historical school, he placed the individual, not the nation, at the center of his philosophy of law, and he was one of the earliest jurists to view law as something that interacts with society, rather than a self-contained system. In *Der Kampf ums Recht*, first published in 1872 and subsequently translated into over twenty languages, he argued that a person is morally obligated to defend his legal rights.

KADETS: See Constitutional-Democratic Party

KHOMIAKOV, ALEKSEI STEPANOVICH (1804-60), was the outstanding philosopher and theologian of the Slavophile group. Khomiakov affirmed Russia's spiritual superiority to the West on the grounds that she had succeeded in uniting the principles of freedom and authority within a context of love. He found the spontaneous harmony of Russian life embodied most fully in the communal spirit (*sobornost'*) of the Orthodox Church. His descendants continued to play a prominent role in Russian intellectual and political life, remaining in the Slavophile camp. In the twentieth century, Nikolai Khomiakov was active in the Octobrist Party and served briefly as president of the Duma.

KHORTITSA, ISLAND OF: See Zaporozhian sech'

KOZLOV, ALEKSEI ALEKSANDROVICH (1831-1901), was the first important Russian philosopher inspired by Leibniz.

KRAUSE, KARL CHRISTIAN FRIEDRICH (1781-1832), was a pantheistic philosopher who argued that social organization should be governed by Right. He subordinated the rights of individuals, groups and nations to the right of humanity.

KROPOTKIN, PRINCE PETR ALEKSEEVICH (1842-1921), gave up the promising military career for which his birth and education had prepared him, and became a professional geologist and then a revolutionary. After a spectacular jailbreak he emigrated to Western Europe, where he established his reputation and where he remained until the revolution of 1917. A follower of Bakunin in his advocacy of collective, socialist anarchism, Kropotkin's views were in general far more gentle and magnanimous. He played down the elements of violence and destructiveness, and stressed instead the cooperative instincts of mankind and the application of modern scientific techniques as the stepping-stones to the future order.

KULAK (literally, "fist") was the colloquial term for a well-to-do peasant, one who might hire other peasants to work for him or serve as the village money-lender.

LASSALLE, FERDINAND (1825-64), was the founder of what became the German Social-Democratic Party. He differed from Marx in advocating a kind of state socialism, in which the socialist goals of the workers' party were to be achieved through the state rather than against it.

LAVROV, PETR LAVROVICH (1823-1900), was one of the chief inspirers of the Populist movement in the late sixties and seventies. His most influential work was the *Historical Letters*, which first appeared in 1868 and 1869. It had a strong ethical and emotional appeal for the young people of the time, telling them that they owed a moral debt to the peasants, whose toil and sufferings had made the higher culture of the intellectual elite possible. (His unfinished, two-volume work, *An Essay on the History of Modern Thought*, 1888-94, traced the history of human thought from the creation of the cosmos.)

LAW [PRAVO] was published weekly in St. Petersburg from 1898 to 1917. It was edited by a group of liberal legal theorists.

LEONT'EV, KONSTANTIN NIKOLAEVICH (1831-91), was a severe and pessimistic critic of nineteenth-century culture. Taking up some of the Slavophiles' themes, he believed that Western Europe was in an advanced state of disintegration and must be prevented from contaminating Russia. To protect Russia from the evils of "Westernism," he advocated the defense of her native institutions, particularly Orthodoxy and autocracy, and—unlike the Slavophiles—he advocated a generally repressive political and cultural regime.

LILBURNE, JOHN (1614?-57), was a leading spokesman for the Levellers, one of the most radical democratic groups in the English Puritan revolution.

LOPATIN, LEV MIKHAILOVICH (1855-1920), was an idealist philosopher who developed Leibniz's metaphysical system, concentrating principally on its ethical dimension.

LOSSKII, NIKOLAI ONUFR'EVICH (1870-1965), was for many years the dean of Russian philosophers in emigration. His system was drawn largely from Leibniz, and he is best known for his doctrine of "intuitivism," an epistemological theory based on intuition.

LUNACHARSKII, ANATOLII VASIL'EVICH (1875-1933), later People's Commissar of Education, studied philosophy under Avenarius and adopted empirio-criticism as an epistemological method. He was also influenced by Nietzsche. He and Maksim Gor'kii were accused by orthodox Marxists of "god-seeking" and a return to religion; the basis for the charge was their belief that traditional religious feeling could be given a new socialist content.

MACH, ERNST (1838-1916), scientist and philosopher, arrived at a positivist doctrine which regarded experience as the sole source of knowledge. He was particularly interested in the methodology of the physical sciences and in purifying them of metaphysical elements. He was the spiritual father of the Vienna Circle and its logical positivism.

"MAXIMALISTS": the extremist wing of the Socialist-Revolutionary Party. In 1906 they broke with the SR's on the grounds that the latter were too moderate and gradualist. The maximalists believed that a full-scale socialist order could be attained in Russia immediately, and that revolutionary activity, particularly in the form of terrorism, should be pressed until that goal was reached.

MENSHEVIKS: See Russian Social-Democratic Workers' Party

MEREZHKOVSKII, DMITRII SERGEEVICH (1865-1941), novelist, critic and philosopher, proclaimed the "Third Testament of the Holy Spirit," which would correct the one-sidedness of both pagan civilization and ascetic Christianity. In the wake of the revolution of 1905, he ceased to be a monarchist and preached a kind of religio-mystical anarchism.

MERKEL, ADOLF JOSEF (1836-96), was a leading German law professor who believed that with the evolution of legal systems the law would come to act as a neutral mediator between conflicting interests.

MIKHAILOVSKII, NIKOLAI KONSTANTINOVICH (1842-1904), was one of the leading theorists of Populism. In his best-known essay, "What Is Progress?", a critique of Herbert Spencer's views that he published in 1869, he formulated his notion of "subjective sociology." Instead of searching for objective, impersonal laws of social development, sociological inquiry must focus on the feelings and aspirations of the individual; progress, therefore, was to be measured not by objective standards but in terms of the happiness and well-being of the individual personality.

MUZHIK: colloquial term for a peasant.

NEKRASOV, NIKOLAI ALEKSEEVICH (1821-77), was one of the leading literary figures in the radical intelligentsia of the 1860s. In addition to his poetry of political and social protest, which enjoyed great popularity, Nekrasov played a key role as publisher of the leading radical magazines. From 1846 to 1866 he directed *The Contemporary*, and after it was closed by the censor he became the publisher of *Notes of the Fatherland* (from 1866 to his death).

NESMELOV, VIKTOR IVANOVICH (1863-1920), studied and then taught at the Kazan' Theological Academy. His thought centered around the question of the meaning of human existence, a question he sought to resolve through a philosophical restatement of the Christian revelation.

NEW WAY, THE [NOVYI PUT'] , was published in St. Petersburg in 1903-04, under the leadership of Dmitrii Merezhkovskii.

NIETZSCHE, FRIEDRICH (1844-1900), was a German philosopher who rejected all the traditional values of middle-class, Christian Europe. He called for a new breed of "blond beast" conquerors who would destroy existing civilization with its mediocrity and limitations and free the human personality.

"NIHILISM" was less a doctrine than the attitude characteristic of Russian radical youth in the 1860s. Nihilists rejected all traditions, all accepted truths, all moral and religious precepts not susceptible to scientific proof, and all the elaborate forms of polite society. Turgenev's Bazarov is the literary image of the nihilist.

NOVIKOV, NIKOLAI IVANOVICH (1744-1818), journalist, publisher, Freemason and humanitarian, was one of the outstanding intellectual figures of the reign of Catherine the Great. Though he did not reject the foundations of the existing order, he found a good deal to criticize in the behavior of Russia's serfowners, officials and dignitaries. Alarmed at his independence, Catherine subjected Novikov to increasingly severe persecution and eventually sentenced him to a long prison term. He was later pardoned by Emperor Paul.

17 OCTOBER 1905, marked the climax of the 1905 revolution. On that day Nicholas II issued the so-called October Manifesto promising civil liberties and a representative, legislative assembly, the State Duma.

OCTOBRISTS, THE (Union of 17 October), were a moderate liberal party to the right of the Kadets. After the franchise was narrowed in 1907, the Octobrists dominated Duma activity. Industrialists and landowners formed their main constituency.

PEOPLE'S WILL, PARTY OF THE, was the terrorist wing of the Populist movement. It functioned from 1878 to 1881, its activity culminating in the assassination of Emperor Alexander II.

PISAREV, DMITRII IVANOVICH (1840-68), who had a brief career as a journalist, was the most extreme exponent of "nihilism" in the sixties. His writings preached materialism, utilitarianism, and the application of the natural sciences to the solution of social problems.

PLEHVE, V. K. von (1846-1904), served as Minister of the Interior in the early years of the twentieth century. He was assassinated in 1904.

PLEKHANOV, GEORGII VALENTINOVICH (1857-1918), known as the "father of Russian Marxism," was Russia's outstanding Marxist theoretician. His first major work, *On the Question of the Development of the Monist View of History*, published in 1895 under the pseudonym Bel'tov, was an attack on the Populists from the Marxist point of view.

POPULAR SOCIALIST PARTY: a small, predominantly intellectual party with moderate Populist views. It formed after the revolution of 1905.

POPULISM was a social and political movement advocating a form of agrarian socialism based on the Russian peasant commune. Inspired to varying degrees by the views of Herzen, Chernyshevskii, Lavrov, and Mikhailovskii, Populism reached the peak of its influence in the 1870s. With the failure of the attempt to spread its views directly to the peasants in the "to the people" movement of 1874, the movement split; some of its adherents turned to political terrorism, creating the People's Will Party which assassinated Alexander II in 1881, while others, including Plekhanov, went on to create the Russian Marxist movement. At the turn of the century, Populism was revived and updated in the form of the Socialist-Revolutionary Party.

PUCHTA, GEORG FRIEDRICH (1798-1846), was a follower of Savigny; he provided the definitive formulation of the historical school's doctrine on customary law. His *Das Gewohnheitsrecht* was published in two volumes in 1828-37.

PUFENDORF, SAMUEL von (1632-94), was a philosopher and historian whose major contribution was his study of international law, *De Jure Naturae et Gentium* (1672). His work is distinguished by its rationalism and awareness of sociological realities.

PUGACHEV, EMEL'IAN ("Emel'ka") (c. 1742-75), was a Don Cossack who led an insurrection in 1773-74, the largest of the great peasant revolts. Claiming to be Peter III, the deposed and murdered husband of Catherine the Great, Pugachev issued "royal" decrees, including one on the abolition of serfdom. He forged a formidable coalition of discontent, which included Cossacks, serfs, and indigenous tribes of the Volga region. The uprising was crushed after a military campaign, and Pugachev himself was publicly executed in Moscow.

RACHINSKII, SERGEI ALEKSANDROVICH (1836-1902), was trained as a botanist but was best known for his theories of popular education and his village school where he developed them. Rachinskii advocated turning all elementary education over to the clergy, and in his own school he introduced an extremely restricted curriculum focused on religious subjects.

RADISHCHEV, ALEKSANDR NIKOLAEVICH (1749-1802), often called the "father of the Russian intelligentsia," was the first critic of Russian conditions to direct his fire at the very principles and institutions of the existing order, rather than at individual abuses. His *Journey from St. Petersburg to Moscow*, published in 1790, was a passionate indictment of serfdom and bureaucratic tyranny. It won him a sentence of exile to Siberia, from which he was pardoned after Catherine's death. He subsequently took his own life.

RAZIN, STEPAN ("Sten'ka") (d. 1671), was a Cossack who led a major peasant insurrection in 1670-71.

RAZNOCHINTSY (literally, "men of diverse ranks") was a term commonly applied in the second half of the nineteenth century to members of the intelligentsia who were of non-noble origin.

RIEHL, ALOIS (1844-1924), was an Austrian neo-Kantian philosopher.

ROZANOV, VASILII VASIL'EVICH (1856-1919), was an author and journalist who exerted a major influence on the symbolist and decadent movements. His main themes were an attack on Christianity for its asceticism, and a glorification of sex as the moving force of the universe.

RUSSIAN SOCIAL-DEMOCRATIC WORKERS' PARTY was Russia's Marxist party. Founded in 1898, at its second congress in 1903 the party split into two factions, the Mensheviks ("members of the minority") and the Bolsheviks ("members of the majority"), the latter under Lenin's leadership. The split arose ostensibly from a dispute over matters of party organization, but in fact it reflected deeper ideological and political disagreements. Despite reunification attempts in subsequent years, the two factions increasingly went their separate ways as two independent parties.

RYLEEV, KONDRATII FEDOROVICH (1795-1826), was a poet, his verse expressing predominantly civic themes. He was among the leaders of the Decembrist rebellion of 1825, which tried to prevent the accession of Nicholas I to the throne. Ryleev was one of the five men hanged for their part in the conspiracy.

SALTYKOV, MIKHAIL EVGRAFOVICH (1826-89), used the pseudonym Shchedrin and is usually referred to as Saltykov-Shchedrin. Most popular as a satirist, he contributed to *The Contemporary* and then to its successor, *Notes of the Fatherland*, which he subsequently edited. His most important work was a novel, *The Golovlev Family*, depicting the decay of a petty gentry family.

SAMARINS, THE, like the Aksakovs, were an old gentry family. In the nineteenth century, three brothers propagated Slavophile ideas in public life. The best known, Iurii Fedorovich (1819-76), was the most politically active of the Slavophiles. He was a high-ranking civil servant and played a major part in working out the peasant emancipation laws.

SANIN: a "decadent" novel by Mikhail Petrovich Artsybashev, first published in 1907. It created a sensation with its ridicule of political activism, acceptance of non-marital sex, somewhat Nietzschean hero, three suicides, and a dash of incest. "Saninism" became a pejorative term for a bohemian life-style, and especially for a "decadent" interest in sexuality, mental and physical abnormality, and amorality.

SAVIGNY: See Thibaut

"SCHISMATICS," or Old Believers, opposed the reforms of the Russian church rituals introduced by Patriarch Nikon in the mid-seventeenth century. Although the dispute concerned the forms of worship and not dogma, it led ultimately to the excommunication of the adherents of the "old belief" from the official church.

SERGEI OF RADONEZH, ST. SERGEI (1314?-92, canonized 1452), was one of the outstanding Russian churchmen of the fourteenth century and one of the most revered figures in Russian religious history. He was the founder and abbot of the Trinity-St. Sergei Monastery, to the north of Moscow, which became a model for Russian monastic life as well as the richest monastery in the country. As a sign of his blessing of Prince Dmitrii's campaign against the Tatars in 1380, Sergei sent two of his monks to accompany the army; they subsequently fell on the battlefield.

SHELGUNOV, NIKOLAI VASIL'EVICH (1824-91), was a Populist writer who remained a lifelong exponent of the ideas of Chernyshevskii and the other "men of the sixties." He was a principal contributor to, and later editor of, *The Cause* [Delo], a radical journal founded in St. Petersburg in the 1860s and continuing for about twenty years.

SHUL'GIN, VASILII VITAL'EVICH , a right-wing journalist and editor, sat in the Second, Third and Fourth Dumas.

SIMMEL, GEORG (1858-1918), philosopher and sociologist, concerned himself primarily with the interaction between men and the culture they create.

SIPIAGIN, D. S. (1853-1902), was a Minister of the Interior at the beginning of the twentieth century. He was assassinated in 1902, as was his successor, von Plehve, two years later.

SLAVOPHILES: a group of thinkers of the 1830s and 1840s who rejected Western secularism and liberalism, believing that the peasant commune and the Orthodox Church offered Russia the foundations for her own unique community life based on love.

SOCIAL DEMOCRATS: See Russian Social-Democratic Workers' Party

SOCIALIST-REVOLUTIONARIES, PARTY OF (SR's): one of Russia's major political parties in the early twentieth century. Drawing mainly on the traditions of Populism, but with some borrowing from Marxist doctrine, the SR's spoke for the interests of the peasantry.

SOLOV'EV, VLADIMIR SERGEEVICH (1853-1900), was the most original and influential Russian philosopher of the nineteenth century. His writings ranged broadly over religion, history, and all aspects of philosophy. His chief philosophical objective was the synthesis of all aspects of reality, a union of science and philosophy, on the one hand, and theology on the other.

STATE DUMA: the lower house of the legislature introduced after the revolution of 1905. Although its powers were decidedly limited, and it was not elected by universal suffrage (and the suffrage was sharply restricted after June 1907), the Duma was the focus of political activity in Russia.

STIRNER, MAX [Johann Kaspar Schmidt] (1806-56), was the outstanding philosopher of individualistic anarchism. In his major work, *The Ego and His Own* [Der Einzige und sein Eigentum], published in 1845, he denied the validity of all transcendent values claiming to provide sanctions for the individual's behavior. In addition to religious beliefs, he rejected ethical, philosophical, and political standards. The "egoist" whose sovereignty he proclaimed is frequently regarded as a forerunner of Nietzsche's "superman."

THIBAUT, ANTON FRIEDRICH JUSTUS (1772-1840), a German jurist, in 1814 issued a call for the codification of German civil law. He was opposed by Friedrich Karl von Savigny (1779-1861), the founder of the historical school of jurisprudence. Savigny stressed the social origins of law: it is not the product of abstract reason but an organic part of a nation's life, formed by popular custom and tradition. He therefore denied the "vocation" of his own or any age for legislation on the grounds that law, as an emanation of the *Volksgeist*, must not be exposed to the arbitrary interference of law-makers.

"THIRD ELEMENT," THE, was the name given to the *zemstvo*'s professional staff (doctors, teachers, agronomists, statisticians, etc.). By and large, this technical personnel was more radical than the elected *zemtsvo* delegates.

THOMASIUS, CHRISTIAN (1655-1728), was the first important thinker of the German Enlightenment. Like Pufendorf, he was a natural law theorist. He argued against Lutheran orthodoxy in legal theory, theology and church organization, and advocated state control of the church. A Pietist himself, Thomasius' major influence was on Pietist thought.

"TIME OF TROUBLES": a period of political disintegration and social upheaval extending from 1598 to 1613. The death without issue of Tsar Fedor, the last of the Rurik dynasty, inaugurated a prolonged dynastic crisis. The political unrest unleashed a social revolution, led by Cossacks. Intervention by Sweden and, more seriously, Poland, added an international dimension and threatened the dissolution of the Russian state. After an abortive attempt to effect a dynastic union between Poland and Muscovy under the Polish royal house the Poles were defeated, order was restored, and the Troubles came to an end with the election of Michael Romanov to the throne in 1613.

TIUTCHEV, FEDOR IVANOVICH (1803-73), a professional diplomat, produced a small corpus of poetry that was almost unknown during his lifetime but later enjoyed high esteem. In addition to his love and nature poetry, Tiutchev wrote remarkable philosophical lyrics and political poems expressing his Slavophile, nationalist, and monarchist political views.

TRUBETSKOI, PRINCE SERGEI NIKOLAEVICH (1862-1905), was a friend and follower of Solov'ev. He developed Khomiakov's doctrine of *sobornost'* in his notion that every individual consciousness is rooted in a cosmic conscious-ness. Trubetskoi was also a moderate spokesman in the revolution of 1905, and became the first rector of the newly reorganized Moscow University.

UNION OF LIBERATION, THE, was a conspiratorial liberal and moderate socialist group founded in 1904. It provided the nucleus for the Kadet Party. Of the *Vekhi* group, Berdiaev, Bulgakov, Frank, Struve and Kistiakovskii took an active part in its formation.

USPENSKII, GLEB IVANOVICH (1843-1902), was an author whose sketches of Russian rural life were partly fiction, partly journalistic reports. Although generally classified as a Populist, Uspenskii did not idealize the peasantry but portrayed the grim reality of peasant life.

WEININGER, OTTO (1880-1903), Viennese-born, wrote *Sex and Character* [Geschlecht und Charakter] , a study of the relationship between sexual traits and personal and national character. Weininger's principal thesis was that all characters show a mixture of masculine and feminine traits. He applied his sexual theories to national types as well, exalting the "masculine" "Aryan race," and condemning the "feminine" Jews. The book enjoyed enormous popularity at this period.

WINDELBAND, WILHELM (1843-1915), was concerned with the philosophy of values and made a major contribution to developing a distinction between the natural and the "historical" sciences.

WOLFF, CHRISTIAN (1679-1754), was a rationalist Enlightenment philos-opher. Not an original thinker, he was a brilliant systematizer and spread the ideas of Leibniz and of modern science. Wolff also established German philo-sophical terminology.

ZAPOROZHIAN SECH': a Ukrainian Cossack community of the sixteenth to eighteenth centuries. It drew its name from its location "beyond the rapids" of the Dnepr River below Kiev. Semi-independent, first under Polish and then under Russian suzerainty, its members lived primarily by raiding the lands around them. The permanent camp was on the Island of Khortitsa in the Dnepr River.

ZEMSTVA (sing. ZEMTSVO) were established in 1864 as institutions of limited local self-government. They existed on the district and provincial level, and were elected by the local population on a class franchise. Their major areas of activity were public health, roads, and education.

A *VEKHI* BIBLIOGRAPHY

The following bibliography is in three parts. Part I lists the editions of *Vekhi* in Russian and English that have been published to date. Part II is the bibliography that appeared in the fifth edition of *Vekhi*, under the heading: "Bibliography of *Vekhi*. An alphabetical index of books, articles and notices on *Vekhi*. From 23 March 1909 through 15 February 1910." The list was by no means complete, and the entries contain a number of errors and inconsistencies. Since it was impossible to check them all, however, the bibliography has been reprinted here as originally published, with only a few minor corrections and with modernized orthography and punctuation. Items are listed in alphabetical order according to the Russian alphabet. Part III both supplements the list in Part II and brings up to date the bibliography of published writings on *Vekhi*. For works on the historical and philosophical contexts of *Vekhi*, see the notes to the Introduction to this volume.

I

The first edition of *Vekhi* appeared in March 1909. Second, third, and fourth editions followed in 1909, and a fifth edition in 1910. In the first edition, Izgoev's article had been printed last; in the second and later editions all the articles were printed in alphabetical order (according to the Russian alphabet) by the authors' last names, and some notes by the authors were added. The fourth edition appended a bibliography of books and articles about *Vekhi*, and in the fifth edition this bibliography was considerably enlarged.

In 1967 *Vekhi* was reprinted by the Posev publishing house in Frankfurt, using the second edition of 1909.

Since 1990, four editions of *Vekhi* have been printed in Russia.

(1) *Vekhi: sbornik statei o russkoi intelligentsii* (Novosti: Moscow, 1990). This is a reprint of the first edition.

(2) *Vekhi: sbornik statei o russkoi intelligentsii* (Sverdlovsk: Izdatel'stvo Ural'skogo universiteta, 1991). This is a reprint of the fourth edition, with an Afterword and notes by B. V. Emel'ianov and K. N. Liubutin.

(3) *Vekhi; Iz glubiny* (Moscow: Izdatel'stvo "Pravda," 1991). This edition,

a supplement to the journal *Voprosy filosofii*, reprints the fifth edition of *Vekhi* as well as *Iz glubiny*. Edited by A.A. Iakovlev, it is the most scholarly of the Russian editions and contains extensive introductions and annotations.

(4) *Vekhi; Intelligentsiia v Rossii: Sborniki statei 1909–1910* (Moscow: "Molodaia gvardiia," 1991), edited by N. Kazakova, with a Preface by V. Shelokhaev. *Vekhi* is reprinted from the first edition, along with the Kadet volume of 1910 that responded to *Vekhi*.

The first complete English translation, "*Vekhi* (Signposts): A Collection of Articles on the Russian Intelligentsia," translated and edited by Marshall Shatz and Judith Zimmerman, appeared in serialized form in *Canadian Slavic Studies*, vol. 2, no. 2 (Summer 1968) to vol. 5, no. 3 (Fall 1971). A second, revised edition appeared in 1986, published by Charles Schlacks, Jr., Publisher, Irvine, California. There is also a translation titled *Landmarks: A Collection of Essays on the Russian Intelligentsia, 1909,* translated by Marian Schwartz, edited by Boris Shragin and Albert Todd (New York: Karz Howard, 1977).

In the present volume, the revised translation of 1986 has been reprinted unchanged, but the introduction, the notes, and the bibliography have been brought up to date.

II

1909

A. P. K. "Poiski novogo ili vechno-starogo." *Vil. vestn.*, 14 maia.
A-r. "Nashumevshaia kniga." *Novoros. krai*, 27 maia.
A.T. "Po povodu 'Razdum´ia u Vekh'." *Sibirsk. zhizn´*, 4 iiulia.
A. Ch. "Obzor zhurnalov." *Severnoe siianie*, No. 8.
Avel´o. "Iz dnevnika obyvatelia" (stikh.). *Utro*, 18 maia.
Aivazov, I. " 'Vekhi'." *Kolokol*, 1 maia.
Aleksandrovich, Iu. "Novyi pokhod protiv obshchestvennosti." *Rul´*, 31 marta.
Ego-zhe. "Nigilizm-modern i nashi moralisty." *Posle Chekhova.* T.II.M., 1909.
Amfiteatrov, A. "Zapisnaia knizhka." *Odessk. nov.*, 7 iiunia.
Antonii, arkhiep. "Otkrytoe pis´mo avtoram sbornika 'Vekhi'." *Slovo*, No. 791, 10 maia.
Ego-zhe. "Otvetnoe pis´mo N. A. Berdiaevu o 'Vekhakh': o Tserkvi i dukhovenstve." *Kolokol*, No. No. 1045 i 1046, 3 i sent.
Antonovich, M. "Pokaiavshiisia bludnyi syn i propashchii chelovek." *Nov. Rus´*, 17 maia.
Anchar. "Iz dnevnika." *Nov. Rus´*, 10 iiunia.
Arsen´ev, K. "Prizyv k pokaianiiu." *Vestn. Evropy*, mai.

Baian. "Dva lageria." *Vecher*, 1 iiulia.
Berdiaev, N. "Otkrytoe pis´mo arkhiep. Antoniiu." *Mosk. ezhenedel´nik*, No. 32, 15 avg.
"Beseda o sbornike 'Vekhi'." *Russk. ved.*, No. 86. 16 apr.
Bikerman, I. "Otshchepentsy v kvadrate." *Bodr. slovo*, No. 8.

Boborykin, P. "Oblichiteli intelligentsii." *Russk. slovo*, 17 apr.

Ego-zhe. "Podgnivshie 'Vekhi'." *Russkoe slovo*, No. 111, 17 maia.

Borskii, B. "Svetliachki russkoi zhizni." *Utro* (Khar'kov), No. 111, 1 iiulia.

Botsianovskii, V. "Nechto o truslivom intelligente." *Novaia Rus'*, No. 124, 8 maia.

Brusilovskii, I. "Pis'mo i otvet." *Sovr. slovo*, 14 maia.

Ego-zhe. "Nedovol'nye." *Kievsk. vesti*, 5 iiulia.

Ego-zhe. "Vokrug prazdnestva. *Kievsk. vesti*, 10 iiulia.

Bulatovich, D. " 'Vekhi' i Novovremenskii vestovoi." *Russk. znamia*, 5 maia.

Ego-zhe. " 'Vekhi' ili dymiashchiesia goloveshki." *Russk. znamia*, No. No. 143, 145, 149, 154, 157, 165, 169, 171 i 175.

Ego-zhe. "Antikhristovo navozhdenie." *Russk. znamia*, No. 192, 29 avg.

Ego-zhe. "Ubelennye sedinami." *Russk. znamia*, No. 233.

Bunin, Iu. " 'Vekhi'." *Vestn. vosp.*, okt.

Bednyi Makar. *Pridneprovsk. krai*, 5 maia.

Belyi, Andrei. ["Pravda o russkoi intelligentsii. Po povodu sbornika 'Vekhi'."] *Vesy*, No. 5.

Belorussov. "Vlast' byta." *Russk. ved.*, No. 153.

V. G. " 'Vekhi' . . . i vehki." *Kievsk. vestii*, No. 231, 30 avg.

Valentinov, N. " 'Vekhi'." *Kievsk. mysl'*, No. No. 107 i 110, 19 i 22 apr.

Ego-zhe. "Eshche o 'Vekhakh'." *Kievsk. mysl'*, No. 132, 14 maia.

Vasilevskii, I. Ne-Bukva. "Skazki zhizni." *Vsemirn. panor.*, No. 7.

Vergezhskii, A. "Vekhisty i anti-vekhisty." *Iuzhn. ved.*, No. 259, 6 noiabria. *Golos* (Iaroslavl'), 6 noiabria. *Sarat. list.*, No. 249.

Volkov, L. "Novaia religioznost' i neonatsionalizm." *Most, ved.*, No. No. 249 i 250, 30 i 31 okt.

Volokh, L. "Vtoraia lektsiia K. I. Arabazhina (Dnevnik retsenzenta). *Odessk. obozr.*, No. 607, 24 dek.

Vol'nyi. "Grekh intelligentsii." *Grazhdanin*, No. 51–52, 16 iiulia.

Ego-zhe. "K religioznomu vospitaniiu v nashem obshchestve." *Russk. pravda* (Ekaterinoslav), 29 iiulia.

Ego-zhe. "Stat'ia." *Russk. pravda*, 5 maia.

Vol'skii, V. "Za granitsei." *Utro* (Khar'k.), 15 iiulia.

Ego-zhe. "V osennie sumerki." *Utro*, 4 iiulia.

"V dva knuta." *Sovr. slovo*, 29 apr.

V zashchitu intelligentsii. Sbornik statei K. Arsen'eva, M. Bikermana, P. Boborykina, Vl. Bostianovskogo, N. Valentinova, N. Gekkera, I. Ignatova, Nik. Iordanskogo, D. Levina, F. Muskatblita, Grig. Petrova. Izd. *Zaria*. Moskva, 1909.

"V pechati i obshchestve." *Novaia Rus'*, 11 maia.

"V religiozno-filosofskom obshchestve." *Russk. slovo*, 23 apr.

"Vekhi novykh putei ili predel'naia vekha?" *Slovo*, 23 apr.

Glovskii, M. "Retsenziia." *Izv. kn. mag. Vol'f*, No. 5, mai.

Goi, A. "Literaturnye shtrikhi." *Kharbin*, No. 1116, 30 dek.

Gornyi, Serg. "Istoriia odnogo puteshestviia" (stikh.). *Russk. slovo*, 7 maia.

"Grekhi i vekhi." *Novaia Rus'*, 19 okt.

Grigor'ev, I. "Literaturnye nabroski." *Odessk. obozr.*, 22 apr.

Grosman, I. "Makhaevtsy sverkhu i makhaevtsy snizu." *Kievsk. vesti*, 28 28 maia.

Homunculus. "Shtrikhi." *Kievsk. mysl'*, 18 iiulia.

Denisov, V. "Nel'zia ne soznat'sia, no i nado priznat'sia." *Rossiia*, 13 iiunia.
Derman, A. "Literaturnye zametki." *Iuzhn. ved.*, 13 avg.
Dzhivelegov, A. K. "Na ostroi grani. K voprosu o russkoi intelligentsii." *Severn. siianie*, No. 8.
To-zhe. *Dalekaia okraina*, No. 680, 14 avg.
"Disput o russkoi intelligentsii." *Russk. slovo*, No. 252.

"Za intelligentsiiu." *Novaia Rus'*, 18 apr.
Zaletnyi, I. "Vozvrat k slavianofil'stvu." *Volga*, No. No. 233 i 234, 5 i 6 noiabria.
"Zashchitniki 'Vekh'." *Pridneprovskii krai, 18 iiunia.*
Znamia truda.

I. "Iz knigi i zhizni." *Russk. ved.*, 9 apr.
I.P. "O nashei intelligentsii." *Tifl. list.*, 26 apr.
Ignatov, I. "Literaturnye otgoloski." *Russk. ved.*, No. 69 i 85.
Idealist. "Tsusima literatury, aferizma i fariseistva." *Nov. vecher*, No. 15, 15 okt.
Izgoev, A. S. "Eshche o sbornike 'Vekhi'." *Rech'*, 26 marta.
Ego-zhe. "Otvet D. A. Levinu." *Rech'*, 29 marta, No. 86.
Ego-zhe. "Pis'mo v redaktsiiu." *Rech'*, 19 maia.
Ego-zhe. " 'Sol' zemli'." *Mosk. ezhened.*, No. 46.
"Intelligentsiia i natsionalizm." *Russk. ved.*, 25 apr.
Isakov, E. "Zhizn' i idei." *Kievsk. vesti*, 21 avg.
Iordanskii, N. "Tvortsy novogo shuma." *Sovr. mir*, mai.
Ego-zhe. "Besplodnyi pessimizm. (Politicheskoe obozrenie.)" *Sovr. mir*, noiabr'.

K. " 'Vekhi' i 'Antivekhi'. (Iz peterb. zhizni.)" *Russk. ved.*, No. 255, 6 noiabria.
Kara-Murza, P. "Bor'ba idei." *Kaspii*, No. 80.
Ego-zhe. "Kniga o gor'koi pravde." *Kaspii*, 5 iiulia.
Ego-zhe. "Kritiki 'Vekhi'." *Kaspii*, 12 iiulia.
Kachorovskaia, A. "Sbornik 'Vekhi' pered litsom russkoi deistvitel'nosti." *Sibir. zhizn'*, 21 iiunia.
Kizevetter, A. "O sbornike 'Vekhi'." *Russk. mysl'*, mai.
Kipen, G. "Temy dnia." *Mariupol'sk. zhizn'*, 9 avg.
Kistiakovskii, B. "Pis'mo v redaktsiiu." *Russk. ved.*, No. 87, 17 apr.
K. M. "Priznaki prosvetleniia." *Kolokol*, No. 1109, 21 noiabria.
Kovalevskii, M. M. "Grekhi intelligentsii." [*Zaprosy*] *zhizni*, No. 1.
Kol'tsov, K. "Kaiushchiesia intelligenty." *Vozrozhdenie*, No. [5–6], 7–8.
Korobka, N. " 'Vekhi' na puti k reaktsionnomu kvietizmu." *Pravda zhizni*, No. 21, 20 apr.

L-n, N. "Eshche o sbornike 'Vekhi'." *Khar'k. ved.*, 15 maia.
Lashniukov, V. "Dvoinoe koshchunstvo." *Kievsk. vesti*, 1 maia.
Levin, D. "Nabroski." *Rech'*, No. No. 82 i 86, 25 i 29 marta, i 17 maia.
Leonidov, D. "Iz literatury i zhizni." *Pridnepr. krai*, 21 iiunia.
"Literaturnoe nasilie." *Sovr. slovo*, 16 iiunia.
Lutkin, A., sviashch. " 'Vekhi'." *Tavrich. tserk.-obshch. vestnik*, 20 iiulia.
Lunin, N. "Skorbnye itogi." *Khar'k. ved.*, 30 apr., 5 i 7 maia.
Lur'e, S. V. "O sbornike 'Vekhi'." *Russk. mysl'*, mai.
Ego-zhe. "Zhizn' i idei." *Russk. mysl'*, iiul'.
L'vov, V. "Nestrashnyi sud." *Odessk. nov.*, 24 iiulia.
Liubosh, S. "Duel' Merezhkovskogo i Struve." *Slovo*, 23 apr.

Liusin, P. "Vozhdi." *Poltavsk. vestn.*, No. No. 2056 i 2069.
"Letopis' poslednei nedeli." *Zaprosy zhizni*, No. 4.

M. K. "Kuda idti?" *Spb. otgoloski*, No. 176, 21 avg.
"Malen'kaia bibliograf. spravka." *Khar'k. gub. ved.*, 14 avg.
Malinovskii, I., prof. "Nachal'naia stranitsa iz istorii russkoi intelligentsii." *Sibirsk. zhizn'*, No. No. 254, 255, 256.
Meb. "'Vekhi'" (stikh.). *Rannee utro,* 9 maia.
Mel'gunov, S. "Nashli vinovnika." *Kievskie vesti*, 25 marta.
Merezhkovskii, D. "Sem'smirennykh." *Rech'*, 26 aprelia.
Ego-zhe. "K soblaznu malykh sikh." *Rech'*, No. 244, 6 sent.
Meshcherskii, V. P., kn. "Dnevniki." *Grazhdanin*, No. 51–52, 16 iiulia.
Miloradovich, K. M. "'Vekhi'." *Zhurnal Min. Nar. Prosv.*, [iiul']-avg.
Mishin. "Dve knigi." *Russk. ved.*, 24 iiunia.
Musca. "Tantsklass." *Rannee utro*, 25 apr.
Ego-zhe. "Proniknovennomu." *Rannee utro*, 2 iiulia.

N. "Memuary unter-ofitserskoi vdovy." *Kievlianin*, 7 iiulia.
N-v, B. "Usovershenstvovanie lichnosti." *Otdykh Khristianina*, noiabr'.
N. G. "Literaturnyi dnevnik." *Odessk. nov.*, 9 i 12 apr.
N. F. "'Vekhi'." *Poltavskie vedom.*, 6 avg.
Nadezhdin, N. "Predel skorbi." *Nov. Rus'*, 23 apr.
Nand. "Sezon nachalsia." *Sibir'*, No. 243.
Nezdeshnii. "Mimokhodom." *Sibir'*, 2 iiunia.
Nikolaev, P. "Snova u 'Vekh' i otvet g. A. T." *Sib. zhizn'*, No. 128.
Novomirskii, N. "Po vekham." *Odessk. obozr.*, No. 577, 19 noiabria.
"Novye puti." *Varshavskii dnevnik*, 9 avg.
Nord. "Bol'noi vopros sovremennosti." *Tifl. list.*, 24 apr.

"Obzor pechati." *Slovo*, No. 788, 7 maia.
"O 'Vekhakh'. Otchet o doklade d-ra Petrovskogo," *Kievsk. vesti*, No. 328.
Ognev, N. "O russkoi intelligentsii." *Rech'*, 23 apr.
Ozerosskii, S. "O 'Vekhakh'." *Rech', No. 139, 24 maia.*
O. L. D'Or. "Sud nad intelligentsiei." *Pridnepr. krai*, 12 maia.
Ego-zhe. "Druzheskaia perepiska." *Utro* (Peterb.), 18 maia.
Opiskin, Foma. "'Vekhi'." *Satirikon*, No. 21, 23 maia.
"Otchet o zasedanii v Spb. zhenskom klube (doklad N. A. Gredeskula: 'Perelom v russkoi intelligentsii')." *Rech'*, 2 noiabria.
Otchety o doklade V. I. Gurko: "Intelligentsiia ot Bazarova do 'Vekh'." *Rossiia*, 11 dek. *Novaia Rus'*, 12 dek.

Peredovaia stat'ia. *Vilenskii vestnik*, 2 maia.
Peredovaia stat'ia. *Nash krai*, 6 iiunia.
Peredovaia stat'ia. *Sarat. vestn.*, 18 iiunia.
Pessimist. "Iz zapisnoi knizhki pessimista." *Russk. rech'*, 2 maia.
Petrov, Gr. "Obvinennye sud'i." *Russk. slovo*, No. 111, 17 maia.
"Pechat'." *Kievskie vesti*, 29 maia.
"Pechat'." *Kharbin*, 25 iiunia.
Po Vekham. Sbornik statei ob intelligentsii i "natsional'nom litse". M., 1909. Predislovie.
Poliatskii, A. "Apologiia meshchanstva." *Kievskie vesti*, No. 335, 15 dek.

"Popravka." *Slovo*, 12 maia.
Postoronnii. "Bei intelligentsiiu." *Vsemirn. panorama*, 15 maia.
Peshekhonov, A. "Na ocherednye temy. (Novyi pokhod protiv intelligentsii.)" *Russk. bogatstvo*, aprel´ i mai.
Ego-zhe. "Svobodnaia kooperatsiia." *Kievskie vesti*, 30 apr.

R-a. "O 'Vekhakh'." *Kievskie vesti*, No. 328.
"Referat o 'Vekhakh'." *Kaspii*, No. 211, 22 sent.
"Retsenziia." *Ural´skaia zhizn´*, 30 apr.
Rozanov, V. "Merezhkovskii protiv 'Vekh'." *Nov. vr.*, 27 apr.
Ego-zhe. "Mezhdu Azefom i 'Vekhami'." *Nov vr.*, 20 avg.
Rum-rum. "Chernosotennye 'Vekhi'." *Russk. znamia*, No. 142.

Sarmatov. "Malen´kie zametki." *Rossiia*, 30 apr. i 31 iiulia.
"Sbornik 'Vekhi'. Rezoliutsiia, priniataia v uchebnom otdele O. R. T. Zn. v Moskve." *Russkoe slovo*, 15 apr.
Sementkovskii, R. Retsenziia v *Istor. vestn.*, No. 5.
Spiro, S. "L. N. Tolstoi o 'Vekhakh'." *Russkoe slovo*, 21 maia.
"Sredi gazet i zhurnalov." *Nov. vr.*, 11 maia.
"Stat´ia." *Novaia Rus´*, 26 apr.
"Stat´ia." *Tifl. listok*, 24 maia.
Stolypin, A. "Intelligenty ob intelligentakh." *Nov. vr.*, 23 apr.
Ego-zhe. "Eshche o 'Vekhakh'." *Nov. vr.*, 2[8] apr.
Struve, P. "Slabonervnost´ ili gra na slabykh nervakh?" *Slovo*, 27 marta.
Ego-zhe. "Razmyshleniia." *Slovo*, 25 apr., 7 i 19 maia.
Ego-zhe. "Otvet arkhiepiskopu Antoniiu." *Slovo*, No. 791, 10 maia.
Ego-zhe. "Na raznye temy." *Russk. mysl´*, mai.
"Sud nad avtorami sbornika 'Vekhi'." *Golos Moskvy*, No. 85, 15 apr.
"Sud nad klevetoi." *Novaia Rus´*, 22 apr.
Severnyi, S. " 'Vekhi' i Chekhov." *Slovo*, 13 iiunia.

Tavrichanin, P. "Starye bogi." *Utro* (Khar´k.), 10 maia.
T-n, S. "Intelligentsiia i 'Vekhi'." *Kievskie vesti*, No. 330.
Tolstoi, K. "Gordost´ mysli." *Spb. ved.*, No. 247.
"L. N. Tolstoi o sbornike 'Vekhi'." *Russkoe slovo*, 12 maia.
Ton, N. "Stranichka zhizni." *Kharbin*, 19 iiulia.
Trubetskoi, E. N., kn. " 'Vekhi' i ikh kritiki." *Mosk. ezhened.*, No. 23.

U. T. "Literaturno-obshchestvennye zametki." *Narodnaia letopis´*, 9 avg.

Filevskii, I. "Povorot v nashei intelligentsii." *Tserk. vestn.*, 25 iiulia.
Filosofov, D. "O liubvi k otechestvu i narodnoi gordosti." *Nasha gazeta*, No. 71, 26 marta.
Ego-zhe. "Spor vokrug 'Vekh'." *Russk. slovo*, 17 maia.
Frank, S. " 'Vekhi' i ikh kritiki." *Slovo*, No. 752, 1 apr.
Ego-zhe. "Merezhkovskii o 'Vekhakh'." *Slovo*, 28 apr.
Ego-zhe. "Kul´tura i religiia." *Russk. mysl´*, iiul´.
Fudel´, M. "Kritika intelligentskogo soznaniia." *Mosk. vedom.*, 29 apr.

Khir´iakov, A. "Blizkie teni." *Pravda zhizni*, 23 marta.
Khristianka. *Usloviia vozrozhdeniia Rossii. (Otvet avtoram knigi "Vekhi.")* Moskva, str. 64, ts. 35 k.

Chernov, S. R. "Zigzagi zhizni." *Novaia zhizn'* (Kharbin), 19 iiulia.
Chukovskii, K. "Sovremennye Iuvenaly." *Rech'*, No. 223, 16 avg.

Shaginian, M. "Eshche o 'Vekhakh'." *Priazovsk. krai*, 29 iiunia.
Shakhovskoi, D., kn. "Slepye vozhdi slepykh." *Golos* (Iaroslavl'), 3 apr.
Sh-g, L. "Starye i novye bogoiskateli," *Zaprosy zhizni*, No. 4.

Esasha. "Osuzhdennaia intelligentsiia." *Varshavsk. dnevnik*, No. 312.

Iuzhnyi, V. " 'Vekhi'. (Zhizn' i literatura.)" *Bakinskie vesti*, No. 16, 28 sent.
Iuzhnyi, I. "Doklad Iu. V. Portugalova." *Orenburgskii krai*, No. 380.
Iu-n. " 'Vekhi' i Chekhov." *Nov. vr.*, 13 iiunia.

Iasinskii. I. "Sud nad intelligentsiei." *Birzhevye vedomosti*, No. No. 11245, 11247, 11249, 11251, 11255, 11257.

1910

A. "Zametki zhurnalista." *Kharbin*, 6 ianv.
A. P. " 'Intelligentsiia'. (Lektsiia K. I. Arabazhina.)" *Russk. slovo*, 4 fevr.

Basargin, A. "Techeniia vstrechnye. (Kriticheskie zametki.)" *Mosk. ved.*, No. 4, 6 ianv.
Ego-zhe. "Kompromissy." *Mosk. ved.*, No. 12, 16 ianv.
"Beseda ob intelligentsii." *Russk. ved.*, 4 fevr.

Vengerov, S. "Literaturnye nastroeniia v 1909 godu." *Russk. ved.*, 1 ianv.

Goi, A. "Zametki zhurnalista." *Kharbin.*, 9 ianv.
Ego-zhe. " 'Geroizm i podvizhnichestvo'. (Literaturnye shtrikhi.)" *Kharbin*, 12 ianv.

Ivanov-Razumnik. *Ob intelligentsii*. Spb., 1910.
Izgoev, A. S. "Intelligentsiia i 'Vekhi'." *Russkoe obshchestvo i revoliutsiia*. Moskva, 1910.

Karavaev, N. "Drama russkoi revoliutsii. (Pis'ma iz Veny.)" *Iuzhn. krai*, No. 9902, 30 ianv.

Naumov, Vs. " 'Vekhi'." *Ekho* (Blagoveshchensk), No. 390, 21 ianv.
Niks. "Da budet ei triumf! (Lektsiia K. I. Arabazhina.)" *Utro Rossii.*, 4 fevr.
Nich. "Spor ob intelligentsii." *Golos Moskvy*, 4 fevr.
Novomirskii, N. "Belletricheskaia illiustratsiia s 'Vekham'." *Odessk. obozrenie*, No. 621, 24 ianv.

Petrov., Grigorii. "Knutom po pristiazhnoi." *Iuzhn. krai*, 9 fevr.

Roslavlev. "Mysli." *Spb. ved.,* No. 35, 13 fevr.

Sergei Glagol'. "O cheloveke i mundire. (Moi dnevnik.)" *Stolichnaia molva* (Moskva), No. 107, 15 fevr.
Skhimnik. " 'Geroizm i podvizhnichestvo'." *Sibir'*, No. 4, 6 ianv.

Chebotarev, F. "U beregov svobody." *Russk. pravda*, No. 918.

Sh. P. "Moskva." *Kievskaia mysl'*, No. 38, 7 fevr.

Iablonovskii, S. "K lektsii o 'Vekhakh'." *Russk. slovo*, 4 fevr.

III

Agurskii, Mikhail. *Ideologiia natsional-bol'shevizma*. Paris: YMCA-Press, 1980.

Brooks, Jeffrey. "*Vekhi* and the *Vekhi* Dispute." *Survey*, 19, No. 1 (86) (Winter 1973), 21–50.

Friche, V.M. *Ot Chernyshevskogo k "Vekham."* Moscow: "Sovremennye problemy," 1910.

Gaidenko, P.P. " '*Vekhi*': Neslyshannoe predosterezhenie." *Voprosy filosofii*, No. 2, 1992, 103–22. Trans. in *Russian Studies in Philosophy*, 32, No. 1 (Summer 1993), 16–46.

Intelligentsiia v Rossii. Sbornik statei. St. Petersburg: "Zemlia," 1910.
Iz glubiny. Sbornik statei o russkoi revoliutsii. Moscow-Petrograd: "Russkaia Mysl'," 1918; 2nd ed.: Paris: YMCA-Press, 1967.
Izgoev, A.S. " '*Vekhi*' i 'Smena vekh.' " *Russkaia mysl'*, No. 3 (1922), 176–78.

Kantor, V.K. "Istorik russkoi kul'tury—prakticheskii politik (P.N. Miliukov protiv 'Vekh')." *Voprosy filosofii*, No. 1, 1991, 101–59.
Kogan, L. "M.A. Antonovich i '*Vekhi*.' " *Voprosy istorii*, No. 1 (January 1949), 98–103.

Lenin, V.I. "O 'Vekhakh.' " *Sochineniia*. 4th ed., 45 vols. (Moscow: Gos. izd. politicheskoi literatury, 1941–67), 16: 106–14. Originally published in *Novyi den'*, 13 December 1909.
Levin, Arthur. "M.O. Gershenzon and *Vekhi*." *Canadian Slavic Studies*, 3, No. 1 (Spring 1970), 60–73.

Martov, L. "Iz literatury i zhizni." *Za rubezhom* (December 1909), pp. 106–30.
Meilakh, B. *Lenin i problemy russkoi literatury XIX-nachala XX vv*. 4th ed.: Leningrad: "Khudozhestvennaia literatura," 1970.
Morson, Gary Saul. "Prosaic Bakhtin: *Landmarks*, Anti-Intelligentsialism, and the Russian Counter-Tradition," *Common Knowledge*, 2, no. 1 (Spring 1993), 35–74.
———. "What is the Intelligentsia? Once More, an Old Russian Question." *Academic Questions* (Summer 1993), 20–38.

Novgorodtsev, P.N., ed. *Problemy idealizma: Sbornik statei*. Moscow: Izdanie Moskovskogo psikhologicheskogo obshchestva, 1903.

O Smene Vekh. Prague: "Logos," 1922.
O-v, N. "Piatidesiatiletie 'Vekh.' " *Mosty*, No. 3 (1959), 279–93.
Oberländer, Erwin. "Nationalbolschewistische Tendenzen in der russischen Intelligenz. Die 'Smena Vech'-Diskussion 1921–1922." *Jahrbücher für Geschichte Osteuropas*, 16, No. 2 (June 1968), 194–211.

Oberländer, Gisela. "Die Vechi-Diskussion (1909–1912)." Ph.D. Dissertation, Cologne, 1965.

Poltoratzky, Nikolai P. "Lev Tolstoy and *Vekhi*." *The Slavonic and East European Review*, 43, No. 2 (June 1964), 332–52.

————. "Soviet Literary Criticism on Lev Tolstoj and *Vexi*." *The Slavonic and East European Journal*, 9, No. 2 (Summer 1964), 141–48.

————. "The *Vekhi* Dispute and the Significance of *Vekhi*." *Canadian Slavonic Papers*, 9, No. 1 (Spring 1967), 86–106.

————. "*Vekhi* i russkaia intelligentsiia." *Mosty*, No. 10 (1963), pp. 292–304.

Proskurinaia, B., and V. Alloi. "K istorii sozidaniia 'Vekh.' " *Minuvshee: Istoricheskii al'manakh*, vol. 11 (Moscow–St. Petersburg: Atheneum Feniks, 1992), 249–91.

Read, Christopher. *Religion, Revolution and the Russian Intelligentsia 1900–1912: The* Vekhi *Debate and Its Intellectual Background*. London and Basingstoke: Macmillan, 1979.

Schapiro, Leonard. "The *Vekhi* Group and the Mystique of Revolution." *The Slavonic and East European Review*, 34, No. 1 (December 1955), 56–76.

Sirotkin, V. " '*Vekhi*': K 80-letiiu 'Sbornika statei o russkoi intelligentsii,' " *Uchitel'skaia gazeta*, 25 November 1989, p. 4.

Smena Vekh. Sbornik statei. Prague: "Politika," 1921; 2nd ed., 1922.

Struve, Petr. "Proshloe, nastoiashchee, budushchee. Mysli o natsional'nom vozrozhdenii Rossii." *Russkaia mysl'* (January–February, 1922), pp. 222–31.

Tolstoi, L.N. ["O 'Vekhakh.' "] *Polnoe sobranie sochinenii*. Jubilee ed., 90 vols. (Moscow: Gos. izd. khudozhestvennoi literatury, 1928–58), 38: 285–90.

Tompkins, Stuart R. "*Vekhi* and the Russian Intelligentsia." *Canadian Slavonic Papers*, 2 (1957), 11–25.

Trifonov, I.Ia. "Iz istorii bor'by kommunisticheskoi partii protiv smenovekhovstva." *Istoriia SSSR*, No. 3 (May–June 1959), 64–82.

Tsipko, Alexander S. *Is Stalinism Really Dead?* Trans. by E.A. Tichina and S.V. Nicheev. San Francisco: HarperSanFrancisco, 1990.

Vekhi, kak znamenie vremeni. Moscow: "Zveno," 1910.

Williams, Robert C. " 'Changing Landmarks' in Russian Berlin, 1922–1924." *Slavic Review*, 27, No. 4 (December 1968), 581–93.

Zernov, Nicolas. *The Russian Religious Renaissance of the Twentieth Century*. New York: Harper & Row, 1963.

Zimmerman, Judith. "The Political Ideas of the *Vekhi* Group." *Canadian-American Slavic Studies*, IX, 3 (Fall 1975), 302–23.

INDEX

Marshall S. Shatz is professor of history at the University of Massachusetts at Boston. He is the author of *Soviet Dissent in Historical Perspective* and *Jan Waclaw Machajski: A Radical Critic of the Russian Intelligentsia* and has translated works by Michael Bakunin, Peter Kropotkin, and Vasily Kliuchevsky.

Judith E. Zimmerman, professor of history at the University of Pittsburgh at Greensburg, is the author of *Midpassage: Alexander Herzen and the European Revolution, 1847–1852.*

Marc Raeff, Bakhmeteff Professor Emeritus at Columbia University, an eminent historian of Russia, is the author of numerous books, among them *Origins of the Russian Intelligentsia: The Eighteenth-Century Nobility; Understanding Imperial Russia: State and Society in the Old Regime; Mikhail Speransky: Statesman of Imperial Russia;* and *Russia Abroad: A Cultural History of the Russian Emigration.*